Jokes in Greek Comedy

Also available from Bloomsbury

Athenian Comedy in the Roman Empire, edited by
C. W. Marshall and Tom Hawkins
Aristophanic Humour, edited by Peter Swallow and Edith Hall
Greek Drama V, edited by Hallie Marshall and C. W. Marshall
Parody, Politics and the Populace in Greek Old Comedy, Donald Sells

Jokes in Greek Comedy

From Puns to Poetics

Naomi Scott

BLOOMSBURY ACADEMIC
LONDON • NEW YORK • OXFORD • NEW DELHI • SYDNEY

BLOOMSBURY ACADEMIC
Bloomsbury Publishing Plc, 50 Bedford Square, London, WC1B 3DP, UK
Bloomsbury Publishing Inc, 1385 Broadway, New York, NY 10018, USA
Bloomsbury Publishing Ireland, 29 Earlsfort Terrace, Dublin 2, D02 AY28, Ireland

BLOOMSBURY, BLOOMSBURY ACADEMIC and the Diana logo
are trademarks of Bloomsbury Publishing Plc

First published in Great Britain 2023
This paperback edition published 2025

Copyright © Naomi Scott, 2023

Naomi Scott has asserted her right under the Copyright, Designs and
Patents Act, 1988, to be identified as Author of this work.

For legal purposes the Acknowledgements on p. viii constitute
an extension of this copyright page.

Cover image © Antikensammlung, Staatliche Museen zu Berlin –
Preussischer Kulturbesitz. F 1697. Photographer: Johannes Laurentius

All rights reserved. No part of this publication may be: i) reproduced or transmitted in any form, electronic or mechanical, including photocopying, recording or by means of any information storage or retrieval system without prior permission in writing from the publishers; or ii) used or reproduced in any way for the training, development or operation of artificial intelligence (AI) technologies, including generative AI technologies. The rights holders expressly reserve this publication from the text and data mining exception as per Article 4(3) of the Digital Single Market Directive (EU) 2019/790.

Bloomsbury Publishing Inc does not have any control over, or responsibility for, any third-party websites referred to or in this book. All internet addresses given in this book were correct at the time of going to press. The author and publisher regret any inconvenience caused if addresses have changed or sites have ceased to exist, but can accept no responsibility for any such changes.

A catalogue record for this book is available from the British Library.

Library of Congress Cataloging-in-Publication Data
Names: Scott, Naomi (Classicist), author.
Title: Jokes in Greek comedy : from puns to poetics / Naomi Scott.
Description: New York : Bloomsbury Publishing Plc, 2023. |
Includes bibliographical references and index.
Identifiers: LCCN 2023008742 (print) | LCCN 2023008743 (ebook) |
ISBN 9781350248489 (hardback) | ISBN 9781350248502 (pdf) |
ISBN 9781350248519 (ebook)
Subjects: LCSH: Greek drama (Comedy)—History and criticism. |
Classical wit and humor—History and criticism.
Classification: LCC PA3166 .S47 2023 (print) | LCC PA3166 (ebook) |
DDC 882/.0109—dc23/eng/20230510
LC record available at https://lccn.loc.gov/2023008742
LC ebook record available at https://lccn.loc.gov/2023008743

ISBN: HB: 978-1-3502-4848-9
PB: 978-1-3502-4849-6
ePDF: 978-1-3502-4850-2
eBook: 978-1-3502-4851-9

Typeset by RefineCatch Limited, Bungay, Suffolk

For product safety related questions contact productsafety@bloomsbury.com.

To find out more about our authors and books visit www.bloomsbury.com
and sign up for our newsletters.

For Tamara and Misha, the funniest little people I know.

Contents

Acknowledgements	viii
Note on Texts and Translations	ix
List of Abbreviations	x
Introduction	1
1 Playing with Words: Jokes and Poetic Language	17
2 Playing with Theatre: Jokes and Dramatic Performance	57
3 Playing with Plot: Jokes and Storytelling	87
Conclusions: Comedy and the Avant-Garde in the Fifth Century and Beyond	117
Notes	125
Bibliography	155
Index	171
Index Locorum	179

Acknowledgements

This book has its origins in a PhD thesis on Aristophanes, completed in 2016 in the Department of Greek and Latin at University College London, and funded by the Stephen Instone PhD Studentship for Greek Literature. I am immeasurably grateful to my supervisors, Chris Carey and Peter Agócs, as well as my examiners, Niall Slater and Oliver Taplin, for their guidance, and I hope that they are able to recognize at least some of the better bits of that thesis in this book.

I spent 2016 to 2023 happily ensconced in the Department of Classics and Archaeology at the University of Nottingham. My thanks must go to my colleagues there for their support and encouragement, as well as to my students for tolerating my constant supply of terrible Greek jokes, and for letting me try my ideas out on them on occasion.

While the Covid-19 pandemic has inevitably limited opportunities for travel in recent years, I am nevertheless grateful to audiences in Vancouver, London and Basel for their feedback on my work earlier in the development of this book, before the world went into meltdown *c.* February 2020.

My thanks must also go to my editors at Bloomsbury, Alice Wright and Lily Mac Mahon, and to the press' anonymous readers, whose insightful comments have most certainly made this a better book. I'm grateful to editors and readers alike for their unerring support of this project.

Finally, to family. My brother Sacha, who generously proofread my entire manuscript, and made a far better job of it than I would have done. (Any remaining errors and infelicities are of course my own, especially if they have to do with using the wrong length of dash.) My mother Tal, without whose hands-on support with first one and then two small children this book would never have been finished. And above all my husband Bobby, whose own scholarly interests tend more towards the sublime than the ridiculous, but who reads every word I write nevertheless. I cannot imagine this book without his input.

Note on Texts and Translations

All comic fragments are cited from Kassel and Austin's *Poetae Comici Graeci* (PCG), and all tragic fragments from Snell's *Tragicorum Graecorum Fragmenta* (TrGF). The text of Athenaeus follows Kaibel's Teubner edition. All other texts, including those of Aristophanes' extant plays, are cited in their most recent Oxford Classical Text edition except where otherwise indicated.

All translations are my own except where otherwise indicated.

Abbreviations

LSJ   Liddell, H. G. and Scott, R., eds (1996), *Greek–English Lexicon: With a Revised Supplement*, 9th edn, rev. Stuart Jones, H. and McKenzie, R., P. G. W., Oxford: Clarendon Press.

Montanari Montanari, F., Goh, M. and Schroeder, C., eds (2015), *The Brill Dictionary of Ancient Greek*, Leiden: Brill.

PCG   Kassel, R. and Austin, C., eds (1983–2001), *Poetae Comici Graeci*, 5 vols, Berlin: De Gruyter.

PMG   Page, D. L., ed. (1962), *Poetae Melici Graeci*, Oxford: Clarendon Press.

TrGF   Snell, B., Kannicht, R. and Radt, S. L., eds (1971–2004), *Tragicorum Graecorum Fragmenta*, 5 vols, Göttingen: Vandenhoeck & Ruprecht.

Introduction

Ξα: Εἴπω τι τῶν εἰωθότων, ὦ δέσποτα,
ἐφ᾽ οἷς ἀεὶ γελῶσιν οἱ θεώμενοι;
Δι: νὴ τὸν Δί᾽ ὅ τι βούλει γε, πλὴν "πιέζομαι,"
τοῦτο δὲ φύλαξαι· πάνυ γάρ ἐστ᾽ ἤδη χολή.

Xanthias: Shall I say one of the usual things, master,
that the audience always laugh at?
Dionysus: Oh anything you like, except 'I'm hard pressed'.
Watch that one, it's really, truly vile.

Ar., *Ran.* 1–4

This exchange, spoken by the slave Xanthias and his master Dionysus at the start of the prologue to Aristophanes' *Frogs*, will be familiar to many readers. The play is a stalwart of undergraduate syllabuses, and for many Classicists these lines are therefore their first encounter with the world of Old Comedy. For my own part, this encounter was accompanied by the distinct sensation of having stumbled on an in-joke to which I was not quite privy. Dionysus' reply to Xanthias is clearly meant to be funny. Exactly why it should be funny, however, requires no small amount of explanation.

The gag rests first and foremost on a pun. The Greek word πιέζομαι ('I'm hard pressed') may refer either to the weight of a heavy load, or, rather disgustingly, to the pressing sensation of a descendent turd when a person badly needs to shit. For the original audience of 404 BC, this crass wordplay was embedded in the dramatic scenario; as we read on, it becomes clear that Xanthias is carrying his master's baggage (12: τὰ σκεύη) on a pole (8: τἀνάφορον), and that it is the sight of the heavily laden slave that sets up Dionysus' response in lines 3–4. Furthermore, Dionysus' repeated prohibition of this scatological pun in any of its various forms turns out to be a response to its status as a stock joke of comic baggage carriers (12–15: τί δῆτ᾽ ἔδει με ταῦτα τὰ σκεύη φέρειν, / εἴπερ ποιήσω μηδὲν ὧνπερ Φρύνιχος / εἴωθε ποιεῖν; καὶ Λύκις κἀμειψίας / σκεύη φέρουσ᾽ ἑκάστοτ᾽ ἐν κωμῳδίᾳ. 'Well why should I carry all this stuff if I can't do the jokes that Phrynichus always does? And Lycis and Ameipsias, they've always got baggage-carriers in their comedies!'). This joke, in other words, allows Aristophanes to get one over his competitors by suggesting that the god of the theatre himself finds their jokes distasteful. In turn, the audience get all the fun of these apparently conventional *double entendres* while also ridiculing them as old hat. Aristophanes' comic rivals aren't, however, the only butt of the joke. Dionysus is surely also subject to ridicule as, in the process of forbidding them, he spells out over and over again the very jokes he supposedly doesn't want to hear. The god's status as a comic target is reinforced by his costume; in lines 46–7, we discover that, from the start of the play, he has been wearing the hero Herakles' lion skin and club over the top of his conventional saffron gown, creating a pleasingly comic contrast between the hyper-masculine and the exaggeratedly effeminate. In sum, a quite extraordinary amount of literary, linguistic, cultural and dramatic knowledge is required to get this joke.

It perhaps goes without saying that jokes are central to Greek comedy's poetics. I use the term 'poetics' here pointedly, since this is a book not only about jokes, but specifically about jokes as a literary and poetic phenomenon. This is to say that the present study is interested in jokes not (only) as a source of humour, nor (primarily) as socio-cultural artefacts. Rather, this is a book about what jokes *in* poetry, and indeed jokes *as* poetry, can tell us *about* poetry. This book's central contention is that jokes in Greek comedy are a critical site of engagement with the language and convention of poetic representation. More than this, I suggest that jokes and poetry share a kind of kinship as two modes of utterance which specifically set out to flout the rules of ordinary speech. Neither jokes nor poetry are straightforwardly communicative; both in different ways privilege form over content, to the extent that (as anyone who has heard a joke mangled into obscurity, or read a 'plain English' summary of a Shakespeare soliloquy, knows only too well) to alter their form beyond a certain point is to destroy it. Without the correct choice of words, a joke becomes mere nonsense, and poetry ceases to be poetry at all. In combining these two contiguous forms of speech, comic poetry serves to underscore their formal similarities. Starting with bad puns, and taking in crude slapstick, vulgar innuendo and frivolous absurdism, this book suggests that the apparently inconsequential jokes which pepper the surface of Old Comedy in fact amplify the impossible and defamiliarizing qualities of standard poetic practice, and reveal the fundamental ridiculousness of treating make-believe as a serious endeavour. In this way, jokes form a central part of comedy's contestation of the role of language, and particularly poetic language, in the truthful representation of reality.

Aristotle and the 'incongruity' theory of humour

In the *Rhetoric*, Aristotle at times seems anxious about this potential slippage between the poetic and the humorous. The *Rhetoric*'s remarks on jokes (1406b6–7: τὸ γελοῖον, 1412a19: τὰ ἀστεῖα) are popular among contemporary theorists because they are widely held to anticipate 'incongruity theory', which has in turn assumed a fairly dominant place within the field of joke studies.[1] It is certainly true that Aristotle's suggestion that jokes make links between words or ideas which are surprising and yet on some level apposite (if only retrospectively) has much in common with the incongruity-based models of humour to which this Introduction will shortly turn (1412a20–2: μᾶλλον γὰρ γίγνεται δῆλον ὅ τι ἔμαθε παρὰ τὸ ἐναντίως ἔχειν, καὶ ἔοικεν λέγειν ἡ ψυχὴ "ὡς ἀληθῶς, ἐγὼ δ᾽ ἥμαρτον." 'For [in jokes] it becomes more evident to the listener that he has learned something when the conclusion turns out contrary to his expectation, and the mind seems to say, "Yes indeed, but I missed it."'). What is less commented upon, however, is the way that Aristotle situates this theory of jokes within a more general discussion of figurative speech.[2] In particular, Aristotle sees jokes and metaphors as adjacent forms of utterance; metaphors may easily tip themselves over into the ridiculous (1406b6–7: εἰσὶν γὰρ καὶ μεταφοραὶ ἀπρεπεῖς, αἱ μὲν διὰ τὸ γελοῖον, 'there are metaphors that are inappropriate, some because they are laughable'), and in turn he suggests that 'many jokes are themselves derived from metaphor' (1412a19: ἔστιν δὲ καὶ τὰ ἀστεῖα τὰ πλεῖστα διὰ μεταφορᾶς).

Aristotle insists that the best metaphors serve to teach the listener something (1410b10–13: τὸ γὰρ μανθάνειν ῥᾳδίως ἡδὺ φύσει πᾶσιν ἐστί ... ἡ δὲ μεταφορὰ ποιεῖ τοῦτο μάλιστα, 'For everyone, it is naturally pleasant to learn something effortlessly ... and metaphor especially performs this function.') Accordingly, they must be neither too obvious and superficial (1410b33: ἐπιπόλαιον), nor too strange and obscure (1406b8: ἀσαφεῖς, 1410b32: ἀλλοτρίαν). They must be, in other words, just defamiliarizing enough to make us see the world afresh, but not so defamiliarizing as to lapse into the ridiculous (1406b8, as above), or worse, the excessively poetic (1406b10–11: ποιητικῶς γὰρ ἄγαν).[3] Implicit in Aristotle's discussion, therefore, is the suggestion that both jokes and poetry are forms of figuration in which, in contrast to other forms of speech, the defamilarizing to some degree takes precedence over the straightforwardly communicative.

While Salvatore Attardo, one of the most prominent voices in the scholarship of jokes and the current editor-in-chief of the discipline's leading journal, *Humor*, has questioned whether Aristotle's comments in the *Rhetoric* truly amount to a theory of incongruity, he is in no doubt as to Aristotle's importance for theories of humour in the Classical, Renaissance and Early Modern periods and beyond.[4] In his 1994 book *Linguistic Theories of Humor*, Attardo suggests that the *Rhetoric* is particularly critical because of its focus on the precise verbal mechanisms which generate humour (1994: 20). In this regard, Aristotle's approach corresponds conveniently with Attardo's own, since, along with his doctoral supervisor Viktor Raskin, Attardo has been at the forefront of developing a theory of humour grounded in linguistics.

In comparison to Attardo, Raskin's work places more emphasis on formal semantic analysis. Raskin's core argument (1985: 99) is that 'A text can be characterized as a single-joke-carrying text if both of the conditions are satisfied: i) The text is compatible, fully or in part, with two different scripts; ii) The two scripts with which the text is compatible are opposite', where a 'script' is defined as a 'large chunk of semantic information surrounding the word or evoked by it. The script is a cognitive structure internalized by the native speaker, and it represents the native speaker's knowledge of a small part of the world' (Raskin 1985: 81).

The details of this so-called Script-based Semantic Theory of Humor (or SSTH for short) have been much quibbled over, not least by Raskin himself. In 1991, Raskin and Attardo published an updated version of SSTH, named the General Theory of Verbal Humor (GTVH), in which his earlier model is critiqued as excessively binary and it is suggested that jokes rely not on a single opposition between scripts, but on a hierarchy of interrelated inputs of script, logic and language. Studies of absurd humour by Jerry Palmer (1987) and Alexander Brock (2004) further challenge theories of the joke which rely on models of binary opposition, and suggest that we should instead see 'constellations' (Brock 2004: 359) of multiple oppositions working simultaneously alongside one another. Palmer, for example, cites a graffito where, to the words 'JESUS SAVES', a second author, using a different hand, has added the words 'and Keegan scores on the rebound!' (Palmer 1987: 53). In his analysis of this joke, Palmer suggests that it relies not on a single opposition between two scripts (Jesus versus goalkeeper), but rather on a cluster of simultaneous oppositions between church and sport, religion and iconoclasticism, earnestness and triviality, and so on. To Palmer's observations, I might add that the attitude of fervent pseudo-religiosity which attends football in the UK makes the joke funnier still; against this background, the juxtaposition of Christ and Kevin Keegan, and the subsequent elevation of the latter to the realm of the former, is simultaneously absurd yet apposite.

The observation that the clashes in jokes must be at least notionally apposite is central to the work of Elliott Oring. Oring's theory of 'appropriate incongruity' is primarily a critique of Raskin's language of 'opposition', which Oring argues is insufficient to describe the range of clashes and incongruities created by jokes.[5] Oring's model instead suggests that in a joke, two incongruent ideas are mapped onto each other through some (often spurious) linking word or idea, such as a double meaning; in this way, the incongruity is made temporarily 'appropriate'. For example, the joke, 'Q: Why should you wear a watch in the desert? A: Because a watch has springs', is based on an incongruity between the scripts DESERT and WATCH, with the double meaning of 'spring' as both a body of water and a mechanical device providing the linking mechanism through which the two scripts are made temporarily appropriate to one another.[6]

While Oring's approach to jokes as a cultural anthropologist is arguably more flexible and less prescriptive than models rooted in linguistics and script analysis, he has in common with Raskin and Attardo a tendency to focus almost exclusively on standalone jokes, often in a question–answer format. By contrast, Jerry Palmer's work on absurd humour, which in its focus on the balance between congruity and incongruity (or sense and nonsense) in jokes is in many ways complementary to Oring, is unusual for its emphasis on narrativity.[7] This emphasis is twofold. First, Palmer's background is in film and television, and as a result his analysis stresses the ways that jokes may be enmeshed in narrative, so that incongruity may be the product not only of the joke as isolated phenomenon, but also of the expectations and realities set up by the fictional world as a whole (1994: 118–19). Secondly, Palmer's understanding of even isolated jokes underscores their temporality. In his book *The Logic of the Absurd*, Palmer suggests that jokes operate as miniature narratives constructed around a moment of Aristotelian *peripeteia*. Palmer argues that jokes are made up of 'two moments': first 'a peripeteia, a shock or surprise that the narrative constructs for us', and then 'a pair of syllogisms, leading to contradictory conclusions a) that the process is implausible, b) that the process nonetheless has a certain measure of plausibility' (1987: 43). Palmer even goes so far as to suggest that *peripeteia* is no less important to comedy than to (Aristotle's understanding of) tragedy (Palmer 1987: 39–44).[8]

Palmer's emphasis on jokes as a mode of storytelling experienced sequentially in a series of narrative 'moments' makes his analysis especially attractive in the study of Greek comedy, and Isabel Ruffell's 2011 work on the absurdist and anti-realist qualities of the Aristophanic universe deploys Palmer's work to good effect. However, as one might expect given his background in film and television, Palmer's focus on jokes within (and indeed as) narrative fiction is skewed towards the world of prose storytelling. Greek comedy, needless to say, is not written in prose, and the specific qualities of humour in verse have received comparatively little scrutiny. There has been some small amount of attention paid by joke theorists, including Palmer, to the potential contiguity of jokes and poetic language. In particular, Aristotle's observations on the similarities between jokes and poetic metaphor in *Rhetoric* 3.11 have been picked up in a number of discussions;[9] and Aristotle's remarks (as well as Cicero's discussion of jokes in *De Oratore* 2.240-255) appear to have influenced Freud, who likewise comments that metaphors and jokes are both forms of indirect representation (Freud [1905] 2002: 76).

However, the majority of theorists who comment on jokes' relationship to metaphor are interested in articulating not the similarities but the differences between these modes of speech. For Aristotle, jokes are distinct from metaphor due to the addition of a deception (*Rhetoric* 1412a: προσεξαπατᾶν) whereby the speaker's expectations are contradicted (1412a21: παρὰ τὸ ἐναντίως). Kant, perhaps following Aristotle, also emphasizes this quality of surprise in jokes;[10] and Freud similarly describes the joke's ability to make unexpected and surprising links between usually disparate categories, taking us 'from one sphere of ideas to another, remote, one' (Freud [1905] 2002: 118). Like Aristotle, Oring and Palmer are also at pains to prise apart the joke and the metaphor. Both claim that the associations made by jokes are fundamentally more spurious or implausible than metaphorical comparisons.[11] This language of plausibility recalls Aristotle's own insistence that metaphors must compare two objects only in ways that are 'suitable' (1412a11–12: οἰκείων).

Aristotle's terminology here is worth commenting on. The term οἰκεῖος, derived from οἶκος ('house, household'), specifically implies that which is familiar, even domestic. However, to describe poetic language, metaphorical or otherwise, as domesticating seems almost laughably inapposite. Indeed, poetry is more often described in precisely the opposite terms as 'estranging' or 'defamiliarizing'.[12] It might even be described, as per Aristotle's definition of jokes, as 'surprising'. This is doubly true of comic poetry. In one of the best (perhaps the best) detailed analyses of Aristophanes' poetic style, Michael Silk concludes that 'the comic vision quite specifically recalls the modern literary-theoretical principle of defamiliarization' (Silk 2000: 157).

It is not only in their mobilization of the unexpected, even discomfiting, abilities of language that jokes and poetic language overlap. They also share an emphasis on linguistic form. One shortcoming of Raskin and Attardo's approach(es) to analysing jokes is that both SSTH and GTVH look more to the underlying categories which structure jokes than to their specific iteration and form. As Oring puts it: 'This conceptualization of opposition is several degrees removed from the operation of actual joke texts' (2011: 218). By contrast, Oring's approach emphasizes granularity and linguistic form; humour, in his reading, is not only operative at the semantic level, but is 'a syntactic affair. To be sure, it depends on semantic domains, but it is the particular *arrangement* (the original sense of the word "syntax") of those domains that creates humor' (Oring 2016: 52).

Jokes, in other words, are not a matter merely of abstract ideas, but of language. Like poetry, they therefore operate at the level of the signifier as much as (or perhaps even more than) at the level of the signified. By way of an example: the joke, 'time flies like an arrow, fruit flies like a banana', is not only reliant on the double meaning of the word 'like', which functions as a preposition in the first clause and a verb in the second. It also relies on the opposition between (cod-)poetic language and colloquialism, metaphor and literality, abstraction and specificity. The use of the second indefinite pronoun ('a banana', not just 'bananas') is, I think, crucial to the humour, since it is instrumental in the colloquial tone of the second clause, as well as in the move from the abstract and general to the comically specific; it also adds to the pleasing sense of symmetry between the two clauses. While the wordplay on 'like', and the general incongruity between the domains of time and fruit flies, would survive its removal, the joke would be far less funny for it. This example perfectly demonstrates how important the minutiae of linguistic form may be to a joke's success.

Puns and poetics

As two modes of language in which form is pre-eminent, even at the expense of clarity of meaning, both jokes and poetry are also characterized by a high degree of interpretative openness. Freud's observation that both jokes and metaphor are forms of indirect representation is again pertinent here, since it is precisely this indirectness which leaves space for the listener's interpretative work.[13] This openness is accompanied by a high degree of multiplicity; in poetry and humour alike, meanings proliferate. To unpack a single one-liner relies on a huge amount of inference; in *Semantic Mechanisms of Humor*, Raskin's enumeration of the inferences required to 'get' a single, straightforward joke (in this case about a patient visiting his doctor) runs to no fewer than nine pages (1985: 118–27). The listener may laugh on the basis of any one, or any combination, of the potential meanings catalogued by Raskin. My own analysis of the opening joke in Aristophanes' *Frogs* with which this Introduction began also serves to prove this point. The sources of humour in these lines are, as we saw, numerous; while the audience may experience their laughter collectively in the theatre, no one can be sure that his neighbour's laughter is occasioned by quite the same thing(s) as his own.[14]

In both jokes and poetry, this interpretative openness combines with the primacy of linguistic form to create an almost endlessly recursive polyvalence. To put it more simply, as two forms of speech founded on ambiguity of meaning, and in which multiple – even contradictory – things may be true simultaneously, jokes and poetry similarly threaten to uncouple language from communication. Indeed, Raskin specifically defines jokes as a non- *bona fide* form of communication, one in which the speaker's purpose 'is not to convey any information contained in the text he is uttering but rather to create a special effect with the help of the text, namely to make the hearer laugh' (1985: 101). Absent his final clause, Raskin's comment might just as easily apply to poetry, which is similarly concerned with the 'special effect' of the text as much as (or perhaps even more than) the meaning contained within it.

It is in this potential gap between form and meaning, or in other words between the world as we experience it and our ability to represent it through the abstractions of language, that Schopenhauer in fact located the essence of humour. Schopenhauer's comments on humour feature only quite sporadically in modern theoretical discussions; he is sometimes credited as one of the earliest proponents of an incongruity theory of jokes, but his comments are rarely discussed in much detail.[15] Schopenhauer argues in *Die Welt als Wille und Vorstellung* ('The World as Will and Representation') that '[t]he cause of laughter in every case is simply the sudden perception of incongruity between a concept and the real objects which have been thought through it in some relation, and laughter itself is just the expression of this incongruity' ([1844] 1907–9: I §13).[16] While this formulation has some similarities with that of Kant, who also uses the language of incongruity in his discussion, Kant, as we saw above, has more in common with Aristotle in his emphasis on the reversal of expectation in jokes. Schopenhauer's incongruity, by contrast, is not the result of strained expectation, but of an incongruity between two modes of perceiving the world. He suggests (I §13) that we all exist in a state of incongruity between our sensuous and abstract knowledge of the world, the former formed through bodily experience, and the latter through our conceptualization of it in rational thought. Schopenhauer argues that abstract thought at best approximates sensuous knowledge, in the manner of a mosaic's approximation of a painting. Abstract, rational knowledge is surely the domain of language; Schopenhauer's theory of humour suggests therefore that jokes are funny because they draw attention to the gap between the world and our ability to represent it in thought and word.

We have now reached a point where we can make some observations about the fundamental relations between jokes and poetry, and, more specifically, about the role jokes may play in unlocking our understanding not only of comic poetry, but of poetry more generally. Both jokes and poetry are, as we have seen, modes of language in which form is pre-eminent; neither is straightforwardly communicative, and both depend upon, and even actively exploit, the ambiguities inherent in language. However, whereas poetry is characterized primarily by a surfeit of potential meaning, jokes exploit the fact that language may simultaneously mean both too much and too little. By exposing the gap between language and representation, form and meaning, jokes are then able to exploit their contiguities with poetic language in order to undermine it, and to present it as a mode of communication no more serious or communicative than their own.

This is especially true of jokes in poetry. The poets of Old Comedy were evidently obsessed with 'serious' literature.[17] Comedy's engagement with tragedy has been the subject of extensive scholarship.[18] The initial focus on Aristophanic paratragedy has in more recent years been broadened out to include other poets of Old Comedy; work by Emmanuela Bakola (2010) and Matthew Farmer (2017) has shown that this kind of critical interest in tragedy was by no means confined to Aristophanes' plays.[19] Comedy's engagement with lyric poetry is somewhat less well served by the scholarship; however, Donald Sells' recent work on this topic has added fruitfully to the discussion (2019: 147–80)[20] and Matthew Wright has also shown the abundance of literary-critical terminology in Aristophanes, and argued that Old Comedy pitched itself at least in part to an audience of educated literati (2012).

Jokes are, of course, the perfect medium through which to make a mockery of these kinds of serious poetic modes. The majority of scholarship on comedy's antagonistic relationship to other poetic genres has focused on overt parody and metaliterary play. Comedy's metapoetic discursivity is often seen primarily as a localized phenomenon, concentrated in the parabasis or in otherwise pseudo-parabatic stretches of text.[21] Niall Slater has been a notable exception in showing how deeply metatheatrical discourse is embedded in Aristophanes' plays (2002 *passim*). However, this explicit, parabatic mode of metapoetics has often been seen as a paradigm for parodic interactions elsewhere, and even the most recent (albeit excellent) work by Farmer (2017) and Sells (2018) on comic parody has focused almost exclusively on this kind of overt mockery of other genres.

Some of the jokes which appear in subsequent chapters of this book certainly fall into this category of overt intergeneric parody – for example, Chapter 2 will see jokes which target tragic stagecraft, and Chapter 3 shows how comedy uses jokes to disrupt traditional, 'serious' storylines drawn from tragedy and epic. The aim of this book is, however, to show that Old Comedy's granular engagement with serious poetic convention is also embedded in the genre's comic fabric. Many of the jokes in this book seem at first glance to be fairly inconsequential, and to have little by way of parodic force. Indeed, many of these jokes are not part of any kind of obvious engagement, sustained or otherwise, with another genre. They do, however, demonstrate a deep-seated concern with how language functions, and, perhaps more importantly, how, when pushed to its limits, it does not. Like poetry, jokes are inherently rule-breaking, or at least rule-bending, kinds of speech (and poetic jokes doubly so). In joking about with these forms of representation, Old Comedy therefore emphasizes the affinities between jokes and poetic speech, and shows up the potential ridiculousness inherent in the latter when it may so easily, in the comedian's hands, be tipped over into the former.

The idea that jokes and poetry, low humour and high art, may be not so much opposites as contiguous forms of speech perhaps seems counterintuitive. However, in Greek, as Stephen Kidd has convincingly argued, the same terminology might comfortably encompass both these activities. In his book *Play and Aesthetics in Ancient Greece* (2019), Kidd outlines the close relationship between play (*paidia*), a category which would seem to comfortably contain jokes, and mimesis in Greek language and thought. Kidd argues that the Greek *paidia* denotes primarily the feeling of delight which motivates such diverse actions as game playing, joke telling and music making, and that even the production of visual art was, by the late fifth century, increasingly understood as a form of *paidia* (2019: 1–9). Kidd further suggests that in Plato's late works, mimesis is presented as merely one subset of the broader category of 'play' (Kidd 2019: 49–73). This understanding of mimesis, and particularly those performative forms of mimetic activity such as drama, dance and song which are regularly denoted by the Greek verb παίζω, as an act of play is not completely alien to English either, given that the term 'play' may also refer to drama. If dramatic mimesis especially is construed as an activity born from play, then it is not so great a leap to see tragic poetry and jokes as affiliated modes of speech.

As we might expect, comedy's framing of non-comic discourse is heavily influenced by tragic practice. Comedians seem drawn to forms of speech such as metaphor and ekphrasis which, while not exclusive to poetry, are certainly strongly suggestive of poetic mimesis. These are, in other words, kinds of language which, even while they might appear in other forms of speech (such as rhetoric or philosophy), nevertheless have an inherently poetic quality. Aristotle himself recognizes this, when he cautions in the *Rhetoric* that a metaphor which is too estranging is at risk of making prose seem too much like poetry (1406b10–11: ποιητικῶς γὰρ ἄγαν). Comedy's focus on language which at the very least gestures towards the poetic is accompanied by a parallel interest in modes of representation which are characteristically (if again not exclusively) dramatic: costume, staging and plot all come in for ridicule. When taken as a corpus, jokes in Old Comedy suggest a genre whose very idea of seriousness is shaped around a tragic paradigm, and whose concern with tragicness courses through its own language and idiom.

Focusing on jokes as a site of metaliterary discourse does not only help in demonstrating just how deeply engrained these concerns are within Old Comedy's poetics. It also has the added benefit of maximizing what the fragmentary comic corpus has to offer. Due to their very quotability, jokes and one-liners make up a large proportion of 'book' fragments passed down to us by authors such as Athenaeus and Julius Pollux. A study of comedy which places jokes at its centre is therefore well positioned to expand beyond Aristophanes, and to sketch a picture of the genre as a whole. This kind of non-Aristophanocentric approach to comedy has become increasingly fruitful in recent decades. Since the publication in 2000 of *The Rivals of Aristophanes* (Harvey and Wilkins, eds), studies of Old Comedy have increasingly looked beyond Aristophanes towards other poets,[22] and the ongoing work of the Freiburg 'KomFrag' project to publish commentaries on the fragments of Greek comedy makes this work more practicable with every passing year.

In addition to allowing us to focus on the very sorts of texts most over-represented in the secondary tradition, it is my contention that, by focusing on jokes, fragmentariness may become not a drawback, but an asset. A joke constitutes a kind of complete, 'closed' text which is in some ways independent of its wider context. This is, of course, not to say that jokes are *only* standalone texts; Ruffell (2011), for example, has shown how there may be thematic constellations of jokes in Aristophanes' plays, and Lowe (2020) makes a persuasive case for how multiple comic pay-offs may be set up and then detonated in a single punchline.[23] However, I would suggest that in reading jokes in the fragmentary corpus *as* jokes, we are to some degree more able to take these fragments on their own terms, and to treat them each as a kind of comic miniature, rather than just as evidence for the larger whole from which they were originally extracted.

In its selection of fragments, this book makes no claims of comprehensiveness. The reader who hopes to find a collection of and commentary on every joke in the comic corpus will, I fear, be disappointed; chapters are not set out as an exhaustive (or even semi-exhaustive) catalogue. Rather, I have tried to find what I think are the best examples of jokes which engage in interesting ways with the ideas set out so far in this Introduction. Such judgements, especially in the realm of humour, are by nature subjective, even personal. I can report, for example, that I find Cratinus' jokes to be on the whole better and cleverer than those of Eupolis, whose more political, *ad hominem* style of comedy means he is less often engaged with the kinds of literary and linguistic phenomena which are this book's subject; Pherecrates' jokes are, to my eye at least, pleasingly virtuosic in their poetic style, and Archippus' puns have a so-bad-they're-good sort of quality. My specific focus on jokes as and jokes about poetry means that my selection is different in emphasis from prior studies of humour in Greek comedy by, for example, Robson (2006), who focuses on obscenity, and Ruffell (2011), whose interest is in the interaction between the political and the absurd. These books, as well as the recent collection of essays by Swallow and Hall (2020), are also first and foremost books about Aristophanes. While Aristophanes will inevitably loom large in any study of Greek comedy, I aim at least to place him more thoroughly in the context of his contemporaries and competitors.[24]

As a whole, this book makes the case for jokes as a site of poetic experimentation whose creative force expressly rivals that of serious literature. My central contention is that comedy uses jokes to show that humorous and poetic language share fundamental structures; in operating at the fault lines of language, both have the potential to prise apart the gap between language and meaning. As a mode which expressly sets out to create impossibilities of language and logic in which multiple incompatible things must be held to be true simultaneously, jokes amplify language's anti-representational potential. Moreover, by redeploying in exaggerated form the defamiliarizing mechanisms of poetic language, jokes in comedy defamiliarize poetic convention itself, presenting serious poetry as ultimately no less ridiculous or full of impossible contradictions than their own comic idiom. In other words, comedy vies for position with serious literature not only by insisting that it, too, is serious (cf. Ar., *Ach.* 500: τὸ γὰρ δίκαιον οἶδε καὶ τρυγῳδία. 'For comedy *too* knows what's right!'), but also by suggesting that serious literature is absurd.[25]

The following chapters look to how comedians use jokes to play about with the major building blocks of their own poetic production: imagery, performance and plot. Chapter 1, 'Playing with Words: Jokes and Poetic Language', takes as its starting point two of the most obvious hallmarks of poetic discourse: metaphor and ekphrasis. I argue that while neither of these tropes is exclusive to poetry, together they encapsulate what is arguably the central ambition of poetic language, namely to use words to summon up an image before the eyes (cf. Aristotle *Rhetoric* 1411a26: πρὸ ὀμμάτων) of the listener. This element of poetic instantiation, and the way that these tropes accordingly attempt to mediate between the abstract and concrete, is obviously attractive to comedians interested in interrogating the potential gap between language and representation. I argue that comedians took a particular interest in playing about with these specific modes of poetic language, and that jokes about metaphor and ekphrasis were a frequent feature of the genre. Comic metaphors and ekphrases often deploy puns whose double (and even triple or quadruple) meanings emphasize the potential polyvalence of language, and its subsequent inability to be singly denotive or straightforwardly representative. The chapter contends that as comedy plays around with conventional tools of 'serious' poetry, tropes such as metaphor and ekphrasis are absorbed into the the genre's own absurd aesthetics. In turn, the listener is asked to see the inherent absurdity of even 'serious' poetry, which claims to navigate the space between abstract utterance and concrete materiality by setting images before our eyes.

Chapter 2, 'Playing with Theatre: Jokes and Dramatic Performance', turns its attention to metatheatre. Comedy's metatheatrical tendencies, and its parallel interest in paratragedy, have been comparatively well served by scholarship.[26] While previous scholarship has inclined towards emphasizing the serious political and poetical qualities of comic metatheatre, this chapter by contrast emphasizes the way that jokes may be used precisely to dismantle drama's pretentions towards seriousness. Building on the work of this Introduction and Chapter 1, which together suggest that poetry and jokes are affiliated forms of language, Chapter 2 argues that puns and dramatic performance are similarly characterized by an inherent doubleness of representation where two clashing realities are superimposed on top of one another. The chapter shows how puns cluster at precisely those moments of comedy which are most fantastical, and which therefore are most likely to expose the gap between the fictional world of the play and the reality of its performance within the real space of the stage. The chapter looks first at non-human characters in plays such as Archippus' *Fishes* and Eupolis' *Cities*, and suggests that puns are used to expose the doubleness of such figures, whose human bodies exist in parallel with their fantastical identities. The second part of the chapter moves on to examine the more overt jokes which target the performance of tragic-like special effects using the *mechane* and *ekkyklema*. As a whole, the chapter shows how comic metatheatre is embedded in the genre's poetic language through jokes. More than this, however, it demonstrates that comedy conceives of metatheatricality not as a breach of its fictional world, but as a part of it. Like a pun which briefly places two oppositional forces in balance, comedy can, unlike tragedy, make the sheer ridiculousness of theatrical make-believe part of its fictional (hyper-)reality.

The third and final chapter, 'Playing with Plot: Jokes and Storytelling', turns its attentions to the causal structures which underpin the comic world. This chapter is somewhat broader in scope, as it turns its focus outwards from individual jokes to the storylines in which they are situated. The chapter suggests that in many comedies, the narrative conceit itself constitutes a kind of joke based on the collision between two (or more) scripts: plays such as Cratinus' *Dionysalexandros* and Aristophanes' *Aeolosicon* are founded on a single, joke-like incongruity, as two characters, and therefore two competing stories, are disruptively spliced together. The chapter begins by discussing

Aristotle's comment in the *Poetics* (1453a35) that in comedy, Aegisthus and Orestes may leave the stage hand in hand as friends, and notes that while such storylines might not feature in Aristophanes' eleven extant plays, mythic plots were common in Old as well as Middle Comedy. I argue that the jokes embedded in these plots make a feature of their multiple scripts to interrupt the chains of cause and effect which underpin the 'serious' storytelling tradition. In turn, comedy suggests that its polyvalent poetic structures, characterized by the same erratic and insoluble multiplicity which structures all joke-carrying texts, are in fact better placed to negotiate the messy political realities of the fifth-century Greek world at war.

Some of the phenomena discussed in this book have been treated independently elsewhere. Aristophanes' poetic style and his use of metaphor are dissected in detail by Michael Silk;[27] comic metatheatre and paratragedy are the subject of studies by Niall Slater (2002), Matthew Farmer (2017) and Stephanie Nelson (2016);[28] and the genre's sometimes equivocal relationship with meaning is teased out by Stephen Kidd in his analysis of comic nonsense (2014) – though it is worth noting that with the exception of Farmer and Kidd, these studies are limited to Aristophanes alone. By bringing these features together and viewing them through the specific prism of jokes, we are able to see the intersections between these apparently disparate facets of the genre, and to understand how comedy engages in a sustained exploration of the role of incongruity both in its own poetics, and in poetic language in general. Perhaps most importantly, this book offers a reading of Greek comedy in which jokes are not incidental, but in which they in fact structure the genre's relationship with poetic and dramatic representation. As a whole, I want to suggest that jokes are artistically and indeed philosophically significant, and to demonstrate that the more we prise apart their many layers of meaning, the funnier they become.

1

Playing with Words: Jokes and Poetic Language

In the mid-fifth century BC, an otherwise-obscure comedian whom Athenaeus calls 'Callias the Athenian' (Ath., 276a, 448b, 453c), wrote a play entitled *The Tragedy of Letters*, in which the letters of the alphabet themselves appeared as characters on stage.[1] The fragments preserved by Athenaeus suggest that portions of the play's choral song consisted of letter sounds, chanted out one by one:

βῆτα ἄλφα βα, βῆτα εἶ βε, βῆτα ἦτα βη, βῆτα ἰῶτα βι, βῆτα οὖ βο, βῆτα ὖ βυ, βῆτα ὦ βω ...

Beta alpha ba, beta ei be, beta eta bee, beta iota bi, beta oo bo, beta u bu, beta oh boh ...

Ath., 453d

The play also featured a 'speech by the vowels' (Ath., 453f: ἐκ τῶν φωνηέντων ῥῆσιν), in which one of the vowels appears to instruct the female chorus in pronunciation, and Athenaeus' discussion finishes with what he deems a slightly salacious joke (Ath., 454a: ἀκολαστότερον) from the play whereby a rude word is spelled out by describing the shape of its letters.[2] While the overall plot of *The Tragedy of Letters* remains uncertain, the strange fragments of this strange play are proof, should we ever have doubted it, that Greek comedy was a genre fundamentally interested in playing about with words.

This chapter will focus on comedy's playful approach to two specific modes of poetic language: metaphor and ekphrasis.[3] Metaphorical comparisons and extended descriptive passages are two of the most obvious hallmarks of poetic discourse,[4] and they are also (in a perhaps not unrelated fact) the two kinds of poetic language which comic poets seem most drawn to playing around with.[5] It is not, however, merely their prevalence in serious poetic language which seems to draw comedy towards these tropes. Metaphor and ekphrasis have in common a specifically visual quality: they are key ways in which a poet may summon up the fictional world before their audience's eyes. This aspect of what we might term poetic instantiation, the way in which these tropes navigate a space between abstract utterance and concrete materiality, makes metaphor and ekphrasis fertile ground for comedians interested in interrogating the representational force of poetic language. Indeed, if Schopenhauer is correct in his assertion that all humour is ultimately derived from the incongruity between our perception of reality and our attempts to conceptualize it through language, then poetic forms such as metaphor and ekphrasis which explicitly attempt to close the gap between visual perception and poetic representation are ripe for ridicule.[6]

The visual qualities of both metaphor and ekphrasis have been remarked upon from Aristotle onwards. In the *Rhetoric*, Aristotle specifically comments on the ability of metaphorical language to bring something 'before the eyes' of the listener (*Rh.* 1411a27–8: καὶ τοῦτο τρόπον τινὰ μεταφορὰ καὶ πρὸ ὀμμάτων) and this same act of 'bringing before the eyes' is in the *Poetics* associated with *enargeia*,[7] the very property used by later rhetorical theorists to define ekphrasis (cf. e.g. Theon *Progymnasmata* 118, 1.7: ἔκφρασις ἔστι λόγος περιηγηματικὸς ἐναργῶς ὑπ' ὄψιν ἄγων τὸ δηλούμενον).[8] This ambition of making the unseen, and even the unseeable, visible through language is, of course, catnip to comedians, who humorously construe it as a classic case of poetic overreach: where serious poetry attempts the impossible, comedy is always quick to mock its efforts. Moreover, the visuality of these poetic tropes makes them especially promising in the context of a dramatic genre which, as we shall see more fully in the next chapter, is always interested in what can and cannot be meaningfully represented on stage.

This is not to say that so-called 'serious' poetry is not also attuned to the impossible and improbable, and particularly to the tensions between abstract language and the concreteness of visual representation. Studies by Zeitlin (1994) and Torrance (2013: ch. 2) have shown, for example, that Euripidean tragedy is alert to the interplay between ekphrastic description and staged representation, and to the potentially metapoetic role of the former in the context of the latter; and outside of drama, lyric often shows a similar concern for the interaction between the verbal and visual in poetic language.[9] I do not wish to suggest, in other words, that comedy is unique in creating, or even in exploiting, this potential gap between language and representation. Rather, this chapter will suggest that comedy amplifies the incongruities inherent in poetic language, thereby presenting jokes and even the most serious poetry as contiguous forms of speech grounded in incongruity. As a result, comedy is able to generate humour at the expense of 'serious' poetic convention. In other words, comedy vies for equal status with 'serious' literature not only by declaring that it, too, is serious, but also by claiming that supposedly 'serious' literature is ultimately absurd.[10]

Comic metaphors

Metaphors are prime territory for comic joke making, not only due to their centrality within poetic discourse, but also because metaphors and jokes share similar underlying structures: at their core, both involve taking two apparently disparate ideas and mapping them onto one another.[11] In metaphors, this mapping takes the form of the comparison drawn between the vehicle and the tenor (or source and target), whereby one is understood in terms of the other. From the 1990s onward, there has been a particular interest in understanding this relationship between vehicle and tenor from the perspective of cognitive linguistics. This cognitive approach takes as its starting point the idea that metaphorical comparisons involve the mapping not only of linguistic categories, but of underlying conceptual domains. Cognitive approaches stress the embeddedness of metaphorical language in everyday speech. For example, common idiomatic expressions such as 'the foundations of a theory' or 'constructing an argument' are understood to be the linguistic manifestations of an underlying conceptual metaphor THEORIES ARE BUILDINGS.[12]

In contrast to cognitive theories of metaphor which argue that the impossibilities of metaphorical language are de-emphasized in the process of cognition, joke theorists are specifically interested in the impossibilities and disjunctures generated when two domains are mapped onto one another. The idea that jokes, like metaphors, are structured by mapping two different and apparently incompatible frames of reference onto one another is central to the work of many joke theorists, most notably Victor Raskin and Elliott Oring, whose respective theories of 'opposition' and 'appropriate incongruity' are discussed in the Introduction.[13] While the specific nuances of their analyses may differ, they are ultimately in agreement that jokes derive humour from the collision of incompatible domains.[14]

With the honourable exception of Aristotle, who in *Rhetoric* 1412a19 designates jokes (τὰ ἀστεῖα) as a kind of subset of metaphor, joke theorists have traditionally been more alert to the similarities between jokes and metaphors than those approaching the problem of metaphor from a more serious perspective.[15] Aristotle's remarks, as well as Cicero's discussion of jokes in *De Oratore* II.240,[16] appear to have been influential on Freud, who in *The Joke and Its Relation to the Unconscious* likewise comments that metaphors and jokes are both forms of indirect representation ([1905] 2002: 76).[17] In Oring's concise formulation, both metaphors and jokes involve mapping two 'clashing conceptual categories' onto one another; and metaphors, like jokes, involve a degree of absurdity due to their suggestion that one thing is not only like another, but in fact actually *is* something else – 'a logically absurd proposition', in Oring's terms (2003: 5).[18]

While the observations of joke theorists concerning the structural overlaps between metaphors and jokes are surely correct, there is a tendency towards overly schematic distinctions between the two categories. For example, Oring suggests that in a metaphor the connections between conceptual categories are not fundamentally spurious, as they are in jokes, and that the terms of comparison therefore provide a clear basis for differentiating between jokes and metaphors.[19] Palmer (1989: 69–70) similarly argues that in a joke implausibility dominates over plausibility, while in the metaphor plausibility dominates over implausibility, again suggesting that the balance of plausibility or implausibility rests in the comparison per se. These analyses I think underestimate the sheer *strangeness* of metaphorical language, and particularly of poetic metaphors, whose power often lies in their ability to make new and unusual connections between categories.[20]

By contrast, poets of Old Comedy are highly alert to the peculiar qualities of even the most standard, clichéd poetic metaphors. Playwrights regularly exploit the potential slippage between metaphors and jokes; indeed the 'oppositional' quality of Aristophanic metaphor is noted by Taillardat, albeit that he does not make the link between the poet's metaphorical collisions and jokes.[21] Unlike Aristotle (*Rh*. 1410b), who suggests that metaphorical comparisons must be neither too obvious nor too obscure (in other words, that successful metaphors are sufficiently, but not excessively, defamiliarizing), comedians actively delight in amplifying the incongruities, and even impossibilities, inherent in a mode of speech which claims that one thing is in fact something else entirely. In their mockery of serious poetry, the playwrights of Old Comedy provide us almost with a how-to guide, laying bare exactly how such serious poetic language works.

From water into wine: Metaphors and poetic speech in Aristophanes and Cratinus

Aristophanes' *Knights*, which took first prize at the Lenaia festival in 424 BC, is perhaps the poet's most overtly aggressive play. In addition to its almost relentless attack on the politician Cleon, the play's parabasis famously features an extended takedown of Cratinus (*Eq.* 526–36), who at the time of the *Knights*' premiere was a dominant force on the Athenian comic stage. Cratinus is condemned as a poetic has-been, whose once-unstoppable powers have thinned to a trickle: gushing river has become piddling drunk. The following year, Cratinus took his revenge. His play *Pytine*, in which the poet presented himself on stage as a character torn between the charms of Drunkenness and Comedy (personified as his mistress and wife, respectively), turned Aristophanes' criticisms on their head, and Cratinus beat his younger rival into third place.[22]

The competitive intertextual relationship between these two plays has been well established by a number of scholars, most notably Rosen (2000), Biles (2002) and Ruffell (2002). What has been less commented upon is the two plays' structural and thematic similarities. Both plots are organized around a central metaphor: in the *Knights*, this takes the form of a *polis*-as-*oikos* comparison, in which the state of Athens is imagined as a household whose ageing master, Demos, has been taken under the thrall of his new slave, the Paphlagonian (Cleon);[23] and the *Pytine* construes its poet's relationship to the two competing forces of comedy and wine in sexual terms.[24]

Both plays also engage extensively with stock metaphors in which speech, and particularly poetic speech or song, is compared to liquids. Such a comparison is relatively well embedded in Greek poetic idiom, in which words are commonly described as 'flowing', as for example in this passage from the *Iliad*:

> τοῖσι δὲ Νέστωρ
> ἡδυεπὴς ἀνόρουσε, λιγὺς Πυλίων ἀγορητής,
> τοῦ καὶ ἀπὸ γλώσσης μέλιτος γλυκίων ῥέεν αὐδή·

> And among them Nestor
> Sweet of speech leapt up, the clear-voiced speaker of the Pylians,
> And from his tongue honey-sweet speech flowed.
>
> *Il.* 1.247–9

The metaphor here is fairly unremarkable – a passing phrase which might escape the notice of all but the most attentive of listeners. However, Cratinus and Aristophanes appear to have seen the comic potential of this comparison, and the humour which might therefore be derived from exposing the absurdities which lurk in even the most standard metaphorical poetics.[25] *Knights* and *Pytine* each exploit the ambiguous space between metaphors and jokes, and deploy it in combination with puns which actively confront us with the incongruities that are created when abstract and concrete collide.

The parabasis of the *Knights* itself is relatively restrained, even subtle, in its use of puns. The passage as a whole oscillates between abstract and concrete, as Cratinus' poetry is imagined as a physical torrent, tearing up everything in its path:[26]

> εἶτα Κρατίνου μεμνημένος, ὃς πολλῷ ῥεύσας ποτ' ἐπαίνῳ
> διὰ τῶν ἀφελῶν πεδίων ἔρρει, καὶ τῆς στάσεως παρασύρων
> ἐφόρει τὰς δρῦς καὶ τὰς πλατάνους καὶ τοὺς ἐχθροὺς προθελύμνους·

> Next he recalled Cratinus, who flowed with much praise,
> gushing through the stoneless flatlands, he swept up from their roots the oaks and planes and carried off enemies from their foundations.
>
> Ar., *Eq.* 526–8

In some ways the metaphor here is fairly conventional, and line 526 even employs the very same verb used in the *Iliad* passage above to describe Nestor's 'flowing' speech (*Eq.* 526: ῥεύσας, cf. *Il.* 1.249: ῥέεν). However, where in the *Iliad* passage above it is the speech which is described metaphorically as 'flowing', here the verb has been transferred from the speech to the speaker, so that it is not the poetry but the actual poet himself who becomes liquid. This peculiar image is followed immediately by a pun which not only acts as a 'linking device' between the two fields of the joke, but also serves as a kind of link between joke and metaphor by encapsulating the latter within a single double meaning. The adjective ἀφελής (527: τῶν ἀφελῶν πεδίων) literally means 'stoneless', but is commonly used to mean 'artless' or lacking in intricacy.[27] Taken in this second sense, a description emerges of Cratinus gushing his way through a barren poetic wasteland, tearing up what few decorative features exist along his way.

This imagery whereby a speaker physically takes on the liquid properties of his speech and spills out into the space around him is also central to the *Knights'* characterization of its primary antagonist, the Paphlagonian. In contrast to Cleon's designation as 'the tanner' (cf. *Eq.* 44), there appears to have been no prior association between Cleon and Paphlagonia.[28] Rather, this alias seems designed almost exclusively to set up a pun on the verb παφλάζω (meaning 'seethe' or 'boil'), which is finally deployed in lines 919–22 of the play:

ἀνὴρ παφλάζει — παῦε παῦ᾽ —
ὑπερζέων· ὑφελκτέον
τῶν δαλίων ἀπαρυστέον
τε τῶν ἀπειλῶν ταυτηί.

The man's seething, stop! Stop! He's boiling over, let's reduce the fuel and draw off some of the threats with this.

Ar., *Eq.* 919–22

Again, while the metaphorical characterization of speech as liquid is conventional, the transference of the metaphor from speech to speaker results in a more absurd image in which the Paphlagonian becomes a cauldron, his words palpably spewing into the theatrical space. Even more than the Cratinus-as-river comparison in the parabasis, this formulation foregrounds the element of physical metamorphosis inherent in metaphorical language. The metaphor begins with an emphatic juxtaposition of the two fields of reference (ἀνὴρ παφλάζει, 'the *man* is seething') which actively confronts us with the collision between the two. These lines also seem to imply that there was some accompanying action, transforming the abstract metaphorical language into something which is physically enacted within the space of the stage: the two -τέον endings ('we must') suggest a flurry of comic activity, and the final pronoun ταυτηί ('with *this*') a stage prop used to act out the process of taking the bubbling Paphlagonian off the boil.

In the *Knights*, puns act to bridge the gap between metaphorical fields of reference, as Aristophanes plays about with the comic possibilities of transferring standard metaphors of speech-as-liquid to the speakers themselves, thereby amplifying the qualities of physical metamorphosis inherent in metaphorical language. In the *Pytine*, Cratinus seems to pick up this thread of Aristophanic metaphor, and to further amplify both the metaphor itself and its potential for joke-like impossibility. Indeed, given the play's Dionysiac themes, and its apparent assertion (via the embodiment of Drunkenness on stage as a character) of the essential connection between wine and poetic production, the *Pytine*'s reliance on the metaphorical language of speech-as-liquid is perhaps unsurprising. One substantial fragment from the *Pytine* features a fairly extended expression of this metaphor:

> ἄναξ Ἄπολλον, τῶν ἐπῶν τοῦ ῥεύματος,
> καναχοῦσι πηγαί· δωδεκάκρουνον <τὸ> στόμα,
> Ἰλισὸς ἐν τῇ φάρυγι· τί ἂν εἴποιμ' <ἔτι>;
> εἰ μὴ γὰρ ἐπιβύσει τις αὐτοῦ τὸ στόμα,
> ἅπαντα ταῦτα κατακλύσει ποιήμασιν

> Lord Apollo, what floods of words!
> Splashing streams, a twelve-springed mouth,
> An Ilissus in his gullet. What can I say?
> If someone won't stop up his gob,
> He'll flood everything here with his poetry.
>
> Cratinus fr. 198 PCG

The first thing to note here is that, in contrast to the passages of *Knights* above, the metaphor of speech-as-liquid is far more sustained. Descriptions are piled up on top of one another, with the two fields of reference repeatedly juxtaposed (1: ἐπῶν ... ῥεύματος, 2: δωδεκάκρουνον ... στόμα, 3: ἐπιβύσει ... στόμα, 4: κατακλύσει ποιήμασιν), so that this excess of description itself takes on an absurd quality.[29] The words-as-liquid metaphor here turns on the double meaning of στόμα in line 2, which (like the English 'mouth') may refer to either the mouth of a person or animal, or metaphorically to the opening of a river or stream. As in a joke, this double meaning is used to bridge the gap between two disparate fields of reference.

Importantly, the passage makes no attempt to smooth over this disparity, but rather amplifies the collision between the abstract (speech) and the concrete (water). Speech is not just described verbally or adjectivally as 'flowing', but is overtly embodied in a series of nouns as 'floods' (1: ῥεύματος), 'streams' (2: πηγαί), and even as one particular river, the Ilissus in Attica (3: Ἰλισός).[30] This final proper noun caps the previous two plurals with its greater specificity, increasing yet further the gap which has opened up between the abstract (speech) and concrete (a specific river which exists in a specific geographical space). This embodiment of speech as a physical body of water builds up to a final *reductio ad absurdum*, as in the last line of the fragment, where speech even takes on the destructive powers of water, flooding everything around it (5: ἅπαντα ταῦτα κατακλύσει). This image of something so abstract as speech spilling into, and indeed filling up, the physical space around the speaker pushes the impossible and absurd qualities of the speech-as-liquid metaphor to the forefront, and the two fields of reference collide much as they would in a joke.

An additional element of humour is potentially opened up by the prayer to Apollo which opens this fragment. In the *Homeric Hymn to Apollo*, the god is warned that the spring at Telephusa may make the location unsuitable for a temple, due to the noise of passing horses, and of mules being watered (*Hymn. Hom. Ap.* 261–3). The god responds by stopping up the spring with stones (*Hymn. Hom. Ap.* 379–87) and building an altar there anyway. The prayer to Apollo therefore arguably adds further emphasis to the collision between concrete and abstract in this passage, as the speaker asks a god known in the mythic tradition for stopping up a *literal* noisy spring to here stop up a metaphorical one.

Cratinus' joke-like explorations of the comic possibilities of speech-as-liquid metaphors are not confined to the *Pytine*. The potential absurdities of the speech-as-liquid metaphor are also highlighted in a short fragment from the *Didaskaliai*. While very little is known about this play, since only the title and this single fragment survive, the title alone, which Storey translates as

'Dramatic Rehearsals', strongly suggests a metapoetic theme not unlike that of the *Pytine*, and this fragment would seem to fit comfortably within such a context:[31]

ὅτε σὺ τοὺς καλοὺς θριάμβους ἀναρύτουσ' ἀπηχθάνου

When you were hated for drawing up from a well beautiful *thriamboi* [i.e. songs for Dionysus].[32]

Cratinus fr. 38 PCG

The metaphorical language here is in some ways appropriate and conventional, with the poetry-as-liquid metaphor again fitting the apparently Dionysiac theme. However, as in the previous fragment, the clash between the abstract and concrete is increased by an almost ridiculous level of specificity, here created through the rare verb ἀναρύτω.[33] The more common form would be ἀρύω, meaning 'to draw water' (itself an oddly specific action in this abstract context), and the addition here of the prefix ἀν- ('up') locates the action even more firmly in physical space, thereby increasing the clash between the concreteness of this action and the abstract notion of 'gaining inspiration for song' for which it seems to stand. Further, by insisting that the water is 'drawn up', the verb inserts the rather everyday image of a well (since it is only from a well that water can be drawn specifically upwards), whose insistent physicality as an object sits rather uncomfortably in this otherwise-abstract phrase. This further emphasizes the contrast between the 'high' act of poetic composition and the 'low', everyday action of drawing water to which it is compared. These multiple collisions in this line between concrete and abstract, spatial and non-spatial, banal and poetic seem to flaunt the ultimate spuriousness of the conventional poetry-as-liquid metaphor, and the result is playful and silly – funny, even.

The inherent peculiarities of the standard metaphorical language used to discuss poetry are similarly foregrounded in a fragment of the *Archilochoi*, which strays even further into the territory of jokes. The fragment appears to come from the play's *agon*, in which the iambic poet Archilochus faced off against either Homer or perhaps both Homer and Hesiod, and in which Archilochus was most probably declared the victor.[34] The fragment begins with the speaker(s) – most likely the chorus[35] – apparently passing judgement on Archilochus' performance in this agon:

εἶδες τὴν Θασίαν ἅλμην, οἷ᾽ ἄττα βαΰζει;

Did you see this Thasian pickle-juice, what sort of thing he's barking?

Cratinus fr. 6.1 PCG

Hiding in this rather peculiar line is a fairly conventional metaphor whereby invective or unpleasant language is referred to as 'salty'[36] or 'vinegary'.[37] However, here again it is not an adjective that is used, but rather a substantive with a highly specific semantic range, namely ἅλμη, meaning brine, and used most frequently in comedy with relation to food preparation and particularly pickling.[38] Adding to the obscurity is the fact that, as in the earlier examples from *Knights*, there has been a transference of the metaphor from speech to speaker, so that it is not the poetry but the poet himself who is referred to as being ἅλμη. This attribution is particularly jarring given the noun's feminine gender (τὴν ... ἅλμην). The obscurity is further compounded by the fact that this metaphor of Archilochus-as-pickle-juice is followed almost instantly by a second metaphor in which the poet is described as 'barking' (βαΰζει; cf. the noise that dogs make in Greek, βαὺ βαύ). Again, this metaphor of human-speech-as-dog-bark is fairly conventional (indeed, such a representation of human speech as dog-barks is central to the trial scene in Aristophanes' *Wasps*),[39] and a description of Archilochus as 'barking' would not be particularly unusual. However, the combination of these two metaphors results in the extremely peculiar image of barking pickle-juice, as Archilochus becomes both brine and dog simultaneously. The accumulation of incompatible images here results in an exaggerated sense of incongruence, as two altogether different fields of reference are mapped onto one another. The link is entirely spurious: the fragment does not seem to propose any real shared characteristics or structural similarities between the 'dog' and 'pickle-juice' themselves; rather, the mapping is created on the level of their linguistic usage, since both are implicated in conventional metaphors concerning harsh speech. In this regard, the double metaphor is in its structure almost indistinguishable from wordplay jokes which use abstract coincidences of language (such as double meanings) to map ideas whose similarities exist only on the level of their signifiers, but which are at the level of the signified entirely unconnected. Taillardat has argued (1965: 501–2) that much of the liveliness of Aristophanes' metaphorical language comes from the way the poet combines common metaphors in unusual ways. This fragment suggests that the same is true of Cratinus, who similarly reanimates these stock metaphors through unusual combinations, and makes apparently conventional language appear suddenly strange and unusual through his joke-like metaphorical formulations.

Comedy, of course, does not limit itself to familiar metaphorical language. As we shall see in the next section, comic playwrights often exploit highly inventive metaphorical comparisons which create new and unusual connections between different fields of reference. However, where comedy does engage with those metaphors which are standard, even commonplace, in poetic speech, it tends to amplify the absurd qualities which are latent in these supposedly serious comparisons. To put it simply, when Homer describes words as 'flowing', this is not a particularly funny formulation, and the impossibility of the comparison of words and liquids passes all but the most observant listener by. When a comedian takes this same comparison, and describes words not just as 'flowing', but as uncontrollably flooding the physical space around the speaker, drowning everyone in the process, the absurdity of the comparison becomes clear, and the metaphor assumes a joke-like quality. The absurdity was always there in Homer, but comedy asks us to notice it, and to take our newfound appreciation of the ridiculousness of metaphor back to our reading of more 'serious' poetry. In turn, comedy asserts the fundamental contiguity between the humorous and the poetic, and casts even the most conventional poetic metaphor as illogical and ridiculous. Poetic metaphors which are themselves already metapoetic seem to lend themselves especially well to this comic approach. Cratinus and Aristophanes in particular display a marked interest in the standard metaphorical language of speech and poetry. The inbuilt metapoetic qualities of such metaphors allow them to become a gateway for a wider comic deconstruction of the aesthetics of 'serious' poetry, as the serious becomes comical under the comedian's gaze.

Between euphemism and metaphor

As we might expect, a fair proportion of comic metaphors have an obscene element. The confrontational, and often highly visual, qualities of comic obscenity make it a useful tool for comedians seeking to induce a further confrontation with the absurd potential of comic language.⁴⁰ The element of collision and defamiliarization which is central to comedy's use of metaphor may be amplified by obscene double meanings, which in turn involve impossible incongruities between incompatible fields of reference. Comic metaphors in fact often pile up multiple *double entendres* to create imagery which is both vividly obscene and outrageously impossible. The impossible excess of obscene comic metaphors at times creates a degree of interpretative ambiguity: we know there's a dirty joke in there somewhere, but it can be difficult to pin down precisely what it is. By contrast, humour sometimes lies in the removal of ambiguity: euphemisms are stripped of their metaphorical force, and we are confronted with the absurdities of their literal meanings. By filtering this play between ambiguity and crude clarity through the prism of something so unmistakably comic as obscenity, playwrights place their own specifically comic brand of poetics at the centre of a conversation about how language may flit between interpretative openness and denotive simplicity, and yet retain a fundamentally absurd quality either way. As with the speech metaphors discussed in the previous section, puns and double meanings play a central role, as poets exploit the slippage between jokes and metaphors, laughing at the expense of the latter while also asserting the literary and poetic virtuosity of the former.

Obscenity lurks in the margins of a fragment, variously attributed to either Cratinus or Eupolis,⁴¹ which combines an unusual series of metaphors in close succession:

ἔχων τὸ πρόσωπον καρίδος μασθλητίνης

He has the face of a shrimp like a leather thong.
Cratinus fr. 314 PCG / Eupolis fr. 120 PCG

Packed into this short fragment is a double metaphor, where someone is described as having a face like a shrimp which is itself then likened to a leather thong in its appearance. The collision between three separate frames of reference, and the resultant excess of imagery, makes the language difficult to process; this difficulty is compounded by the presence of an apparently new coinage, unattested elsewhere, μασθλήτινος, which itself uses a relatively obscure word for leather (μάσθλης, as opposed to more commonly attested words such as e.g. σκῦτος and its many related compounds) as its basis.

There seems also to be an additional, obscene meaning which adds a fourth field of reference to the multiplicity of imagery here. As Carl Shaw has persuasively argued, the sexual overtones of fish imagery in Old Comedy have been previously underappreciated, and it seems that crustaceans in particular, on account of their shape and colour, were a particularly rich source of phallic euphemism.[42] While the shrimp alone is not in itself enough to indicate the presence of a sexual euphemism here, its combination with the adjective μασθλήτινος does perhaps suggest a reference to the comic phallus, which was stitched from red leather and which is even referred to by Aristophanes as 'the leather thing' (Ar., *Nub.* 538–9: σκυτίνον καθειμένον, / ἐρυθρὸν ἐξ ἄκρου, παχύ). The obscene double meaning of 'shrimp' here adds a striking visual element to the already excessive imagery compacted into these short few words, and this excess compounds the inherent absurdities of metaphorical language by insisting not only that 'one thing … is something other than itself',[43] but that it is in fact three or four different things all at once. In jokes, as in poetry, meanings proliferate, and the listener is left to untangle the results to the best of their ability.

Metaphorical ambiguity is also a feature of a fragment of Cratinus' *Pytine* in which the poet's love of wine is imagined in sexual terms:

νῦν δ᾽ ἢν ἴδῃ Μενδαῖον ἡβῶντ᾽ ἀρτίως
οἰνίσκον, ἕπεται κἀκολουθεῖ καὶ λέγει
"οἴμ᾽ ὡς ἁπαλὸς καὶ λευκός · ἆρ᾽ οἴσει τρία;"

Now if ever he sees a little Median first-blush-of-youth
winelet, he follows, trailing after it and saying,
'Oh lordie, how tender and fair, will it take three?'

Cratinus fr. 195 PCG

Unlike in the previous fragment, where the difficulties of the metaphorical imagery were a result of the multiple fields of reference packed one on top of another, here the mapping is relatively straightforward: a young wine is imagined as an adolescent youth, and drinking therefore becomes a kind of metaphorical pederasty. However, the metaphor begins to break down in the final clause of the fragment. The meaning of 'three' (τρία) in the context of drinking is clear, in that it must refer to the ratio of water mixed to each part of wine.[44] It is also clear from the context that there is a sexual double meaning in play here, but the precise nature of that double meaning is more ambiguous. Storey (2011: 368) suggests the possibility of an oblique cock-and-balls reference, or an allusion to a *ménage à trois*, both of which seem persuasive interpretations. However, this is clearly not an established innuendo with a set meaning, and indeed half the fun of the joke seems to be in asking the listener to use their imagination to fill in the gaps. As in the 'shrimp' joke above, the sexual tone encourages us to read in additional double meanings which in turn complicate the metaphorical language, so that the imagery becomes somewhat fuzzy round the edges. As a result, the metaphorical mapping which started out so straightforwardly in this fragment is made to seem awkward, and we are confronted with the incompatibility of the two fields of reference.

Whereas some of comedy's sexual metaphor-jokes derive their comic force in part from their very ambiguity, others delight in (as it were) de-euphemizing euphemism. A fragment of Cratinus' *Nomoi* combines euphemism with a rather gloriously terrible joke:

τυρῷ καὶ μίνθῃ παραλεξάμενος καὶ ἐλαίῳ

After lying with cheese and mint and oil.

Cratinus fr. 136 PCG

The metaphorical convergence between sex (παραλεξάμενος) and eating (τυρῷ καὶ μίνθῃ ... καὶ ἐλαίῳ) in this fragment seems appropriate for a play whose title and fragments suggest that it imagined a new Golden Age in Athens, perhaps ushered in by the return of the politician Solon.[45] The connection between the two fields here rests on a pun, since Tyro and Minthe were also the names of heroines who slept with gods.[46] Indeed, this line could easily be reformulated as a joke (Q: What do Greek gods do when they're hungry? etc.). The pun is made funnier still by the inclusion of ἐλαίῳ ('oil'), placed at the end like a kind of punchline, which unlike τυρῷ and μίνθῃ does not have a double meaning as a name, and which therefore confronts us more fully with the impossibility of having sex with foodstuffs.[47] The imagery is made more vivid by the possibility, given the association between oils and sex, of reading ἐλαίῳ as a dative of instrument.[48] Within the course of a single line, therefore, we have moved from a fairly gentle euphemism (common in comedy) where eating is construed in sexual terms, to a potentially rather graphic image which challenges us to recognize the peculiarity of this standard metaphorical mapping.[49]

A joke in Aristophanes' *Clouds* goes even further in confronting the audience with the literal meaning of a commonplace obscenity. The term εὐρύπρωκτος, meaning 'wide-arseholed' (i.e. someone who engages in passive homosexual behaviour), is often used in comedy as a generic insult (e.g. Ar., *Ach.* 716: εὐρύπρωκτος καὶ λάλος χὠ Κλεινίου, 'that son of Cleinios, a bugger and a babbler'). The word (and its associated vivid imagery) therefore undergoes a process of semantic sublimation, so that it in practice functions as a metaphor whereby a nogoodnik of any kind is imagined as a sexual degenerate; in particular, misbehaviour in the public and political arena is assimilated metaphorically to private perversion.[50]

The *Clouds*' comic centrepiece, the *agon* between Good and Bad Argument, concludes with an extended joke which plays on the literal versus metaphorical meanings of this term. Bad Argument promises that, under his tutelage, a young man can learn to be so proficient a speaker that he can talk himself out of any situation, even should he be caught red-handed in adultery (1071–82). Good Argument responds that this seems a risky strategy, since its failure would result in 'getting the radish treatment' (1083: ῥαφανιδωθῇ),[51] and becoming quite literally εὐρύπρωκτος as a result. Bad Argument, naturally, fails to see the problem:

Ητ: φέρε δή μοι φράσον·
    συνηγοροῦσιν ἐκ τίνων;
Κρ: ἐξ εὐρυπρώκτων.
Ητ: πείθομαι.
    τί δαί; τραγῳδοῦσ' ἐκ τίνων;
Κρ: ἐξ εὐρυπρώκτων.
Ητ: εὖ λέγεις.
    δημηγοροῦσι δ' ἐκ τίνων;
Κρ: ἐξ εὐρυπρώκτων.

Bad Argument: Come on then, tell me from what class of men are the prosecutors drawn?
Good Argument: From the wide-arseholed.
Bad Argument: I quite agree. Right, and what of the tragedians?
Good Argument: From the wide-arseholed.

> Bad Argument: You've nailed it. And what of the politicians?
> Good Argument: From the wide-arseholed.
>
> Ar., *Nub.* 1088–94

Seeing that wide-arseholedness is no barrier to public life, Good Argument concedes defeat and flees with a final parting shot, 'I've lost, you buggers!' (*Nub.* 1101: ἡττήμεθ'. ὦ κινούμενοι). The joke here relies on a collision between the metaphorical and literal usage of the term εὐρύπρωκτος, as the audience are made to confront (rather graphically, thanks to the radish) the true meaning of this widespread insult applied to men whose performance in the public life of the *polis* is found wanting.

In addition to being a key part of the genre's overall aesthetics, obscene double meanings are a particular asset to comic language which straddles the line between joke and metaphor, since the element of obscenity places greater emphasis on the joke-like qualities of metaphorical language. In playing about with obscene double meanings, comedians are able to amplify the absurd and humorous qualities of metaphorical language, while also taking this supposedly serious poetic trope down a peg by suggesting that metaphor is only ever a skip and a hop away from becoming a dirty joke. Whether by creating novel and at times ambiguous *double entendres* which confront the listener with the absurd impossibilities of their metaphorical mappings, or, conversely, by confronting us with the literal meaning of obscene terms which have through conventional use come to lose their shock value, comic metaphor has the potential to be outrageously impossible, or simply outrageous.

Acorns, spiders, sprats: Metaphorical invention in comedy

So far in this chapter, we have seen how comedians may use the structural similarities between jokes and metaphors to amplify the inherent absurdities of conventional metaphorical language. From words-as-liquids, through to political-misbehaviour-as-sexual-misbehaviour, comedy uses puns and double meanings as a means of defamiliarizing standard metaphorical idiom, and asserts the fundamentally comic qualities of even the most 'serious' poetic tropes. However, not all comic metaphor adheres to this pattern, and there is a large subset of examples which create new and unusual metaphorical mappings. As with comedy's forays into more conventional metaphor, double meanings are often used to create links between disparate fields of reference. This generates a decidedly comic metaphorical aesthetic, in which the line between poetic description and humour becomes increasingly blurred.

A fragment of Cratinus' *Drapetides*, which describes a set of libation cups, magnifies the incongruities inherent in metaphorical language by collapsing multiple fields of reference within a single short phrase:[52]

δέχεσθε φιάλας τάσδε βαλανειομφάλους

Receive these libation cups with acorn/bath-shaped bellybuttons.

Cratinus fr. 54 PCG

The compound word here is rather ambiguous, since its first section could derive from either βαλανεῖον ('bath'),[53] or βάλανος ('acorn').[54] Acorn might perhaps make more sense in the compound word itself, since it is easier to see a comparison (in shape at least) between navel and acorn than navel and bath; however, in the context of libation cups, baths are not wholly irrelevant, since both baths and cups are containers of liquid (and the resultant comparison implied between libation wine and bathwater is rather gloriously grotesque). This ambiguous word, and its jumble of potential acorn/bath/navel imagery, adds to the absurd impossibility of the metaphor, as the cups take on multiple characteristics at once, becoming human bodies with navels, whilst also sharing features with acorns (in shape) and/or baths (in function). This impossible, almost nonsensical,[55] accumulation of metaphorical imagery is further increased by the possible sexual meaning of 'acorn', which was an apparently standard metaphorical term for the *glans penis* used not only by comedians,[56] but also by technical writers.[57]

A similarly obscure metaphor, in which laws are compared to spider webs, appears in fragment 21 of Plato Comicus. Plato's career seems to have overlapped with both Cratinus and Aristophanes, and his plays apparently had a political bent.[58] The play from which fragment 21 is taken, *Greece* or *Islands*,[59] has in particular drawn comparisons with Eupolis' *Cities*, and seems likewise to have engaged with the topic of Athens' relationship to its empire (Pirrotta 2009: 88–9).[60] Indeed, fragment 21 itself is clearly political in tone:

εἴξασιν ἡμῖν οἱ νόμοι τούτοισι τοῖσι λεπτοῖς
ἀραχνίοις, ἂν τοῖσι τοίχοις ἡ φάλαγξ ὑφαίνει

Our laws are just like these fine spider webs,
which a spider weaves on the walls.

Plato Comicus fr. 21 PCG

The comparison between laws and spider webs is certainly novel, and it seems unclear on what grounds, exactly, it is made. The adjective λεπτός ('fine') perhaps suggests a speaker condemning their city's legal framework as somehow flimsy, although it is possible to interpret this description as more complimentary, given the word's accompanying implications of subtlety and fine-craftedness. Whether one takes λεπτός in a positive or negative sense, however, it seems at odds with what follows. The speaker describes the webs as those woven by a φάλαγξ. Given the context, this word must be taken primarily to mean 'spider'; this alternate form of the more usual φαλάγγιον appears also in Aristophanes (Ar., *Vesp.* 1509: τουτὶ τί ἦν τὸ προσέρπον; ὀξὶς ἢ φάλαγξ; 'What's this creeping up on me, a vinegar cruet or a spider?').[61] However, no listener would surely be able to discard the principal definition of φάλαγξ as a battle line, and this double meaning creeps into the edges of the metaphor to quite transformative effect. The initial image of law as a fine-spun web gives way to a secondary, and considerably more threatening, image of a garrison stealing spider-like across a city, and in turn the domestic walls (τοίχοις, line 2; the term refers specifically to the internal walls of a house) which are home to the spider metamorphose into city walls under occupation. As the first metaphor shifts into the second via the double meaning of φάλαγξ, laws which were first described (whether positively or negatively) as somehow light-touch are suddenly associated instead with military enforcement. The resultant tension between these two images seems fitting, given this play's apparent engagement with Athenian imperial rule, which might be variously characterized as benign and detached, or actively oppressive, depending on the perspective of the speaker. The fragment as a whole therefore reads rather ambivalently, and the double metaphor (laws-which-are-webs woven by spiders-who-are-soldiers) is difficult both to visualize and to interpret.

A double meaning is similarly used in Aristophanes' *Acharnians* to create novel connections between apparently unrelated fields of reference. The play's hero, Dicaeopolis, is in the process of creating his own private peace treaty with the Spartans, and this process of peacemaking is imagined metaphorically as wine tasting:

Δ: οἱ δ' οὖν βοώντων. ἀλλὰ τὰς σπονδὰς φέρεις;
A: ἔγωγέ φημι, τρία γε ταυτὶ γεύματα.
αὗται μέν εἰσι πεντέτεις. γεῦσαι λαβών.
Δ: αἰβοῖ.
A: τί ἐστιν;
Δ: οὐκ ἀρέσκουσίν μ', ὅτι
ὄζουσι πίττης καὶ παρασκευῆς νεῶν.
A: σὺ δ' ἀλλὰ τασδὶ τὰς δεκέτεις γεῦσαι λαβών.
Δ: ὄζουσι χαὗται — πρέσβεων εἰς τὰς πόλεις,
ὀξύτατον, ὥσπερ διατριβῆς τῶν ξυμμάχων.
A: ἀλλ' αὑταιὶ τοί σοι τριακοντούτιδες
κατὰ γῆν τε καὶ θάλατταν.
Δ: ὦ Διονύσια,
αὗται μὲν ὄζουσ' ἀμβροσίας καὶ νέκταρος
καὶ μὴ 'πιτηρεῖν "σιτί' ἡμερῶν τριῶν",
κἀν τῷ στόματι λέγουσι "βαῖν' ὅπη 'θέλεις".
ταύτας δέχομαι καὶ σπένδομαι κἀκπίομαι,
χαίρειν κελεύων πολλὰ τοὺς Ἀχαρνέας.

Dicaeopolis: They [i.e. the Acharnians] can shout away, but have you brought the treaties?
Amphitheos: I should say so, three for you to sample.
Here's the five-year, take it and have a taste.
Dicaeopolis: Yeurgh!
Amphitheos: What is it?
Dicaeopolis: It's no good, it reeks of pitch and ships assembling.
Amphitheos: Well take this ten-year and taste it, then.
Dicaeopolis: Urgh, this one smells all vinegary, of embassies to allied cities, like time-wasting.
Amphitheos: Alright, take this thirty-years-on-land-and-sea one.
Dicaeopolis: Oh Lord Dionysus, this one smells of ambrosia and nectar, of not keeping watch for three day's rations, it says to my mouth 'go wherever you want', I'll take it and offer it up and drink it down and tell the Acharnians to go do one.

Ar., *Ach.* 186–203

The unusual metaphor here is facilitated by a pun: σπονδαί can mean either libations poured to the gods, or, due to the role of libations in the process of swearing an oath, a peace treaty. This in turn creates a further set of double meanings, whereby 'three-year', 'five-year' and 'thirty-year' come to signify simultaneously the vintage of the wine and the length of the truce offered to Dicaeopolis. These double meanings are, however, used not so much to bridge the gap between these two fields of reference as to bring them into collision. The passage piles up clashes between abstract and concrete which amplify the incompatibility of the two meanings of σπονδαί. Dicaeopolis' wine tasting starts off on relatively firm ground. He complains that the first 'treaty' tastes of pitch (190: πίττης), which might be used to waterproof both the interiors of wine jars and the hulls of ships, and which does at least have a distinct odour.[62] However, the metaphor quickly becomes more peculiar: what, exactly, should we imagine 'ships assembling' (190: παρασκευῆς νεῶν), 'embassies to allied cities' (192–3: πρέσβεων εἰς τὰς πόλεις ... τῶν ξυμμάχων), and, most abstract of all, 'time-wasting' (193: διατριβῆς) smell like? The structure of the metaphor further increases this sense of incompatibility. Rather than using the pun on σπονδαί to smooth over the metaphor's rough edges, the passage flits between its two fields of reference,[63] and the repeated juxtapositions of these abstract and impossible smells with more reasonable and quantifiable descriptors – tarry (190: πίττης), vinegary (193: ὀξύτατον), ambrosial nectar (196: ἀμβροσίας καὶ νέκταρος) – only serves to emphasize the sheer oddness of the comparison between peacemaking and wine tasting.[64] In this way, a standard double meaning which we might usually take for granted becomes newly absurd.

From metaphors to ekphrasis

A fragment of Antiphanes shows how a joke-like reversal may be deployed to expose the underlying absurdity of a metaphor which initially seems unproblematic. Fragment 123 comes from a play variously named as *The Man from Mt Cnoethideus* or *The Potbelly*,[65] about which very little is known, but which Athenaeus quotes in his discussion of a small fish known variously as the βεμβράς or μεμβράς:

ἄτοπά γε κηρύττουσιν ἐν τοῖς ἰχθύσι
κηρύγμαθ᾽, οὗ καὶ νῦν τις ἐκεκράγει μέγα
μέλιτος γλυκυτέρας μεμβράδας φάσκων ἔχειν.
εἰ τοῦτο τοιοῦτ᾽ ἐστίν, οὐδὲν κωλύει
τοὺς μελιτοπώλας αὖ λέγειν βοᾶν θ᾽ ὅτι
πωλοῦσι τὸ μέλι σαπρότερον τῶν μεμβράδων

They're making absurd proclamations in the fish market,
some bloke bellowing that he has anchovies sweeter than honey.
If that's so, what's to prevent the honey-sellers crying out
that they're selling honey more putrid than anchovies?

Antiphanes fr. 123 PCG

As Olson notes in his discussion of this fragment (2007: 361–2), the shouty fish-seller making overblown claims for his wares is something of a comic cliché.[66] The 'absurd' (ἄτοπά) claim described by this fragment's speaker is in fact no less clichéd, relying as it does on a completely standard figure of speech whereby honey is the benchmark of sweetness both literal and metaphorical. Indeed, far from being strange or unnatural (cf. ἄτοπος), the claim is frankly unremarkable. The comparison's underlying absurdity is, however, revealed by its inversion, as the speaker points out that while every fish-seller boasts of the honey-like qualities of his wares, the honey-sellers are not equally proud of the fish-like qualities of theirs! As Olson observes, the joke is augmented by the punning use of σαπρός ('putrid, fermented'), which when used in relation to wine may indeed signify sweetness, but which in the context of fish is decidedly less appetizing. In showing how quickly a comparison between A and B can be made to seem ridiculous simply by comparing instead B to A, this example from Antiphanes reveals in typical comic style how closely standard figurative language skirts the edges of the absurd. Such figurative language is one of the major building blocks of literary expression, and so to target it in this way is to attack the very foundations of poetry.

Comedy's interest in the potentially risible qualities of usually serious poetic metaphor is accompanied by a parallel interest in another foundational poetic technique, namely ekphrasis, which is to say a vivid description bringing the subject matter 'before the eyes' of the listener.[67] While metaphor may decorate or flesh out poetic description, the act of description itself is arguably poetry's central conceit, the means by which the imaginary is made manifest in language. In this way, ekphrasis sits within a nexus of language, vision and space. This is especially true in a theatrical setting, where this intersection of description, sight/watching, and the physical space of the stage means that ekphrasis may form a focal point for thinking about how theatre creates meaning, and how it summons up its fictional world for the audience.

Although the above definition of ekphrasis, and indeed the word's usage as a piece of critical terminology, stems from much later rhetorical handbooks, the idea of language which has the ability to 'place before the eyes' goes back at least to Aristotle. In both the *Rhetoric* and the *Poetics*, Aristotle emphasizes the poetic quality of visuality and vividness. In the *Rhetoric* (1411b) he links this to metaphor, arguing that good metaphorical language has the ability to place an image before the eyes of the listener, and in the *Poetics* (1455a22–5), he suggests that this quality belongs to any kind of poetic style (λέξις) which makes the audience feel as if they are really present and witnessing the story being told. Aristotle's comments in the *Poetics* are particularly pertinent for the present discussion, relating as they do to the specifically visual qualities of dramatic poetry. Furthermore, his terminology of vividness (ἐναργέστατα) is notable for its overlap with later rhetorical definitions of ekphrasis which similarly stress the role of *enargeia* as a defining quality of ekphrastic speech:[68]

> δεῖ δὲ τοὺς μύθους συνιστάναι καὶ τῇ λέξει συναπεργάζεσθαι ὅτι μάλιστα πρὸ ὀμμάτων τιθέμενον· οὕτω γὰρ ἂν ἐναργέστατα [ὁ] ὁρῶν ὥσπερ παρ' αὐτοῖς γιγνόμενος τοῖς πραττομένοις εὑρίσκοι τὸ πρέπον καὶ ἥκιστα ἂν λανθάνοι [τὸ] τὰ ὑπεναντία.

> It is necessary to arrange the story and to finish it in speech so that it is placed especially before the eyes. Thus seeing it most vividly (ἐναργέστατα) just as for those present as things are happening, one might find what is appropriate (πρέπον) and not miss that which is least contradictory.
> Arist., *Poetics* 1455a22–5

This potential for poetic language to assume a spatial quality (to create, in other words, the illusion of *thereness*),[69] while central to later ekphrastic discourse, is also a clear concern for comic dramatists, whose relationship with the *thereness* of poetry is in practice decidedly ambivalent.[70] On the one hand, drama is a poetry of presence: the audience really *are* there, watching the action unfold in front of their eyes. On the other hand, however, the physical space of the stage and the action which takes place within it represents only a small slice of the spatial possibilities of the theatre. The fictional world is always imagined as extending beyond the stage, both into the immediately contiguous space just outside its boundaries, and more broadly into an imaginary universe into which the action of the stage is conceptually embedded. This extension is partly dramatized physically, through entrances and exits which insist on the existence of a further fictional space beyond that which is immediately visible to the audience;[71] and also, crucially, through the use of descriptive language which summons up the world beyond.

This is, of course, true not only for comedy, but for tragedy. Rush Rehm, in his book *The Play of Space* (2002), emphasizes the role of contiguous spaces, both what he calls 'extrascenic' (just offstage) and 'distanced' (far off), in tragedy's spatial poetics. Indeed, David Carter (2006) has made a convincing case that in many tragedies, there is a pattern whereby the real action of the plot takes place precisely within these offstage spaces (either within the stage building, just out of sight; or just beyond the boundaries of the city), with the stage space which represents the city itself seeing the consequences of these actions, rather than the actions themselves. These imaginary dramatic spaces are loaded with metapoetic potentiality. While landscape may hold metapoetic, and literary-critical, promise outside of dramatic poetry,[72] such discourses take on particular force in drama, where they may form a focus for 'thematising the implications both of vision and of the interplay between illusion and reality' (Zeitlin 1994: 142; Zeitlin refers here specifically to Euripides, but her observation is no less true for other dramatic poets). In summary: in a genre embedded in the act of spectatorship, to summon up through poetic description an offstage landscape 'before the eyes' of your audience is implicitly to critique the relationship between the spoken word and the act of viewing, between poetic utterance and the sight (un)seen. In this way, ekphrasis taps into the same tension between perception and representation which Schopenhauer, as we saw in the Introduction, argues is central to the operation of jokes.[73]

The metapoetic potential of poetic ekphrasis, and the apparent quality (or at least illusion) of real *thereness* it claims, seem something of a draw for comic playfulness. Much like comic metaphors which draw attention to the latent absurdity of claiming one thing is another, comic ekphrases pinpoint the illusion of physical presence as a potential site of both representational failure and risible poetic falsehood. The fragments of Greek comedy are brimming with fantastical landscapes, as playwrights use extended descriptive passages to evoke an impossible, absurd world which is always happening – with typical comic wryness – just offstage where you can't see it. In this way, comedy gently interrogates the quality of *thereness*, teasing out the absurdities, and even deceptiveness, of a poetic project which seems to summon up tangible presence through words, which intrinsically lack any tangible or spatial quality.

Other genres of poetry and drama, of course, also allude to these tensions of illusionism. Even outwardly 'serious' ekphrases often contain an element of playful disobedience, as the poet, in a typical act of one-upmanship, describes with words things which cannot be detected by eye. I borrow here the terminology of 'disobedience' from Andrew Laird. As Laird has argued in relation to Catullus 64, while 'obedient' ekphrasis 'limits itself to the description of what can be consistently visualized', 'disobedient' ekphrasis (such as, Laird suggests, that found in Catullus' epyllion) 'breaks free from the discipline of the imagined object and offers less opportunity for it to be consistently visualized' (Laird 1993: 19). Such 'disobedience' can be found in poetic ekphrasis from Achilles' shield,[74] through to the ekphrastic epigrams of the Hellenistic period,[75] and into the Latin poets[76] and beyond.[77] However, in contrast to even the most elaborate ekphrastic passages of 'serious' poetry, comedy is characteristically less subtle, and is liable to hit us over the head with things which other genres merely hint at. As such, comic ekphrases are defiantly disobedient, poetically, logically, and, most crucially, dramatically. This disobedience is often key to their humour, as comedy summons up impossible landscapes which bring to life (sometimes literally) the abundance of the mythical Golden Age.

In this section, I want to make the case for these comic Golden Age narratives as not only, as has been well established, an exploration of comedy's typical political nostalgia, as well as a site of engagement with the genre's characteristic celebratory, agrarian poetics,[78] but also as a central way in which comedy engages with the relationship between description and reality, illusion and representation, language and space. The fragments of Golden Age plays are full of reported landscapes whose magical unreality strains at the edges of dramatic representation. These landscapes, in their combination of the mythic past and imagined future, have a quality of timelessness which maps onto the similar temporal qualities of ekphrasis, which represents a kind of pause in poetic narrative.[79] While comic Golden Age plays promise to bring these mythical pasts/futures temporarily into the present,[80] they ultimately fall short: comic landscapes of the Golden Age almost always exist just out of sight, just offstage, just out of reaching distance, and are thus never quite truly present in the manner they purport to be. In this way, comedy playfully exposes the falseness of ekphrasis, which promises, but never delivers, an act of viewing and of spatial presence in words. In its focus on the absurd untruth which lies at the heart of ekphrasis, comedy anticipates later anxieties about the art of vivid description, and its ability not to reveal, but rather to conceal, and to lead the listener away from the factual towards the emotional and experiential.[81]

Ekphrasis and the comic 'Golden Age'

As with the metaphor-jokes earlier in this chapter, comic ekphrases play about with joke-like incongruities. Some of these incongruities take the form of puns, while others rely on more diffuse contrasts between the logic of the 'real' world and the topsy-turvy landscape of the comic imagination. At the heart of their humour, however, lies a fundamental incompatibility between the limitlessly inventive marvels described by the comic poets and the realities of what can and cannot be brought to life within the stage space. Comedy promises its audience all kinds of wonders, from sausages that blossom on the treetops, to rivers flowing with wine, and foods that spring to life out of the landscape and beg to be eaten. While the genre primes its audience to accept this kind of magical unreality as part of the fictional world of the play, at the same time the audience understand that the conventions of the ancient theatre, and its relatively basic options with regard to scene changes and *skenographia*, mean that these will always be relegated to the offstage space.[82] In other words, comedy can promise its spectators all kinds of fantastical sights, safe in the knowledge that they will never expect actually to see them. There is, therefore, a kind of humour inherent to this gap between the outlandish world of the comic imagination and the more prosaic realities of the ancient theatre. The more extravagant comedy's descriptive poetics, the more ludicrously obvious this gap becomes.

A long fragment of Pherecrates' *Miners* (fr. 113 PCG) preserved by Athenaeus (268d–269c) illustrates well this quality of Old Comic ekphrases.[83] Athenaeus groups the play with Cratinus' *Wealth-Gods*, Crates' *Wild Beasts*, and Teleclides' *Amphictyons*, which seem to be Golden Age plays in a similar vein.[84] The title, along with the indication in fragment 113 that the dead are enjoying the play's paradise (113.7: τοῖς νεκροῖς), suggests a plot in which a utopia is discovered by digging down into the underworld. The fragment's gentle humour derives from a simple act of substitution, in which features of the natural world are replaced with foodstuffs. This bizarre integration of food into the landscape seems something of a running joke in comic ekphrasis. A fragment of Cratinus' Golden Age play *Nomoi*, for example, sees the gods literally raining down food from the heavens, in a manner which perhaps might be seen as echoing the comic convention of throwing dried fruit and nuts to the audience:[85]

ὁ δὲ Ζεὺς ὀσταφίσιν ὕσει τάχα

Any moment now and Zeus will shower us with raisins.

Cratinus fr. 131 PCG

By humorously reimagining the condensation that settles on hot food as dew, a further fragment of this play even more explicitly makes food into a kind of feature of the natural landscape:

καὶ δρόσον βάλλων ἕωθεν χλιαρὸς ταγηνίας

A warm pancake giving out dawn's dew.

Cratinus fr. 130 PCG

Pherecrates in the *Miners* makes this into a more extended joke, and drives home the incongruities created through the comic *topos* of the edible landscape. The *Miners* sets its Golden Age landscape in the underworld, and Farioli has suggested (2001: 92–104) that Pherecrates may well have exploited the incongruity between the usual rather bleak picture of the afterlife in the Greek imagination and the play's utopian vision.[86] In the poet's underground utopia, rivers run with porridge and soup (fr. 113.3: ποταμοὶ μὲν ἀθάρης καὶ μέλανος ζωμοῦ πλέῳ);[87] the initial swap of liquid for liquid becomes more absurd when bread and cake are added into the mix (fr. 113.5: μυστίλαισι, καὶ ναστῶν τρύφη), and the rivers are described as 'running babbling through the straits with actual croutons' (fr. 113.3–5: ποταμοὶ ... / διὰ τῶν στενωπῶν τονθολυγοῦντες ἔρρεον / αὐταῖσι μυστίλαισι).[88] This humorous shift between liquid and solid also features later in the fragment, as the inhabitants of this Golden Age landscape are described as 'drinking down' (fr. 113.24: καταπιεῖν) the thrushes which fly around ready-roasted. Lines 8 to 9 bring a clever double meaning into play:

φύσκαι δὲ καὶ ζέοντες ἀλλάντων τόμοι
παρὰ τοῖς ποταμοῖς σίζοντ᾿ ἐκέχυτ᾿ ἀντ᾿ ὀστράκων.

And instead of shells, sausages and steaming slivers of blood pudding
were poured out sizzling on the riverbanks.

Pherecrates fr. 113.8–9 PCG

The word used here for shell, ὄστρακον, primarily means a potsherd, and this meaning is reanimated by its context within the description: we might well expect that a soup-river would shed fragments of soup-bowl in place of shells. However, Pherecrates' landscape defies even this playful joke-logic, as the pot-shells are in turn substituted for sausages, and the imagery retreats further and further into absurdity.

At one point, the fragment seems to hint jokingly at the ultimate non-existence of its fantastical landscape:

τὰ δὲ μῆλ᾿ ἐκρέματο, τὰ καλὰ τῶν καλῶν ἰδεῖν,
ὑπὲρ κεφαλῆς, ἐξ οὐδενὸς πεφυκότα.

And the loveliest of lovely apples hung
over their heads, blooming out of nothing.

Pherecrates fr. 113: 26–7 PCG

This image of apples appearing not on the ends of branches, but out of thin air is funny in and of itself. The description does, however, also seem to have a wry, knowing quality; much like Aristophanes' *Birds*, which, as we shall see later in this chapter, conjures its fictional world quite literally out of the ether,

Pherecrates here seems to nod to the physical unreality of comedy's magical landscapes, which, though they may appear almost before our eyes through description, never quite make their physical appearance on stage.

Aristophanes' *Seasons* seems similarly to play about with the gap between what is described and what is actually seen on stage. According to Cicero (*De Leg.* 2.37), the play satirized the introduction of foreign gods into Athens; however, little is otherwise known about the plot.[89] Fragment 581 sees a conversation in which an unidentified divine figure, perhaps one of the play's new gods, promises the city of Athens year-round plenty.[90] The fragment begins as follows:

Α: ὄψει δὲ χειμῶνος μέσου σικυούς, βότρυς, ὀπώραν,
στεφάνους ἴων Β: οἶμαι δὲ καὶ κονιορτὸν ἐκτυφλοῦντα.
Α: αὐτὸς δ' ἀνὴρ πλωλεῖ κίχλας, ἀπίους, σχαδόνας, ἐλάας,
πυόν, χόρια, χελιδόνας, τέττιγας, ἐμβρύεια.
ὑρίσους δ' ἴδοις ἂν νειφομένους σύκων ὁμοῦ τε μύρτων.

A: And in the middle of winter you'll see cucumbers, bunches of grapes, summer fruits, coronets of violets —
B: — and I suppose clouds of dust that will completely blind us.
A: And the same guy will sell thrushes and pears,
honeycomb and olives,
beestings, blood sausage, swallows, crickets, embryonic meat,
and you'll see snow-covered baskets of figs and myrtle berries.

Ar., fr. 581 PCG

While for those of us used to modern supermarkets selling strawberries in December these lines may appear insufficiently remarkable, for an agrarian society bound to the seasons, the promise of winter cucumbers is quite as fantastical as anything found in Pherecrates' underworld utopia. Bagordo identifies this fragment as most likely coming from the play's *agon*, with one of the play's new gods facing off against a traditional Olympian deity, and offering the human characters a better world under their watch (Bagordo 2020 ad loc.). If Bagordo is correct, then this fragment suggests that the argument of the *agon* also had a metapoetic inflection, as the second speaker's failure to embrace the play's new comic utopia is couched as a kind of refusal to believe in the fiction of its enactment on stage. The god's promises are repeatedly couched in the language of sight (581.1: ὄψει ... σικυούς, 'you will see ... cucumbers'; 581.5: ὑρίσους δ' ἴδοις, 'you will see baskets'), inviting the audience to visualize the fantasy world described. In turn, the interlocutor's scepticism is framed in terms of blindness. Not only does he flatly refuse to imagine the scene described to him, and so to participate in the fantasy, but he blots it out, summoning up a dust cloud to obscure its wonders. In his unwillingness to accept the presence of the imaginary, the speaker reveals the ultimate tenuousness of comic fantasy. If the listener refuses to play along, and to accept as manifest the fantastical world described, then it will simply fail to materialize, disappearing, as it were, into so much dust.

A fragment of Crates' *Wild Beasts* makes more of a game of the interplay between onstage description and offstage action, and, as so often, a pun is central to the humour. The plot of the *Wild Beasts* seems to have concerned a power grab by the beasts in question, and the play's subsequent Golden Age utopia apparently imposed vegetarianism upon the human characters.[91] The fragments suggest that, in common with many comic utopias, the play also had a strong element of automatism.[92] Fragment 16 is very much in this mode, as the speaker promises that there will no longer be any need for slaves, since the whole kitchen, from the utensils to the food itself, will operate of its own accord:

πρόσεισιν αὔθ' ἕκαστον
τῶν σκευαρίων, ὅταν καλῇ τις "παρατίθου, τράπεζα·
αὐτὴ παρασκεύαζε σαυτήν. μάττε θυλακίσκε.
ἔγχει κύαθε. ποῦ 'σθ' ἡ κύλιξ; διάνιζ' ἰοῦσα σαυτήν.
ἀνάβαινε μᾶζα. τὴν χύτραν χρῆν ἐξερᾶν τὰ τεῦτλα.
ἰχθύ βάδιζ'." "ἀλλ' οὐδέπω 'πὶ θάτερ' ὀπτός εἰμι."
"οὔκουν μεταστρέψας σεαυτὸν ἁλὶ πάσεις ἀλείφων;"

Why, every bit of equipment will come when you call! 'Come here, table, and lay yourself! Bread-basket, get kneading! Spoon, get pouring! Where's the wine-cup? Come here and wash yourself out. Come up here, barley-cake, the pot needs to start dishing out the beetroot. Step it up, fish!' 'But I'm not yet roasted on my other side.' 'Well then flip yourself and trickle over some oil and salt.'

Crates fr. 16.4–10 PCG

The fragment leans heavily into the language of physical presence. In addition to its numerous verbs of motion ('come here', 'come up', etc.; the walking fish is a particularly nice comic touch), the passage is littered with prepositions (16.4: πρόσεισιν, 16.5: παρατίθου, 16.6: παρασκεύαζε, 16.7 ἔγχει ... διάνιζ', 16.8: ἀνάβαινε ... ἐξερᾶν, 16.10: μεταστρέψας), which create an illusion of spatial presence in words. This language is accompanied by a pun: the word used for kitchen utensils (16.5: σκευαρίων) is also the technical term for theatrical props.[93] This lends the fragment a metatheatrical edge, as it jokingly suggests that the theatre's props may come to life and invade the stage. This metatheatrical reading, however, undercuts the promise of stage presence, as our attention is directed away from the world of the imaginary towards the more prosaic logistics of its dramatization. While the Greek theatre did have some clever special effects (and these are discussed in the next chapter), their possibilities did not extend to walking tables and self-washing cups. The joke therefore makes a contrast between comedy's almost limitless possibilities for the world it can describe, and the rather more limited possibilities for what can actually be brought on stage. As with the fragment of Aristophanes' *Seasons* which promises its audience wondrous sights never to be delivered, the pun here draws our attention to the gap between descriptions which always promise to bring a scene before our very eyes, and the reality in which it never truly appears. As a result, these comic ekphrases exploit the very same disjunct between language and perception, figuration and reality, which, as we saw in the Introduction, is a fundamental component of jokes; in turn, ekphrasis is positioned as an inherently ridiculous poetic undertaking.

Describing Cloud Cuckoo Land: Ekphrasis in Aristophanes' *Birds*

The Cloud Cuckoo Land of Aristophanes' *Birds* is surely the most famous example of a comic landscape constructed out of thin air. The transformation of the boundless sky into the walled city of Nephelokokkygia is notoriously effected through a pair of puns.[94] The opening of the *Birds* finds the hero and his companion going ἐς κόρακας (*Av.* 28, 'to the crows'; the phrase has roughly the same force as the English 'go to hell'), following a raven and a crow who seem to be leading them into the wilderness and towards the birds. This typically comic literalization is followed by a second crucial pun. When Peisetairos first has his idea to found a city in the clouds, he suggests that they simply turn the πόλος (celestial sphere) into a πόλις (city): a letter is swapped, and just like that the world is transformed.[95]

In addition to their role in the creation of the play's fictional world, puns are also central to its description. A series of choral songs towards the end of the play employs the language of far-off wonders to describe a parallel fantasy-Athens which, from the perspective of Nephelokokkygia, lies at the edges of the world.[96] Of the four vignettes, two are fairly broad in their humour. These parody the infamous Athenian mugger Orestes, who was perhaps something of an urban legend (*Av.* 1482–93),[97] and the philosopher Socrates (*Av.* 1553–64), by reconfiguring them as strange, pseudo-mythical figures instead of unremarkable daily nuisances. The other two are, by contrast, rather more granular in their humour, as they use a series of puns to describe the 'foreign' landscape of Attica. The first of these conjures up some fabulous botany in its description of the Cleonymus tree:

πολλὰ δὴ καὶ καινὰ καὶ θαυ-
μάστ' ἐπεπτόμεσθα καὶ
δεινὰ πράγματ' εἴδομεν.
ἔστι γὰρ δένδρον πεφυκὸς
ἔκτοπόν τι Καρδίας ἀ-
πωτέρω Κλεώνυμος,
χρήσιμον μὲν οὐδέν, ἀλ-
λως δὲ δειλὸν καὶ μέγα.
τοῦτο <τοῦ> μὲν ἦρος ἀεὶ
βλαστάνει καὶ συκοφαντεῖ,
τοῦ δὲ χειμῶνος πάλιν τὰς
ἀσπίδας φυλλορροεῖ.

We have winged our way
over many new and wondrous things,
and seen strange goings-on.
Beyond Kardia grows
a peculiar tree,
the Cleonymus,

good for nothing,
big but feeble,
in spring it buds with summonsfruit,
and in winter
drops its shieldleaves.

Ar., *Av.* 1470–81

Like the mugger Orestes, Cleonymus is something of a running joke in Aristophanes, supposedly for dropping his shield in the line of battle.[98] The passage is packed full of puns which splice together the botanical with the political, and the fantasy world with the real one. Καρδίας ἀπωτέρω (1474–5) may mean either 'far from Kardia' (a distant Greek colony in Thrace), or, since καρδία means the heart, 'far from courage'; the description δειλὸν καὶ μέγα (1476, 'big but feeble' in my translation above) plays on the more usual pairing of δεινὸν καὶ μέγα ('strange and great'); συκοφαντεῖ (1478, 'summonsfruit') alludes both to figs, which do indeed grow on trees, and to the practice of sycophancy (vexatious prosecution);[99] and the final punchline sees the tree shedding not leaves, but shields (1481; the verb φυλλορροεῖ means 'drops its leaves').[100] For the purposes of this discussion, however, the most interesting double meaning in the passage is the adjective ἔκτοπόν, which in line 1474 introduces the description of the Cleonymus tree. Used here to denote something foreign or strange, ἔκτοπος literally means 'out of place'. The word seems to hint knowingly at the play's ekphrastic game. Just like Nephelokokkygia itself, which is fashioned from nothing but air and words, the fantastical places described by the bird chorus are really no place at all.

Lines 1694–705 play a similar game, and punningly reimagine familiar place names as part of the play's fantastical landscape:

ἔστι δ᾽ ἐν Φάναισι πρὸς τῇ
Κλεψύδρᾳ πανοῦργον Ἐγ-
γλωττογαστόρων γένος,
οἳ θερίζουσίν τε καὶ σπεί-
ρουσι καὶ τρυγῶσι ταῖς γλώτ-
ταισι συκάζουσί τε·
βάρβαροι δ᾽ εἰσὶν γένους,
Γοργίαι τε καὶ Φίλιπποι.
κἀπὸ τῶν Ἐγγλωττογαστό-

ρων ἐκείνων τῶν φιλίππων
πανταχοῦ τῆς Ἀττικῆς ἡ
γλῶττα χωρὶς τέμνεται.

There is in Denuncia,
by the clock-springs,
a race of no-good tonguebellymen,
they reap and sow and gather
and pluck figs
with their tongues,
a barbarous race,
Gorgiases and Phillips,
and from these tonguebellyphillips,
everywhere in Attica,
they cut the tongue apart.

Ar., Av. 1694–705

The passage makes a play on the Chian harbour Phanae and the verb φαίνειν, meaning to denounce (1694: ἐν Φάναισι), and on the name of a fountain at the base of the Athenian acropolis, and the water clock used to time speeches in the lawcourts (1695: Κλεψύδρᾳ); it sets up another fig-pun (1699: συκάζουσί) through a more conventional metaphor where the reaping of profit is envisioned as the harvesting of crops and reimagines famous legal orators (1701: Γοργίαι τε καὶ Φίλιπποι) as grotesque monsters, all tongue and stomach, whose disgusting behaviour is offered up as an *aition* for the Athenian practice of cutting out the tongue separately as part of animal sacrifice.[101]

The passage's conclusion lands us squarely in Attica (1704: τῆς Ἀττικῆς), driving home the fact, should it have escaped us thus far, that the fantastical world evoked by the chorus is simply Athens viewed through a distorting lens. By mapping the play's 'reported space' onto the space inhabited by the audience, the bird chorus' imagined landscape takes on a physical presence; and so, in another of the *Birds*' typically literalizing moves, the wonders which in comedy always exist just offstage and out of sight are located in the actual offstage space. However, this physical presence turns out to be just as illusory as any of comedy's ekphrases; by co-opting even the real world into the play's fantastical unreality, the *Birds* asks the audience to reflect on the process of fictionalization, and casts the act of poetic description as a kind of distorted misrepresentation which turns even the most apparently real and tangible into something ultimately false.

The falsehood of the *Birds*' descriptive poetics is actually made explicit earlier in the play, in a sequence which (like the Cleonymus tree, above) emphasizes the underlying placelessness of comedy's imagined landscapes. As part of his creation of the birds' city in the sky, Peisetairos instructs the chorus to encircle it with a ginormous wall. According to Peisetairos, this wall in the air is to be made from solid bricks (πλίνθοις), giving the structure a simultaneous feeling of substance and of impossibility, since the practicalities of locating a brick wall on thin air are, at the very least, somewhat challenging.

> καὶ δὴ τοίνυν πρῶτα διδάσκω μίαν ὀρνίθων πόλιν εἶναι,
> κἄπειτα τὸν ἀέρα πάντα κύκλῳ καὶ πᾶν τουτὶ τὸ μεταξὺ
> περιτειχίζειν μεγάλαις πλίνθοις ὀπταῖς ὥσπερ Βαβυλῶνα.

> Well then first of all I instruct you to build one bird city,
> and to wall round the whole of the air and everything in between
> in a circle with huge, oven-baked bricks, just like they have in Babylon.
>
> Ar., *Av.* 550-2

The description of the bricks as ὀπταῖς (baked) might almost be a pun. The adjective sounds like it could be derived from the verb ὁράω, which would give it a meaning something like 'visible',[102] a funny description for an air-wall which, of course, will be completely invisible to the audience, constructed entirely offstage and out of sight. This (possible) hint at the wall's unreality becomes rather more concrete when its construction is related to Peisetairos by a messenger (Ar., *Av.* 1122-63). The messenger's description is met by Peisetairos with increasing scepticism. The rather improbable measurement of 100 fathoms (1131: ἑκατοντορόγυιον, equivalent to roughly 200m) elicits some surprise:

> ὦ Πόσειδον, τοῦ μάκρους.
> τίνες ᾠκοδόμησαν αὐτὸ τηλικουτονί;

> By Poseidon, that's bloody big!
> Who built such a thing?
>
> Ar., *Av.* 1131-2

To the messenger's account (*Av.* 1133-63) of cranes carrying stones, crakes doing the chiselling, storks making bricks, geese using their feet as spades, and pelicans their beaks for the woodwork, Peisetairos responds with a series of incredulous questions, with each answer from the messenger seeming only to raise still further questions (e.g. 1141–2: 'Ok, but who carried the mortar?', 'The herons, in buckets.' 'Ok, but how could they get it in the buckets?').

On the messenger's departure, the chorus apparently sense Peisetairos' scepticism and ask him, 'well, what do you make of it? Aren't you amazed?' (1164: οὗτος, τί ποιεῖς; ἆρα θαυμάζεις). Peisetairos replies as follows:

νὴ τοὺς θεοὺς ἔγωγε· καὶ γὰρ ἄξιον·
ἴσα γὰρ ἀληθῶς φαίνεταί μοι ψεύδεσιν.

I am, by god, and justly so!
In truth, it seems to me to be a lie.

Ar., Av. 1166–7

This wink towards the wall's unreality hints in turn at the ultimate falseness of the *Birds*' entire ekphrastic edifice. Indeed, one interloper in birdland seemingly fails to encounter the structures that Peisetairos and co. have so carefully constructed in words. No sooner has the first messenger brought news of the completed birdwall, but a second arrives to inform Peisetairos that it has already been breached (*Av.* 1171–4), and the goddess Iris swoops into view (1199). Iris immediately pronounces the whole business of Peisetairos' bird-state to be ἄτοπος (1208: ἄτοπόν γε τουτὶ πρᾶγμα. Cf. 1471 ἔκτοπόν, discussed above), a word which in this context means 'strange' or 'extraordinary', but whose primary meaning as 'lacking place' is surely a nod at the non-spatial qualities of Nephelokokkygia. When Peisetairos interrogates her about how she managed to penetrate the city's defences, she seems to have no idea what he's talking about, and even goes so far as to question whether he is quite right in the head (1210: οὐκ οἶδα μὰ Δί' ἔγωγε κατὰ ποίας πύλας, 'Good god, I don't know which gate'; 1213: τί τὸ κακόν; 'What is this nonsense?', 1214: ὑγιαίνεις μέν; 'are you quite well?'). Much like the fragment of Aristophanes' *Seasons* discussed above, this exchange appears to interrogate the role of audience co-operation in marking out the thin line between real and unreal in the poetic imagination. For all that a poet may conjure up new and extraordinary worlds in words, all it takes is for the listener to refuse to believe in their reality and the entire edifice crumbles. Peisetairos' accusations of falsehood (1167: ἴσα γὰρ ἀληθῶς φαίνεταί μοι ψεύδεσιν) seem to get to the heart of comedy's ambivalent relationship with poetic invention. Peisetairos is himself the architect of the *Birds'* fantastic city in the sky, and yet here he is, wryly joking about the unreality of his own creation.[103] In this way, he stands analogous to the comic poets who similarly build an imaginary world only to playfully deconstruct its foundations.

Conclusions

As Peisetairos takes on the gods, so too do our comic poets have a rather higher target in mind as they joke about the absurdities and unrealities of their own literary language. As we have seen throughout this chapter, the conventions which are often the butt of comedy's poetic playfulness are not purely comic, but are rather those which it shares with more serious literary genres, and which are central not only to comic poetry, but to poetry full stop. By playing about with two of the most fundamental tropes of poetic language, metaphor and ekphrasis, comic poets display a marked ambition to reach beyond their own generic boundaries and comment on the mechanics of serious poetic convention.

Ambition is, however, not the sole reason for comedy's sustained interest in these particular tropes. Both metaphor and ekphrasis have in common a specifically visual quality. Whether by describing, or by embellishing that description, ekphrasis and metaphor aim to bring the poetic world to life, and to set it 'before the eyes' of the listener (cf. Arist., *Rh.* 1411a: καὶ τοῦτο τρόπον τινὰ μεταφορὰ καὶ πρὸ ὀμμάτων. Theon *Progymnasmata* 118, 1.7: ἔκφρασις ἔστι λόγος περιηγηματικὸς ἐναργῶς ὑπ' ὄψιν ἄγων τὸ δηλούμενον). As such, they hold particularly attractive possibilities for a dramatic genre such as comedy, and the comic poets are clearly alert to these tropes' suggestive interplay between the verbal and the visual. The presentation in comedy of language as a visual force is, however, not exactly uncomplicated. Comedy quite literally takes place before the eyes of its audience. And yet, as we have seen, it simultaneously plays about with its own lack of materiality, forever placing its most ambitious imaginings offstage and out of sight in ekphrases which promise wonderment and spectacle, but never quite deliver on the latter. The gap hinted at here between comedy's apparently limitless imagination, and the more prosaic realities of theatrical representation, comes in for more overt scrutiny when it is not just poetic, but specifically dramatic convention at issue. As we shall see in the coming chapter, jokes about costume and staging abound, and it is precisely this disjunct between performance and imagination which often gives these jokes their comic force.

A similarly equivocal relationship to the representational qualities of language is also characteristic of comic metaphors. Like the comic landscapes which make a joke of their non-presence and spatial un-reality, metaphors in comedy often revel in obscurity. Where comic ekphrasis is wry and knowing, metaphors are more overtly joke-like. As we have seen, while puns often lurk at the edges of comedy's descriptive passages, they are structurally integral to its metaphors. Time and again, comedy exploits the potential slippage between metaphors and jokes to uncover the absurdity which underlies even the most commonplace of literary comparisons.

Comedy's play with literary language ultimately grapples with the nature of poetic mimesis. By joking around with the conventional tools of 'serious' poetry, tropes such as metaphor and ekphrasis are absorbed into the genre's own absurd aesthetics. In turn, we are asked to see these tropes as fundamentally ridiculous even in their apparently 'serious' manifestations. More than this, by embedding these poetic figures in its jokes and wordplay, which by nature are more concerned with the fun that can be had with signifiers over and above their actual role in signification, comedy probes their representational value, and asks us to consider (momentarily, at least) whether 'serious' poetry too is more concerned with language's form than its function.

As comedy plays about with the building blocks of poetic language, it ultimately asserts its own contiguity with 'serious' poetry. Comedy's approach to metaphor and ekphrasis demonstrates a sustained concern with how these foundational poetic tropes may be affiliated to jokes as modes of non-normative speech grounded in incongruity. Each to some degree prioritizes linguistic form over and above straightforward communication; each exploits the potential ambiguities and multiplicities of language, and is subject to a high degree of interpretative openness; and each in different ways is attentive to the gap between the world and our ability to represent it in thought and word. However, where 'serious' poetic language, in its attempts to place an imagined reality 'before the eyes' of the listener, strives to bridge this gap, jokes are determined to magnify it. In sum, jokes are not merely an embellishment to comedy's metaphors and ekphrases, but structurally integral to them, as the genre sets about illustrating the ultimate convergence between these forms.

2

Playing with Theatre: Jokes and Dramatic Performance

In an episode of the third series of the British television comedy *Blackadder*, the absurdly stupid Prince Regent is accompanied by his head butler, Blackadder, to the theatre.[1] No sooner has the prince got to grips with the fact that the action of the play is 'just pretend' than a would-be assassin invades the stage and throws a crude incendiary device into the audience. 'It's not a play anymore, sir. Put the bomb down and make your way quietly to the exit', Blackadder explains to his exasperating charge.

This is, of course, all very silly. Hidden in this silliness, however, is a serious, or at least quasi-serious, point about the inherent absurdity of theatrical make-believe. The prince is clearly ridiculous. The action on stage is utterly non-naturalistic (the actors over-emote; the onstage stabbing is frankly farcical; the whole endeavour is, in sum, ludicrous), and yet the prince is completely unable to distinguish between reality and this hyper-stylized theatrical code. In taking the action seriously as if it were real, he reacts in entirely the 'wrong' way. The scene seems to suggest, however, that the audience reacting in the 'right' way are more ridiculous still: they might not, like the stupid prince, shout 'He's behind you!' when Brutus approaches to stab Caesar, but they nevertheless treat the theatre's game of 'let's pretend' as if it were a quite serious enterprise.

Old Comedy is similarly preoccupied with the earnestness with which audiences approach the theatre's act of make-believe. The genre's fixation with 'serious' theatre has been thoroughly explored by Matthew Farmer (among others),[2] who argues that comedy displays a kind of 'culture of tragedy', in which the rival genre is a constant topic of both interest and critique, and comedy's parallel impulse towards revealing its own theatrical workings has been set out in most detail by Niall Slater (2002).[3] Scholarship on this topic has, however, had its own tendency towards earnestness, and both metatheatre and paratragedy are often conceived as having at the very least a political edge.[4] This chapter, in its focus on jokes, attempts to sidestep such seriousness in favour of a greater emphasis on the playfulness with which comedy dismantles its dramatic illusion.[5] As in the previous chapter, however, this interest in jokes is not merely an aesthetic preference for the funny over the serious. At heart, it seeks to contest that comedy's interest in dramatic representation does not exist only in those moments of explicit metatheatrical or paratragic discourse (an address to the audience; a play within a play), but is embedded in the genre's comic texture, playing out at the level of the word, the joke, the pun.

Puns will be a particular focus of this chapter. In the context of a genre which is constantly acknowledging its own artifice, puns offer a unique opportunity through their own inherent doubleness. As we saw in the Introduction, jokes in general, and puns in particular, rely on superimposing two oppositional fields of reference onto one another. According to the script-based model developed by Raskin, and refined by Oring, the comic force of puns derives from the clash between their two incompatible domains, which are (by means of a linking device) made fleetingly to co-exist. To return briefly to Oring's example, the joke, 'Q: Why should you wear a watch in the desert? A: Because a watch has springs', is based on an incongruity between the scripts DESERT and WATCH, with the double meaning of 'spring' as both a body of water and a mechanical device providing the linking mechanism through which the two scripts are made temporarily 'appropriate' to one another (Oring 1992: ch. 1). It is precisely this co-existence of two incongruous, even oppositional,[6] ideas that makes the pun such a productive tool for comedy, which is, as a genre, forever determined to prise apart the relationship between the fictional world and its representation on stage.

The first part of this chapter will look at the puns which cluster around non-human characters in comedy. The comic stage was graced by actors playing fish, insects, islands and cities, as well as even more abstract entities like music, harvest time and of course the famous good and bad arguments of Aristophanes' *Clouds*. Such characters are one of the most conspicuously fantastical – one might say anti-realist – conventions of the comic stage, and this, combined with their obvious visual absurdity, makes them something of a lightning rod for the metatheatrical exposure of dramatic make-believe. In sum, there seems to be both an inherent playfulness and an inherent metatheatricality to the kind of overt play-acting involved in putting non-human characters on stage. It is therefore not surprising to find that such characters attract an unusually high concentration of puns. These puns often rely on a collision between two scripts, one consistent with the character's fictional identity, and the other relating to a specifically human field of reference. As such, these puns allow characters to occupy a dual identity, at once embodying their fictional role whilst also acknowledging the presence of the human body of the actor which lies underneath.

Puns therefore prise open the representational fault line between the fantastical world of the play and its enactment within the 'real' performance space of the theatre. In comedy, the fictional world and the acknowledgement of fictionality are in constant tension, with one never getting the better of the other.[7] This sense of parallelism, in which the metatheatrical acknowledgement of fictionality is not so much a breach of the play's illusion as an integral part of it, mirrors the mechanism of the pun, which likewise allows us to superimpose two apparently mutually exclusive fields of reference, with neither one eclipsing the other. As comedy plays about with the relationship between representation and represented, puns embed this doubleness into the fabric of the genre itself.

Perhaps most crucially, the kind of representational doubleness suggested by comic puns models a very specifically comic kind of metatheatricality. The second part of this chapter will move on to discuss some of the more overt jokes about staging and dramatic representation in Old Comedy. The discussion will focus primarily on jokes which poke fun at devices such as the *ekkyklema* and *mechane*. As with non-human characters, stage technology represents one of the more fantastical tendencies of Greek drama, and these jokes draw attention to the absurdity of presenting such devices as an augmentation of dramatic realism. The jokes often turn on a key difference between comic and tragic stagecraft. Tragedy is presented as a kind of theatre in which the fictional world and its representation on stage exist in an almost hostile opposition to one another: to acknowledge the latter is to undermine the former. By contrast, like the pun which briefly places two oppositional forces in balance, in comedy the fictional world and an acknowledgement of its fictionality may co-exist. These jokes about stagecraft share with the puns discussed in the chapter's first half an insistence on the fictional world's rootedness in the physical and spatial reality of the stage. The puns which accompany non-human characters in comedy frequently draw attention to the presence of the human body as the fundamental building block of drama, and to the consequent physical co-existence of the 'real' world within the fictional dramatic space. Similarly, jokes about stagecraft suggest that in embracing the physical realities of stagecraft, dodgy special effects and all, comedy can make the sheer ridiculousness of theatrical make-believe part of its fictional (hyper-)reality.

Like the scene from *Blackadder* with which we began, Old Comedy is out to present the whole business of dramatic representation as ridiculous. We can take it seriously the 'wrong' way (in the manner of the stupid prince) by mistaking fiction for real life; or (like the rest of the audience) we can take it seriously the 'right' way, and act as if the absurdities of the theatre are in fact deeply affecting high art. Better still, we can refuse to take it seriously at all, and treat the theatre for what it is: a highly silly, if entertaining, piece of make-believe. By allowing the audience to laugh at theatricality itself, comedy ensures that the joke is not, ultimately, on them.

Metatheatrical jokes in comedy are, however, more than just a takedown of serious dramatic convention. As in its approach to poetic language, comedy's use of puns as a mode of metatheatre forms part of its assertion of the structural convergence between jokes and 'serious' fictional representation. In presenting drama as a form of poetry grounded, like jokes, in incongruous doubleness, comedy offers us a new way of understanding the theatre. More than this, it positions jokes as a critical tool in and of themselves which allow us to see with new clarity the mechanisms of poetic and dramatic representation which more 'serious' theatre (in comedy's telling, at least) invites us to overlook.

Non-human characters in Old Comedy: Archippus and the problems of fish with feet

Archippus' *Fishes* premiered in the final years of the fifth century.[8] Although comparatively little of this play remains, it seems that, like Aristophanes' *Birds* and Crates' *Wild Beasts*, the plot revolved around some kind of animal rebellion.[9] The twenty or so[10] fragments which survive from the play suggest that the titular fishes either took over human society, or set up some kind of parallel version of their own.[11] In fragments 15, 17 and 18 PCG the fishes appear to practise some form of religion;[12] fragment 16 sees them aping the procedures of the Athenian democracy; and fragment 28 suggests the fishes even demanded revenge against those who had previously consumed them.[13] Archippus apparently had something of a reputation for his comic wordplay, and the fragments of the *Fishes* are indeed packed with (at times truly terrible) puns.[14] The jokes often rely on a collision between two fields of reference, one fish-based, and the other human, as the 'gentlemen fish' (fr. 30: ἄνδρες ἰχθύες) slip between these two identities. Quite a bit of humour is derived from puns on fish names which sound like human professions, as for example in fragment 15:

A: τί λέγεις σύ; μάντεις εἰσί γὰρ θαλάττιοι;
B: γαλεοί γε, πάντων μάντεων σοφώτατοι

A: What's that you say? There are soothsayers in the sea?
B: Why yes, dogfish, the wisest of all soothsayers.[15]

Archippus fr. 15 PCG

This is, of course, not much of a pun in its English translation. The joke in Greek relies on a similarity between the noun γαλεός (dogfish)[16] and a Sicilian clan of soothsayers, the Galeotai.[17] However, even in Greek, the pun is fairly terrible, the kind of joke which we in English might designate a 'groaner', and which the Greeks called ψυχρός ('frigid'),[18] since the linking device between the two fields of reference is not a true double meaning, but just two words which sound a little bit alike, making the mapping between the two scripts rather forced and unnatural.

Although the primary pun in this line is not a true double meaning, there are some extra potential double meanings packed into the peripheries of this joke. Like the metaphor-puns which we saw in the last chapter, in which authors like Cratinus pile up multiple meanings to the point of near imagistic incoherence, the noun Γαλεῶται which the listener must supply from the similar γαλεοί in order to make Archippus' pun make sense has a series of additional zoological resonances. The soothsaying family of Galeotai were in fact named after a kind of spotted lizard (γαλεώτης),[19] and, as was common in Greek,[20] this land animal name served a double purpose as a fish name, in this case designating the swordfish (Thompson 1947: 43). These triple and even quadruple meanings therefore lurk at the edges of this joke, further adding to the awkwardness of the pun, and making it more difficult for the listener to process.

Fragment 16 plays a similar punning game, and deploys fish names which also have resonances within a more human field of reference. The fragment mimics the procedures of a formal proclamation in Athens, suggesting that in the play the fish either took over the Athenian democracy or set up a version of their own:

> ἐκήρυξεν βόαξ,
> σάλπης δ' ἐσάλπιγξ' ἔπτ' ὀβόλους μισθὸν φέρων

> The grunting-fish made the announcement and the saupe-fish sounded the trumpet taking a fee of seven obols.

Archippus fr. 16 PCG

Again, the puns are fairly weak, deploying words which almost sound alike in place of true double meanings. There is a play between the name of the grunting-fish (βόαξ) and the verb βοάω ('I shout or proclaim'), and between σάλπη (a close relation of the sea bream) and the verb σαλπίζω ('I sound the trumpet'). The emphasis on sound here is notable. Unlike choruses of warbling birds (Ar., *Av.*) or ribbitting frogs (Ar., *Ran.*), both of which animals have strong associations with song,[21] or even buzzing insects (Ar., *Vesp.*) or bleating nanny goats (Eup., *Aiges*), which, while they lack such specific musical associations, do at least make a clear sound, fish (with some very few notable exceptions such as the grunt fish) are entirely mute. While Archippus' *Fishes* is not the only play to feature a singing chorus of songless animals,[22] the active emphasis on the fish characters' sound here is jarring, and raises questions of the suitability of such mute animals for choral song.

As in fragment 15, the puns in fragment 16 act as a kind of gateway for the fish to slip into a new, human-like identity. This instability of identity seems to spread outwards from the play's fish characters to the fictional world's human inhabitants. Fragment 14 labels human political leaders as παλιναίρετος, a term which may refer both to politicians removed from office and subsequently re-elected, and to fish released only to be caught a second time (Storey 2012: 8). In a reversal of fragments 15 and 16, fragments 19, 25 and 27 seem to use names of *hetairai* which might also refer to fish. Just as fish names with potential resonances within the human world were exploited to allow the fish characters of the play to adopt human roles, the fishy names of the *hetairai* in these fragments lead them to be claimed as property of the sea, as the fish appear to accede to their 'return' as part of a peace treaty with the Athenians.[23] Farioli points out in her discussion of these fragments that, just like in Aristophanes' *Birds* (*Av.* 667–74), where Peisetairos ogles the nightingale Procne, difference in species need not have precluded sexual attraction, and indeed it is difficult to see how the transfer of the *hetairai* could have played out without this element (Farioli 2001: 173). As the fish-men directed their gaze on the women's bodies, their own (potentially phallic?)[24] physicality may well have been spotlighted in turn, leading to a comic interplay between the characters' two incongruous identities as the audience's attention is drawn to the conspicuously human bodies behind the actors' fish costumes.

To this end, it is worth taking a moment to consider what the figures delivering Archippus' awkward puns might actually have looked like. Even more than mammals and birds, fish costumes are tricky. We share relatively few physical characteristics with fish, and fundamentally, having an actor with arms and legs play any animal without them is going to cause costuming difficulties. These difficulties are even more pronounced when you need your fish chorus to dance: the more your costume disguises the actor's limbs, the harder this becomes, and it would inevitably have been challenging to find a balance between the visual and the practical.[25] However you try to solve it, the human body of the actor is going to make its presence felt.

When we consider them in tandem with the play's costumes, the 'frigidness' of Archippus' puns begins to seem not so much a failure of poetic power as a literary and dramatic device in itself. The fragments of Archippus' *Fishes* seem almost to trumpet the fact that they are shoehorning the puns in, as they rely not so much on true double meanings as on words which almost, but not completely, sound alike. The sheer groan-inducing awfulness of these puns works to confront us with the incompatibility of our two fields of reference; and when we combine this with a costume which is similarly forced and unnatural (our fish-with-feet), we are in turn confronted with the uncomfortable doubleness of the figures on stage in front of us, whose fish characters and costumes surely cannot disguise the all-too-human bodies underneath. In the *Fishes*, the fictional world and the reality of its performance appear at best to share a kind of uneasy co-existence within the physical space of the stage. In this way, the clash between fiction and reality becomes an active part of the play's comic aesthetics, with bad puns playing a central role.

The pig-girls of Aristophanes' *Acharnians*

While the bad puns of Archippus' *Fishes* work to draw attention to the clash between the characters' fictional identity as fishes and the human identity of the actors playing them, many of the puns which accompany non-human characters in Old Comedy are more direct in their focus on the actor's physical body. This is particularly true when the character is female. In contrast to the majority of animal choruses, which seem to have a default male identity,[26] a punning set-piece in Aristophanes' *Acharnians* brings on stage two pig-girls. After securing his own personal peace treaty with the Spartans, Dicaeopolis sets up a private marketplace in which to trade with those hostile cities whose goods had previously been barred from Athens under the Megarian decree.[27] The first visitor is a Megarian merchant, who tries to pass his daughters off as a pair of piglets in order to sell them to Dicaeopolis:

> ἀλλ' ἔστι γάρ μοι Μεγαρικά τις μαχανά,
> χοίρους γὰρ ὑμὲ σκευάσας φασῶ φέρειν.
> περίθεσθε τάσδε τὰς ὁπλὰς τῶν χοιρία.
> ὅπως δὲ δοξεῖτ' ἦμεν ἐξ ἀγαθᾶς ὑός·
> ὡς ναὶ τὸν Ἑρμᾶν, αἴπερ ἰξεῖτ' οἴκαδις
> ἄπρατα, πειρασεῖσθε τᾶς λιμοῦ κακῶς.
> ἀλλ' ἀμφίθεσθε καὶ ταδὶ τὰ ῥυγχία,
> κἤπειτεν ἐς τὸν σάκκον ὧδ' ἐσβαίνετε.
> ὅπως δὲ γρυλιξεῖτε καὶ κοΐξετε
> χἠσεῖτε φωνὰν χοιρίων μυστηρικῶν.[28]

> But I know a Megarian trick,
> I'll fit you out with piggy props:
> put on these piggy-hooves,
> you must appear good sows,
> or by Hermes, when you come home,
> you will perish most terribly from hunger.

> Fix these snoutlets on,
> and get in this sack,
> grunt and squeak piggylike,
> and make the sound of the Mystery-pigs.
>
> Ar., *Ach.* 738–47

As the Megarian trader costumes his daughters on stage, and instructs them on how best to perform their roles, the very fact of humans pretending to be animals is configured as a kind of play-acting, and an unconvincing kind at that (since, as Compton-Engle has demonstrated in her analysis of this scene, Dicaeopolis is repeatedly shown seeing through their disguise).[29]

The scene's metatheatrical focus on the performance of comic animal roles is accompanied by a series of obscene puns which work to focus the audience's attention on the clash between the pseudo-animal characters on stage and the human bodies of the actors playing them. The daughters' dual pig-girl identity itself derives from a crude play on the double meaning of the word χοῖρος as both 'piglet' and a slang term for the female genitalia (possibly with particular reference to young girls),[30] and the scene as a whole therefore reads simultaneously as marketplace transaction and sexual procurement. The reified χοῖρος pun gets its punchline at lines 781–2, when Dicaeopolis, still not convinced by the girls' disguise, despite the Megarian's insistence, jokes:

> νῦν γε χοῖρος φαίνεται.
> ἀτὰρ ἐκτραφείς γε κύσθος ἔσται.
>
> They might be piglets now,
> But they'll grow up into right cunts.
>
> Ar., *Ach.* 781–2

Sex organs are a continuing visual presence as the scene progresses. Dicaeopolis quizzes the pig-girls about their diet, asking, 'do you munch down on chickpeas ... and figs?' (801: τρώγοις ἂν ἐρεβίνθους; 802: ἰσχάδας), both of which foodstuffs are well attested as phallic euphemisms (cf. Henderson 1991: 117–19).

The collision between the human and animal is increased by the sheer obscenity of the joke. The word κύσθος seems to belong to the strongest class of obscenity in Greek: it appears only very infrequently even in Old Comedy, with only four secure attestations,[31] and although women in comedy are usually no strangers to bad language, there is also no attested usage by a female speaker.³² This is a truly shocking word, one which actively confronts us with the human anatomy, thereby increasing the sense of incongruity between human and animal (Henderson 1991: 130). This series of sexual puns, in addition to the element of disguise and role playing in this scene, therefore construes the presentation of these non-human characters on stage as explicitly and inherently metatheatrical: it becomes a kind of performance, which the audience, like Dicaeopolis, simply cannot fail to see right through. The punchline to the piglet pun makes a confrontation with the human body simply inescapable. In turn, the body becomes a site of representational contestation, and the jokes' double meanings act as an analogy for the doubleness inherent in all theatrical performance.

Playing about with abstraction: The body on stage in Old Comedy

Puns in the comic fragments in fact frequently draw attention to the presence of the human body as the fundamental building block of drama, and to the consequent physical co-existence of the 'real' world within the fictional dramatic space. This confrontation with the human body seems to be a particular feature of scenes which employ abstract non-human characters. With these kinds of characters there is the potential for an even greater disjunct between the character (which is abstract) and the body of the actor playing them (which is unavoidably concrete), and therefore an even greater potential for the exposure of this act of fictionality. As ever, the playwrights of Old Comedy are keen to punningly exploit this disjunct between representation and represented, (fictional) idea and (staged) reality.

As studies by Hall (2000) and Kidd (2014: 77–83) have shown, personified abstractions in Old Comedy seem almost always to have female bodies, with the inevitable result that any increased emphasis on these bodies is often highly sexualized in tone.³³ The entrance of the chorus of Eupolis' *Cities* deploys puns to this effect, drawing the audience's gaze onto the city-women's bodies, and prising open the mimetic gap between their abstract identity and the physical reality of the actors' bodies within the stage space. The fragments suggest an individuated chorus,³⁴ as for example in Aristophanes' *Birds* (267–304),³⁵ but with a slightly more lengthy introduction for each chorus member as they take the stage.³⁶ Fragment 244, for example, sees an unknown character enquire of one city as follows:

πεφυτευμένη δ' αὕτη 'στὶν, ἢ ψιλὴ μόνον;

Is she planted up, or bare land?

Eup., fr. 244 PCG

The pun here turns primarily on the adjective ψιλός, which can refer either to agricultural landscape, or to body hair (presumably in this case to pubic hair).³⁷ This sexualized field of reference also retrospectively casts the verb φυτεύω in a new light. The word means 'to plant', and can therefore be read as simply playing off the hair-as-plants metaphor activated by ψιλός. However, the verb may also mean 'to beget children'. A more apt English translation in this context might perhaps be, 'Has she been seeded?', as the interlocutor enquires not only as to the state of the woman's body hair, but as to her virginity (i.e. plant seed versus human seed) and perhaps also her sexual productivity (i.e. is she barren, or has she proved herself fertile?), thereby mapping sexual and agrarian fertility onto one another.

Fragment 247 draws the audience's gaze towards the cities' human bodies to an even greater degree:

A: ἡ δ' ὑστάτη ποῦ 'σθ';
B: ἥδε Κύζικος πλέα στατήρων.
A: ἐν τῇδε τοίνυν τῇ πόλει φρουρῶν <ἐγώ> ποτ' αὐτὸς
    γυναῖκ' ἐκίνουν κολλύβου καὶ παῖδα καὶ γέροντα,
    κἀξῆν ὅλην τὴν ἡμέραν τὸν κύσθον ἐκκορίζειν.³⁸

A: Where's the last one?
B: She is Cyzicus, full of staters,
A: Ah yes, keeping watch in that city I screwed a woman, a boy, and an old man for an obol. I could have spent the whole day unclogging its cunt.

Eup., fr. 247 PCG

The collision between the abstract and concrete in this fragment is facilitated by the potential sexual resonances of the verb φρουρέω, meaning 'I keep watch or guard', but which is often used specifically of an occupying force, and which therefore construes the act of sexual congress as an assault on the woman's body, with the male speaker literally taking up space within her.[39] As with the *Acharnians*' pig-girls, the sheer obscenity of the word κύσθος actively confronts us with the human anatomy, thereby increasing the sense of collision, as the human bodies beneath the chorus' costumes become shockingly present for the audience.

In common with Archippus' *Fishes*, the chorus of *Cities* raises difficult issues of costuming, which have often been downplayed by the scholarship on this play.[40] Both A. M. Wilson (1977: 282) and Compton-Engle (2015: 125) suggest that the fragments may offer some clues as to some of the cities' costumes, so 'Cyzicus full of staters' (fr. 247 PCG), 'Tenos with many scorpions' (fr. 245 PCG),[41] and 'Chios who sends you ships' (fr. 246 PCG) might each bear these respective attributes as a symbolic totem of their identity.[42] We should not, however, underestimate the level of abstraction at play in such a visual presentation as this. Despite the 'fish with feet' issues of Archippus' play, we can imagine that the chorus did at least in some ways look like fish, costumed with fish masks, fins, and perhaps a bodysuit painted with scales.[43] An actor kitted out with some symbolic scorpions does not in any way resemble a city; even an actor wearing a mask (or perhaps a hat) decorated with buildings (to make only one possible suggestion) does not really look like a city in any meaningful sense. The difference in size alone is a stumbling block, and one which fragment 247, with its imagery of military occupation, arguably draws attention to (since even the most lurid of imaginations surely cannot conceive of an entire army 'stationed inside' a single person all at once). It is perhaps not without cause that the individuated chorus of the *Cities* is introduced at such apparent length, since the audience would most likely be unable to identify them on the basis of their costumes alone. Even more than the fish of Archippus' play, these kinds of abstract characters really strain the limits of dramatic mimesis; but rather than asking the audience to ignore the gap between the fictional world and its representation, the plays make a feature of it, juxtaposing the abstraction of costume with a corporeal physicality which encourages us to acknowledge how the actor's body takes up space on stage, with puns acting as a gateway between these two oppositional forces.

Puns which construe the female body as a space to be occupied and conquered are also a feature of two of Aristophanes' abstract personifications.

The closing scenes of the *Lysistrata*, in which Reconciliation is brought on stage in the form of a naked woman (Ar., *Lys.* 1114),[44] operates in an almost identical manner to Eupolis' *Cities*, deploying similar agricultural puns (Ar., *Lys.* 1173: ἤδη γεωργεῖν γυμνὸς ἀποδὺς βούλομαι, 'I want to strip off naked and get down to ploughing!'), and again using the obscene κύσθος to create a clash between the physicality of the human body and the abstraction of the character embodied by the actor.[45] The puns in both *Cities* and *Lysistrata* are, however, thoroughly capped by a passage in the *Peace*, whose puns are some of the most virtuosic in all extant Greek comedy. After returning from Olympus, where he has rescued the goddess Peace, our hero Trygaeus hands over one of her two attendants, Theoria ('Spectatorship'; the word has particular associations with the theatre and athletic festivals), to the Council:

ἔπειτ᾽ ἀγῶνά γ᾽ εὐθὺς ἐξέσται ποιεῖν
ταύτην ἔχουσιν αὔριον καλὸν πάνυ,
ἐπὶ γῆς παλαίειν, τετραποδηδὸν ἱστάναι,[46]
καὶ παγκράτιόν γ᾽ ὑπαλειψαμένοις νεανικῶς
παίειν, ὀρύττειν, πὺξ ὁμοῦ καὶ τῷ πέει·
τρίτῃ δὲ μετὰ ταῦθ᾽ ἱπποδρομίαν ἄξετε,
ἵνα δὴ κέλης κέλητα παρακελητιεῖ,
ἅρματα δ᾽ ἐπ᾽ ἀλλήλοισιν ἀνατετραμμένα
φυσῶντα καὶ πνέοντα προσκινήσεται·
ἕτεροι δὲ κείσονταί γ᾽ ἀπεψωλημένοι
περὶ ταῖσι καμπαῖς ἡνίοχοι πεπτωκότες.
ἀλλ᾽, ὦ πρυτάνεις, δέχεσθε τὴν Θεωρίαν.
θέασ᾽ ὡς προθύμως ὁ πρύτανις παρεδέξατο.

Right then, now they've got her we can have a first-rate tournament right away tomorrow, wrestle on the ground, get her on all fours, and the guys oiled up for the *pankration* can hit that, dig at her eagerly with fist and cock, and the day after that you can hold the horse races, rider will ride past rider, chariots overturning one another, they'll thrust forward, huffing and puffing; the other drivers will lie on top with their cocks skinned as they attack the curves. Here, Prytaneis, take Theoria. Look at that, how eagerly the Prytaneis took her from me!

Ar., *Pax* 894–906

This highly complex passage (described rather coyly by one mid-century commentator as 'unfortunately in two senses untranslatable')[47] turns on a fairly standard double meaning whereby sex is described as an athletic contest (Henderson 1991: 169–70). This joke is introduced with a pun on παλαίω (896, 'I wrestle'), whose obvious potential for *double entendre* is intensified by the addition of ἐπὶ γῆς ('on the ground'). However, the jokes soon become rather more abstract and difficult to untangle. The passage's imagery slowly builds in scale. What began as a one-on-one contest (the metaphor of the wrestling match) soon becomes more of a group endeavour, with the addition of a plural participle in line 897 (ὑπαλειψαμένοις).[48] Although we briefly return to firm ground with two straightforward puns on παίω ('I hit or strike') and ὀρύττω ('I dig or gouge'), the passage's meaning begins to break down when, in line 899, the idea of chariot racing is introduced. The joke here is again rooted in a conventional double meaning: the language of horse-riding was regularly used in Greek (as indeed in English) to denote sex (Henderson 1991: 165). However, as with the entire army garrisoned inside a single woman in Eupolis' *Cities* fragment 247 above, there are issues of size here; the passage describes whole chariot races taking place within Theoria, with the curves of her body (904: περὶ ταῖσι καμπαῖς) standing punningly for the bends of the racetrack. The spatial dynamics add to the anarchic humour of the joke, but as we gradually up the ante from a wrestling match to a full-on chariot race, the viability of the human body as a means of representing something which seems so abstract ('spectatorship'), while simultaneously requiring the kind of physical space which exceeds the limits of the human body alone ('an athletic festival which includes chariot racing'), begins to seem strained. The passage starts in line 894 with the verb ἐξέσται ('it will be possible'), but by the end of Trygaeus' speech this language of possibility seems in itself something of a wry joke, and by the time Trygaeus physically hands Theoria over to the Prytaneis (905–6), the actor's bodily presence has come to seem entirely at odds with their symbolic and dramatic function.

The physical manipulation of the body is an even greater feature of a lengthy fragment of Pherecrates' *Chiron* (fr. 155 PCG), and puns are again crucial to the effect.[49] The surviving fragments leave us little clue as to the plot of this play, although the title does suggest the possibility of some kind of mythological theme (see Franchini 2020: 239–40). Fragment 155, quoted by Plutarch in his treatise *De Musica*, sees a courtesan-like[50] figure representing Music complain about her treatment at the hands of proponents of the New Music such as Timotheus and Cinesias:[51]

λέξω μὲν οὐκ ἄκουσα· σοί τε γὰρ κλυεῖν
ἐμοί τε λέξαι θυμὸς ἡδονὴν ἔχει.
ἐμοὶ γὰρ ἦρξε τῶν κακῶν Μελανιππίδης,
ἐν τοῖσι πρῶτος ὃς λαβὼν ἀνῆκέ με
χαλαρωτέραν τ' ἐποίησε χορδαῖς δώδεκα.   5
ἀλλ' οὖν ὅμως οὗτος μὲν ἦν ἀποχρῶν ἀνὴρ
ἔμοιγε <   > πρὸς τὰ νῦν κακά.
Κινησίας δέ <μ'> ὁ κατάρατος Ἀττικός,
ἐξαρμονίους καμπὰς ποιῶν ἐν ταῖς στροφαῖς
ἀπολώλεχ' οὕτως, ὥστε τῆς ποιήσεως   10
τῶν διθυράμβων, καθάπερ ἐν ταῖς ἀσπίσιν,
ἀριστέρ' αὐτοῦ φαίνεται τὰ δεξιά.
ἀλλ' οὖν ἀνεκτὸς οὗτος ἦν ὅμως ἐμοί.
Φρῦνις δ' ἴδιον στρόβιλον ἐμβαλών τινα
κάμπτων με καὶ στρέφων ὅλην διέφθορεν,   15
ἐν πέντε χορδαῖς δώδεχ' ἁρμονίας ἔχων.
ἀλλ' οὖν ἔμοιγε χοὗτος ἦν ἀποχρῶν ἀνήρ·
εἰ γάρ τι κἀξήμαρτεν, αὖθις ἀνέλαβεν.
ὁ δὲ Τιμόθεός μ', ὦ φιλτάτη, κατορώρυχε
καὶ διακέκναικ' αἴσχιστα.

I shall tell you, and not grudgingly, since it pleases your heart to hear and mine to tell. Melanippides was the start of my travails, the first to take me and loosen me up, he made me slacker by twelve strings. But he wasn't too bad a sort really, compared to my sufferings now. Cinesias the Athenian, that bastard, he shoved dissonant twists in my strophes and ruined me utterly, so that in his dithyrambs, just like in a mirror, right seems like left. But even *he* was bearable. Phrynis inserted that private whirlwind of his, twisting and bending me he almost killed me with those twelve harmonies on five strings. But even *he* wasn't such a bad guy, he'd hurt me but he'd make it right. But, darling, Timotheus has dug into me and gouged me out *most* horribly.

Pherecrates fr. 155.1–20 PCG

In this passage, the metaphorical abuse of musical tradition by the New Music and its proponents is construed as the physical and sexual abuse of the character's body. A series of puns play on the twisting and turning of strings in play (or in tuning),[52] and the physical manipulation of the body;[53] and this in turn mirrors the metaphorical twistiness of the New Music's harmonic style.[54]

The abstract aesthetic qualities of contemporary music are therefore played out on the actor's body, as Music is loosened (4: ἀνῆκέ, 5: χαλαρωτέραν), twisted and turned (9: καμπὰς, 15: κάμπτων με καὶ στρέφων). As we have seen in other fragments, the imagery of this passage emphasizes the way in which men literally take up space within the female body during sex. Music tells us that Melanippides made her slacker by a measure of χορδαῖς δώδεκα (5, 'twelve strings');[55] while χορδή here primarily pertains to the animal gut used to make strings, it can also mean a sausage or black pudding (likewise due to the role of gut in their production), and in this guise can be read as a fairly transparent euphemism for the phallus (Dobrov and Urios-Aparisi 1995: 155). Phrynis is likewise described as putting his 'private whirlwind' into Music (14: ἴδιον στρόβιλον ἐμβαλών); while the whirlwind is an unusual and rather imaginative euphemism, the use of the preposition ἐν leaves us in little doubt.[56] Further, due to its coiled shape, στρόβιλος may also refer to a pine cone, which is perhaps a more obviously phallic visual image; indeed, there is one example, in Aristophanes' *Women at the Thesmophoria*, of a speaker comparing a penis to a pine cone (*Thesm.* 515–16: τὸ ποσθίον ... στρεβλὸν ὥσπερ κύτταρος. 'His little thingy ... just like a twisted pine cone').[57]

Spatial imagery also features in the fragment's final punchline:

ὥσπερ τε τὰς ῥαφάνους ὅλην
καμπῶν με κατεμέστωσε

Like a cabbage, he stuffed me full of caterpillars/twists

Pherecrates fr. 155.27–8 PCG

This pun plays rather brilliantly on the words καμπή (twist in a musical phrase) and κάμπη (caterpillar), the latter of which, due to its shape, clearly carries an additional sexual double meaning in this context.[58] The fragment as a whole is therefore highly tactile. The twisting/turning puns, which allow Music to slip between her two simultaneous identities as abstract concept and human woman, make the body's presence *felt* in a very concrete way, and one which is at odds with her rather more abstract and symbolic character. The continued graphic emphasis on how her body is not only occupied but stretched out by the vigorous sexual assault of her musical clients further confronts the audience with the conflict between the abstraction of Music's character and the physical role of the actor's body in her dramatic representation.[59]

Jokes which emphasize the role of the actor's body on stage are not always sexual in tone. In Aristophanes' *Islands* and *Clouds*, jokes are used to direct attention to the choreuts' faces. Like the *Islands* of Plato Comicus (discussed in the previous chapter), Aristophanes' *Islands* appears to have engaged with themes of war and empire, and Torchio suggests that it may have been a peace play with a narrative structure akin to the *Acharnians* or *Peace* (2021: 57).[60] The fragments show that the chorus of island-women, like Eupolis' city-women, were introduced individually; the chorus' entry seems to have established an explicitly metatheatrical tone from the outset, as in fragment 403 they are described as entering from the stage's *eisodos*:[61]

A: τί σὺ λέγεις; εἰσὶν δὲ ποῦ;
B: αἱδὶ κατ' αὐτὴν ἣν βλέπεις τὴν εἴσοδον

A: What are you saying? Where are they?
B: They're these ones here that you see at the *eisodos*.

Ar., fr. 403 PCG

A further fragment sees an unknown character comment on the demeanour of one of the Islands as she enters:[62]

ὡς ἐς τὴν γῆν κύψασα κάτω καὶ ξυννενοφυῖα βαδίζει

How she walks stooped down to the ground and all clouded over!

Ar., fr. 410 PCG

The first participle in this fragment (κύψασα) relates only to the actor's body language and movement as they enter. However, the second participle, ξυννενοφυῖα ('clouded over/wearing a gloomy look'),[63] is a pun which plays on the character's dual island/woman identity, and, in conjuring up the image of an island with a face, draws the audience's attention to the incompatibility between the two.

The joke in Aristophanes' *Clouds* is somewhat more extended.[64] When the cloud chorus arrive on stage (similarly introduced in line 325 as entering at the *eisodos*), Strepsiades complains that they don't look at all like clouds, but rather women with noses:

Στρ: λέξον δή μοι, τί παθοῦσαι,
    εἴπερ νεφέλαι γ' εἰσὶν ἀληθῶς, θνηταῖς εἴξασι γυναιξίν;

>   οὐ γὰρ ἐκεῖναί γ' εἰσὶ τοιαῦται.
> Σω: φέρε, ποῖαι γάρ τινές εἰσιν;
> Στρ: οὐκ οἶδα σαφῶς· εἴξασιν δ' οὖν ἐρίοισιν πεπταμένοισιν,
>   κοὐχὶ γυναιξίν, μὰ Δί', οὐδ' ὁτιοῦν· αὗται δὲ ῥῖνας ἔχουσιν.

> Strepsiades: Tell me, if these truly are clouds, how come they look like women? Those ones up there don't look like that!
> Socrates: Well, how do those ones look?
> Strepsiades: I don't really know. They're sort of like wool when it's been spread out. Not like women, no by Zeus, not in the least. And these ones, they've got noses!
>
> Ar., *Nub.* 340–5

This is a rather incongruous image, and one whose humour is increased by the sheer specificity of Strepsiades' description: the clouds have not just faces in general, but noses in particular. On one level, Strepsiades' observations are simply the set-up for a bigger punchline which will follow in lines 345–56. Clouds, Socrates explains, take on different shapes depending on what they see on earth below them; that's why we've all seen clouds which look like a wolf or a bull, and since the effeminate politician Cleisthenes is sitting in the audience, it is only natural that the clouds should take the form of women in response.[65] However, the joke seems also to acknowledge the limitations of dramatic representation, and the particular challenges of using human actors to represent the non-human on stage. Rather than attempt to make the chorus look meaningfully cloud-like, Strepsiades' observations suggest that the production instead embraced the inevitable disconnect between the actors on stage and their fictional identities; in particular, the contrast drawn between the 'fleecy' clouds in the sky and the cloud chorus on stage (who, we must therefore presume, were non-fleecy) implies an approach to costuming which was symbolic rather than actively representational. Anticipating potential audience dissatisfaction, the *Clouds* makes a joke at its own expense, and, as Socrates explains away the clouds' unusual representation and form, we are left to reflect on both the imaginative ambition, and the dramatic limitations, of the comic stage.

In comedy, there is never any such thing as *just* a joke. Jokes are inherently a mode of speech with multiplicities of meaning, and even a passing one-liner therefore packs an awful lot into its highly compact form. The structure of jokes, in which two (or more) opposing scripts run simultaneously, provides playwrights with an opportunity to play about with the co-presence of different worlds on stage, as jokes and puns allow for the fictional world and its dramatic representation to come into constant collision. In prising apart the fault line between representation and represented, jokes and double meanings embed metatheatrical exposure in the language and idiom of comedy.

By training our gaze on the joke in this way, it is not only the embeddedness of metatheatre which is revealed, but also its variability, which is to say which component of theatrical pretence is unmasked at any given moment. A large proportion of the non-human characters discussed in this chapter also contain an element of cross-dressing, in that female characters are being played by male actors. Yet while jokes expose the presence of the actor's human body, and the ways in which this body is at odds with the character's fictional non-human identity, our metatheatrical gaze is not directed towards the mismatch of gender between actor and character. Metatheatre is not just scattergun, but rather tends to tease out one specific aspect of theatrical artifice at a time: to expose every element of fictional and dramatic pretence at once isn't so effective as just offering one specific and focused glimpse behind the curtain. This careful calibration of comic metatheatre, at once acknowledging the fictionality of the comic world without ever fully dismantling it, brings us back to the crucial role of puns in metatheatre. Puns are specifically reliant on a doubleness of meaning: two incompatible things being briefly true at once. Puns allow the actors on stage to at once occupy, and disavow, their human bodies, and to place their fictional identity, and its metatheatrical exposure, in perfect equilibrium. In this way, puns create a world in which the disjunct between actor and character is not a threat to the fictional world, but part of the comic one, and in which therefore metatheatre does not ultimately undermine fictionality, but rather exists in parallel with it.

Double meanings and double identities in Aristophanes' *Wasps*

Old Comedy can be ruthlessly episodic: a joke is picked up, exploited to its fullest potential, and then unceremoniously dropped as the playwright moves on to the next.[66] While the *Acharnians* certainly makes theatrical representation a central theme throughout the play, the same is not really true of *Clouds*, which notably does not make a sustained feature of the disjunct between the chorus' fictional identity and their human bodies;[67] and even in the *Acharnians*, jokes are not central to the metatheatrical project outside of the marketplace scene.

It is unfortunately impossible to know whether the jokes about dramatic representation in plays such as Archippus' *Fishes* or Eupolis' *Cities* were sustained, or whether the gap between the fictional and staged worlds became a thematic feature of the plays as a whole. One play does, however, give us an idea of how a single joke might be spun out throughout the dramatic action, and of how puns and double meanings could be put to sustained use in exposing the double identities of characters on stage. Aristophanes' *Wasps* features a highly unusual animal chorus, who throughout the play occupy two identities as both wasps and old Athenian jurors.[68] Unlike in the *Birds* or *Frogs*, for example, in which the animals, while anthropomorphized to some degree, still maintain an essentially animal quality, the identity of the *Wasps*' chorus is far more liminal. While always (and, I would suggest, correctly) categorized as an animal chorus, the old men of the *Wasps* are not, like Aristophanes' other animal choruses, anthropomorphized (to a greater or lesser degree) animals, but might better be described as theriomorphized men.[69]

The wasp chorus' dual identity turns on a literalization of the double meaning of the word ὀξύς, which can be used both literally to refer to a sharp object (such as a stinger), and metaphorically to denote a harsh temperament or mode of speech.[70] The old men's waspishness is first introduced in a simile:

ἀλλ', ὦ πόνηρε, τὸ γένος ἤν τις ὀργίσῃ
τὸ τῶν γερόντων, ἔσθ' ὅμοιον σφηκιᾷ.
ἔχουσι γὰρ καὶ κέντρον ἐκ τῆς ὀσφύος
ὀξύτατον

You wretch, if anyone angers that tribe of old men,
They're just like a wasp nest,
And they've got a sharp sting in their loins![71]

Ar., *Vesp.* 223–6

This description not only relies on the double meaning of ὀξύτατον, but also mobilises the joke-like ambiguity of the word ὀσφύς. The word in Greek can mean either 'loins', which in itself has metaphorical resonances of masculinity or virility, or 'arse/lower back', the site at which an actual wasp's stinger is located. Despite the description of the chorus in these lines, which might lead the audience to expect some kind of animal costume, the first appearance of the chorus sees them in human guise, dressed in long cloaks. Other than a brief reference to hives in line 241, and an address to Philocleon as 'honeybee' (ὦ μελίττιον) in line 366,[72] there is little hint of their identity as insects, as instead they complain about their poverty, and reminisce about their glory days as soldiers.

It is not until line 408 that the chorus remove their cloaks[73] (ἀλλὰ θαἰμάτια λαβόντες ὡς τάχιστα, παιδία) and expose the wasp costumes they wear underneath.[74] In the aftermath of the punning playfulness of lines 223–6, this moment of visual literalization in which we discover that the wasps have not so much 'a sting in their loins' as 'a stinger on their arses' (225–6, above) acts as something like a punchline, and is marked as such by the exclamation of the slave Xanthias:

Ἡράκλεις, καὶ κέντρ᾽ ἔχουσιν. οὐχ ὁρᾷς, ὦ δέσποτα;

By Heracles,[75] they've got *actual* stingers! Don't you see them, master?

Ar., *Vesp.* 420

The ensuing mêlée sees the chorus use their stage movements to act out their wasp identity. They describe their stings bracing for action (407: κέντρον ἐντατέον ὀξέως), before using their stings as weapons in a stand-off with Bdelycleon and his slaves according to the orders of the chorus-leader (422–5). Bdelycleon and his slaves in turn react to them as wasps, fighting them off using smoke (457: ἀλλὰ καὶ σὺ τῦφε πολλῷ τῷ καπνῷ), a method commonly used against wasp nests.

However, the chorus never discard their primary identification as jurors, but, just as in the puns which first introduced them, hold these two opposing identities in equilibrium throughout the play. Indeed, the chorus go on to claim in the parabasis that their two identities are not oppositional at all, but rather mutually reinforcing. The epirrhema begins with the chorus asserting that, far from undermining or conflicting with their characterization as Athenian men, their wasp sting is in fact a confirmation of this status:[76]

ἐσμὲν ἡμεῖς, οἷς πρόσεστι τοῦτο τοὐρροπύγιον,
Ἀττικοὶ μόνοι δικαίως ἐγγενεῖς αὐτόχθονες

We who have this arse on us
Are by right the only indigenous Attic race.

Ar., *Vesp.* 1075–6

Throughout the epirrhema, the chorus' language brings their two identities into collision. They describe their participation in the Battle of Marathon, using their participation in the Persian wars as a symbol of their status as true Athenians. Given that the battle took place almost seventy years previously, in 490 BC, it seems unlikely that there were many veterans of the Persian wars surviving by the time of Aristophanes' early career. Rather, the Persian wars seem to be used by Aristophanes as an emblem of the golden age of Athenian manhood, and the chorus' waspishness is embedded within this narrative of archetypal Athenian bravery.[77] The Persians are first described as coming upon Athens with smoke and fire (1079: τῷ καπνῷ τύφων ἅπασαν τὴν πόλιν καὶ πυρπολῶν), presumably a reference to the burning of Attica by Xerxes' army (cf. Hdt. 8.50). However, the language quickly shifts from human to animal, when in the next line the Persians are described as attacking not the city but ἡμῶν . . . τἀνθρήνια, 'our nests' (1080), and the fire and smoke which seemed to belong to the chorus' human identity as soldiers under attack instead becomes associated with the act of smoking out a wasp nest (cf. *Vesp.* 457). Similarly, the chorus' description of themselves in battle presents them as hybrid wasp-men, since they are at once human soldiers standing 'man to man' (1083: στὰς ἀνὴρ παρ' ἄνδρ') with shields and swords (1081: ξὺν δορὶ ξὺν ἀσπίδι), and wasps who defend themselves with their stings (1088: κεντούμενοι).

The epirrhema ends in one last pun:

ὥστε παρὰ τοῖς βαρβάροισι πανταχοῦ καὶ νῦν ἔτι
μηδὲν Ἀττικοῦ καλεῖσθαι σφηκὸς ἀνδρικώτερον.

So everywhere among the Barbarians
Nothing is called manlier than an Attic wasp.

Ar., *Vesp.* 1089–90

Like the pun on ὀξύς which first introduced the wasp chorus (Ar., *Vesp.* 223–6), this double meaning plays on the literal versus metaphorical potential of the word ἀνδρικώτερος ('braver, more manly'), whose root in the noun ἀνήρ ('man') jars with its neighbouring noun (1090: σφηκὸς, 'wasp') to create a humorous collision between the chorus' two identities. This final punchline caps the chorus' description of their wasplike military manoeuvres, reinforcing the idea that they do not so much switch between two conflicting identities as inhabit both at once.

The chorus' duality, created and subsequently reinforced through the use of puns, produces a sense that even within the fictional world of the play they are not so much real wasps as men pretending; and the subsequent spectacle of humans-who-also-embody-animals mirrors the very act of choral animal performance, in which human actors take on animal roles. This self-conscious performativity is set against the background of a plot in which human characters repeatedly take on animal roles. The early part of the *Wasps* sees Philocleon taking on a number of guises as he acts out a series of different tricks in an effort to escape from his house and join his fellow jurors. In this scene Philocleon is repeatedly assimilated to different animals in the speech of other characters, who describe the old man as 'like a limpet' (105: ὥσπερ λεπὰς), 'like a bee' (107: ὥσπερ μέλιττ' ἢ βομβυλιὸς), 'like a jackdaw' (129: ὡσπερεὶ κολοιὸς), and 'scurrying like a mouse' (140: μυσπολεῖ). This culminates in a comic skit in which the old man seemingly 'becomes' a sparrow (207: στροῦθος ἀνὴρ γίγνεται), and enacts this new identity by taking to the roof of his house, only to be shooed back inside with a net (208: τὸ δίκτυον).[78]

By flipping the tradition of anthropomorphized comic animals on its head to present instead a chorus of theriomorphic men, the *Wasps* places the idea of theriomorphic embodiment centre stage. The consistent foregrounding of the chorus' status as simultaneously human and animal in turn foregrounds the idea of men-as-animals which is central to the performance of an animal chorus on stage; and the characters' dual human-animal status mirrors the similar status of the actors as men-playing-animals. The comic tradition of the animal chorus is therefore embedded within the parallel comic tradition of self-conscious performativity; by emphasizing the act of theatrical metamorphosis inherent in the performance of animal roles, the play casts the animal chorus as one of the more conspicuous acts of fictionality in the comic tradition. Both at the point of their introduction to the play, and during the epirrhema in which the chorus offer to explain (1074: διδάξω) their appearance to the audience, puns are central to this conceit, as double meanings are used to bring the chorus' dual human-animal identity into collision.

The *Wasps* shows how it is possible to use a single pun as the catalyst for a more sustained exploration of the incongruity between a character's fictional identity and their real human body, and how this opposition can be recast as an augmentation of, rather than a threat to, the fictional world of the play. In turn, puns embed the chorus' overt performativity within the play's comic language and idiom. Whether the puns of Eupolis' *Cities* or Archippus' *Fishes* were deployed to comparable effect, or were just passing jokes analogous to those in the *Acharnians* or *Clouds*, their similar emphasis on the human body serves to ground the fantastical world of the play within the real space of the stage. By embracing the limitations of dramatic representation, comedy is conversely granted greater imaginative freedom, as the increasingly large gap between fictional world and staged reality can simply be made part of the fun.

The outlandishness of a world populated by wasp-men or city-women or fish with feet may seem so quintessentially comic as to bear little relation to anything beyond comedy's own generic idiom. However, on closer inspection, these more conspicuously fantastical elements of comic convention are used to amplify the inherent absurdities of all dramatic representation. Jokes and puns first bring into focus the fact that all drama runs two scripts at once, as performance and reality, fictional world and staged code co-exist within the physical space of the stage; and secondly, embed an acknowledgement of this double script within the comic project itself. Jokes are not surface-level ornamentation, but an integral part of how comedy thinks about, and plays with, the possibilities of the dramatic world. By using puns as a tool of metatheatre, comedy casts theatrical representation as a mode of speech analogous to jokes, a form in which two contradictory realities are forced into uneasy, and even actively incongruent, co-existence.

Flying high: Playing with tragic illusion

The conspicuously fantastical nature of non-human characters on stage provides comedy with ample opportunity to play about with the gap between the fictional world and its representation on stage through the conventional symbolic language of the theatre. However, while such characters are an established convention of comic drama, their generic specificity limits their agonistic potential. The jokes which accompany these figures largely lack competitive force, and any comparison between comedy's punning embrace of the limitations of dramatic realism, and the supposedly more illusionistic ambitions of 'serious' theatre is therefore only ever implicit.

Comedy's attitude towards those theatrical conventions which it shares with tragic theatre is, predictably, rather different. Jokes which target tragedy's stage conventions are not only playful double meanings, but tend towards rather more aggressive jibes which bring comic and tragic stage conventions into opposition. Again, these jokes appear to cluster around the more fantastical elements of tragic stage practice: a character in flight, or, worse, on wheels; the sudden intrusion of a monster or god into the human world. As comedy plays about with dramatic illusion, jokes place a series of oppositions (between fictional world and staged reality; tragedy and comedy; symbolism and naturalism) in dialogue, and call attention to the incompatibility between tragedy's artistic ambitions, and the limitations of dramatic representation in practice.

Not-so-special effects

Few things expose this incompatibility so effectively as stage technology and special effects. Surely intended by tragedians as a moment of awe-inspiring spectacle, the appearance of an actor on the *mechane* is regularly mocked in comedy as an example of how tragedy aims to augment its dramatic illusion, but ends up clumsily puncturing it instead. Such jokes are a mainstay of Aristophanic comedy. The *Peace* most notably contains an extended flight sequence in which the protagonist Trygaeus, modelling himself on the tragic heroism of Bellerophon, sets out for Olympus on the back of a giant dung beetle.[79] The flight is not without incident. As beetle and rider are carried aloft, the *mechane* apparently wobbles, and Trygaeus, startled, interrupts his paratragic anapests (149–72) to cry out in considerably less elevated language and meter:

οἴμ᾽ ὡς δέδοικα, κοὐκέτι σκώπτων λέγω.
ὦ μηχανοποιέ, πρόσεχε τὸν νοῦν, ὡς ἐμὲ
ἤδη στροβεῖ τι πνεῦμα περὶ τὸν ὀμφαλόν,
κεἰ μὴ φυλάξει, χορτάσω τὸν κάνθαρον.

I'm getting pretty scared, and I'm not kidding now.
Pay attention Mr. Crane-Operator!
Some wind is already twisting about round my bellybutton,
And if you're not careful, I'm going to be feeding the beetle!

Ar., *Pax* 173–6

The contrast between the *mechane*'s association with grand tragic set-pieces and its obvious lack of grace here combines with slapstick humour, as the audience laugh at the perilous flight to which Trygaeus (and indeed the actor playing him) is subjected.[80] The humour here is, however, not limited to crude slapstick. Much like the jokes which accompany non-human characters on the comic stage, comedy's forays into fantastical special effects encourage us to see double, and to acknowledge that the gap between the fictional world and its representation on stage makes drama a form not so much mimetic as symbolic. In reality, Trygaeus' flight bears little relation to a hero ascending to the heavens, but rather presents us with an actor dangling precariously from a rope and hoping to god that he comes back down again safely. The joke derives its comic force not only from this disjunct, but also from the opposition between tragic and comic approaches to it: how much more ridiculous to ask the audience to ignore, as tragedy does, this gaping chasm between fiction and reality.

The comedian Strattis twice makes a joke in this vein, but with the addition of a pun. In a fragment of the *Atalantus*, whose overall plot may have had an element of paratragedy, a character appears to complain about the awkwardness and discomfort of appearing on the *mechane*.[81] While the *Peace* focuses on the clumsiness of the *mechane* in flight, here it seems to be the actor's dismount which exposes the device's limitations, as the operator is unable to get him down with the requisite speed, and this causes an intrusive delay in the action of the play:[82]

ἀπὸ τῆς κράδης, ἤδη γὰρ ἰσχὰς γίν[ομαι
ὁ μηχανοποιός μ᾽ ὡς τάχιστα καθελέτω

Have the crane operator get me down from this branch,
And fast! I'm already becoming a fig.

Strattis fr. 4 PCG

The joke here plays on the double meaning of κράδη, which literally means a sprig or branch, but which was commonly used to refer to the *mechane*:[83] so long has the actor been suspended on this 'branch', he has started to become a part of it. The joke is, as usual, funnier in Greek. ἰσχάς means not a fresh fig, but a dried one, with the implication that the actor has been strung up in the sun so long that he has not only sprouted into a piece of fruit, but even become desiccated from his long exposure (Orth 2009 ad loc.).

The intrusive nature of stage technology is also subject to a joke in the concluding scenes of Aristophanes' *Knights*. It is notable that the joke in the *Knights*, like *Peace*, seems to target Euripides' *Bellerophon*, and its use of stage technology. The defeated Paphlagonian makes his final exit from the stage atop the *ekkyklema*, instructing the stagehands:

κυλίνδετ᾽ εἴσω τόνδε τὸν δυσδαίμονα.

Roll me inside, accursed!

Ar., *Eq.* 1249

The line is quoted almost verbatim from the *Bellerophon*, in which the crippled hero seems to have been removed from the stage into the *skene* building via the *ekkyklema*:[84]

κομίζετ᾽ εἴσω τόνδε τὸν δυσδαίμονα

Bring [me/him] inside, accursed!

Eur., *Beller.* fr. 311 TrGF

The joke relies on the substitution of the similar κυλίνδετ᾽ εἴσω for the original κομίζετ᾽ εἴσω, thereby explicitly naming the stage effect through which the now-immobilized tragic hero is removed from view, and exposing the absurd disjunct in tragedy between onstage movement (actor appearing on wheels) and the fictional world of the play (in which we are clearly supposed to imagine that the wheels are not really there).[85]

Jokes about tragic stage technology often centre on the genre's apparent lapses into cliché, and (as in this example from *Knights*) the particular artificiality with which tragic plots are brought to a close through the employment of such special effects.[86] Strattis' branch/fig joke makes a second appearance in a fragment of his *Phoenician Women*, but here the (albeit very poorly preserved) text makes clear that this is a *deus ex machina* appearance (fr. 46);[87] and a fragment from the poet Antiphanes famously complains about the laziness of tragedians who employ the *mechane* to end their plays when they have otherwise run out of ideas:[88]

<ἔπει>θ' ὅταν μηδὲν δύνωντ' εἰπεῖν ἔτι,
κομιδῇ δ' ἀπειρήκωσιν ἐν τοῖς δράμασιν,
αἴρουσιν ὥσπερ δάκτυλον τὴν μηχανήν,
καὶ τοῖς θεωμένοισιν ἀποχρώντως ἔχει.

And then, when they can't say anything else,
And they're completely out of ideas for the play,
They raise the *mechane* like it's a finger,
And that's plenty good enough for the spectators.

Antiphanes fr. 189.13–16 PCG

Jokes about cliché on the one hand suggest imaginative failure, as tragedians are seen to lapse into the same repetitiousness of comedians rehashing an old joke.[89] The language of cliché, however, also characterizes tragic stage action as a system of symbolic convention, rather than anything which approaches meaningful, let alone naturalistic, representation.[90] Tragedy has become a kind of closed loop, whose generic language has come to speak primarily to its own conventions as a system of signification, at the expense of actual mimetic significance.

A joke in Aristophanes' *Wealth* pokes fun at tragic costuming conventions, and the extent to which the genre's devolution into cliché has become so exaggerated as to rob it of its mimetic force. In the play, the hero Chremylus restores the sight of the god Wealth, with the result that riches are distributed more fairly, and a new golden age is ushered in. The middle section of the play features a face-off between Chremylus and Penia ('Poverty'), in which Penia attempts to argue that she is essential to mankind's overall wellbeing and success. As might be expected in comedy, tragedy is associated with the hero's adversary, and when Penia enters, Blepsidemus is quick to label her as a symbol of the rival genre. The hero Chremylus fires back a witty one-liner as follows:

Xp: σὺ δ᾽ εἶ τίς; ὠχρὰ μὲν γάρ εἶναί μοι δοκεῖς.
Βλ: ἴσως Ἐρινύς ἐστιν ἐκ τραγῳδίας·
    βλέπει γέ τοι μανικόν τι καὶ τραγῳδικόν.
Xp: ἀλλ᾽ οὐκ ἔχει γὰρ δᾷδας.[91]

Chremylus: But who are you? You look rather pallid to me.
Blepsidemus: Maybe she's one of the Erinyes out of tragedy; she does look pretty crazy and tragic.
Chremylus: But she doesn't have any torches!

Ar., *Plut.* 422–5

By this point in the early fourth century, torch-bearing Furies seem to have become something of an emblem of tragicness, and it is this cliché which is the subject of Aristophanes' joke here.[92] We are not really meant to suppose that the character's identification as a tragic Fury is dependent on the presence or absence of torches as part of her costume. Rather, the joke rests on the idea that tragic stage practice has become so ossified that it matters less whether its characters look like the things they are supposed to represent, and more whether they conform to the symbolic language of the genre. In this way, the joke draws attention to the gap between tragedy's mimetic aspirations, and its increasing descent into cliché, whereby it is more concerned with its conventions of representation than representation itself.

Conclusions

The innate structural qualities of jokes and puns imbue them with metatheatrical potentiality. By superimposing two opposing fields of reference, jokes embed the doubleness of theatrical performance in comic idiom, and draw attention to the fact that all drama functions according to a dual script in which the world of the play and the world of the stage are in constant dialogue.

Scattered throughout Greek comedy, we find jokes which pick apart the relationship between representation and represented on stage. The more overtly anti-realist conventions of both comic and tragic drama act as something of a lightning rod for this kind of playful self-consciousness. The more comedy strays into the realm of the fantastical, the greater the disjunct between the world of the play and its staged reality becomes, and this in turn can be used to reflect on the inherent gap between fiction and performance in drama. Puns often look inwards towards comedy's own dramatic idiom, as playwrights such as Archippus deploy terrible jokes which practically revel in the incompatibility of comedy's imaginative limitlessness and the awkward realities of performance.

While jokes about tragic performance do sometimes employ puns, they are more likely to have a competitive quality, and to rely on oppositions between comic and tragic convention. Not only the gap between fiction and performance, but also the contrast between comedy's willingness to embrace this double script and tragedy's wish to disavow it, becomes the object of humour. Jokes about tragic performance also home in on the slippage between convention and cliché, and use accusations of the latter to expose the disjunct between tragedy's apparent ambitions towards naturalism, and its reality as a genre whose artificial systems of signification lack true representational value.

By drawing attention to the double script which characterizes all dramatic action, jokes in comedy prise apart the representational fault line between fiction and performance. Whether by punningly playing about with the dual identities of the figures on stage as both characters within the fiction and actors within the stage space; or by mocking tragedy's attempts to gloss over the unreality of its performative language, jokes are a central part of the comedian's metatheatrical toolkit. Whereas the jokes which look inwards towards comedy's own dramatic idiom tend to characterize drama's two scripts as existing in balance, jokes which target tragic stagecraft create a more antagonistic series of oppositions between fiction and performance, tragedy and comedy, representation and represented. The joke's flexibility as an instrument of metatheatre, and its ability to embed multiple meanings and realities within a single word, lends it a unique value as a mode of discourse which is at once funny, but which may also be deployed to make a not-entirely-frivolous point about the ultimate failure of poetic and dramatic representation to truly and truthfully represent the world. In this way, comedy not only insists on the affiliation between poetic and humorous language, but also casts all dramatic performance as a form which, like jokes, is structured around the gap between our perception of the world, and its representational approximation.

3

Playing with Plot: Jokes and Storytelling

The pleasure (ἡδονή) of comedy as opposed to tragedy, so Aristotle tells us in his *Poetics* (1453a35), is that mortal enemies such as 'Orestes and Aegisthus might go off together as friends by the end, and nobody kills anybody' (1453a37–9: Ὀρέστης καὶ Αἴγισθος, φίλοι γενόμενοι ἐπὶ τελευτῆς ἐξέρχονται, καὶ ἀποθνῄσκει οὐδεὶς ὑπ᾽ οὐδενός).[1] Comedy, in other words, is a disruptor of norms, and a genre in which we should expect the unexpected. Indeed, in its subversion of the reader's expectations, and the subsequent collision between the *Poetics*' imagined version of events and what we know to be the 'true' story, in which these characters are practically paradigms of internecine strife, Aristotle's pithy little formulation might almost qualify as a joke.

From our modern vantage point, this summary of the kind of story most at home (1453a36: οἰκεία) in comedy seems slightly counterintuitive, since in Aristophanes' eleven extant plays we in fact find few characters analogous to Aristotle's Orestes and Aegisthus. However, beyond Aristophanes, mythological comedies were commonplace.[2] Titles of plays by Hermippus (*The Birth of Athena*,[3] *Europa*), Pherecrates (*Chiron*), Plato Comicus (*Io*, *Adonis*, *Menelaus*) and Phrynichus (*Cronos*) suggest plots that riffed on familiar myths. While it has sometimes been argued that such 'mythological burlesque' was primarily the preserve of so-called Middle Comedy, these plays were in fact common even in the fifth century.[4] Cratinus regularly turned to the epic cycle for material;[5] and the fragments of Aristophanes include titles such as *Daedalus* and *Lemnian Women*, suggesting plots which adhered more closely to mythic storylines than those of his extant plays.[6]

So far, this book has focused primarily on jokes as localized phenomena, albeit ones which have the cumulative potential to reach beyond their immediate context and comment on literary and dramatic convention more broadly. At most, we have encountered what appear to be running jokes which operate within or even between plays (as was the case for Aristophanes' poetic-speech-as-liquid jokes in the *Knights*, which in turn spilled over into Cratinus' *Pytine*),[7] but which nevertheless function as individual jokes in their own right. However, jokes in Old Comedy were not only discrete units. We know from Aristophanes' extant plays that while there are plenty of standalone gags, each one-liner may also be integrated into an entire nexus of interrelated jokes.[8] Moreover, in addition to these networks of humour, we should not lose sight of the fact that jokes were also embedded in a wider narrative framework.

It is to this narrative framework, and its potential for humour, that this chapter turns. In particular, it will focus on those plays where the narrative conceit itself constitutes a kind of joke based on the collision between two (or more) scripts. The fragmentary corpus attests to a series of plays constructed around a protagonist whose identity is, to a greater or lesser degree, hybrid. The most famous example of this is perhaps Cratinus' play *Dionysalexandros*, whose portmanteau title hints at its central character's double role;[9] and whose hypothesis, first published in 1904, describes a plot in which the god Dionysus disguises himself as the Trojan prince Paris in order to steal Helen in his place.[10] A number of such portmanteaued play titles are attested, including Strattis' *Anthroporestes*[11] and Aristophanes' *Aeolosicon* (of which more shortly), suggesting that this kind of double-scripted plot construction was relatively common. The kinds of hybrid identities suggested by these titles are, of course, not unique to them. Both political satire and paratragedy similarly rely on characters who inhabit two scripts simultaneously. The plot of the *Acharnians*, for example, is at points reliant on the audience reading its main character, Dicaeopolis, as a pseudo-Telephus, and the political metaphor which structures the plot of *Knights* sees a number of characters stand in for contemporary politicians.[12] However, titles such as the *Dionysalexandros* suggest that this device was both more sustained and more prominent in these plays.

It is interesting to note that every single one of our attested 'portmanteau' titles contains at least one name drawn from myth. For the purposes of joke making, working with myth has obvious advantages: each story constitutes a kind of ready-made script (defined, in Raskin's terms, as a cognitive structure which both speaker and audience have pre-internalized),[13] whose multiple tellings and re-tellings have created a wide network of associations and expectations for the comedian to play upon.[14] As the comedian Antiphanes puts it, 'you only need say "Oedipus" and the spectators know the rest' (fr. 189.5–6 PCG: Οἰδίπουν γὰρ φῶ / τὰ δ᾽ ἄλλα πάντ᾽ ἴασιν).[15] A comedy which plants one foot in the mythic universe therefore has the opportunity to take a narrative script which is comparatively stable (in that it comes with a set of predetermined, albeit flexible, characters, events, and so on) and splice this together with elements which are incongruous and disruptive. Comedy's quotidian aesthetics are a particular gift in this regard, and we find in mythological comedies that the world of gods and heroes bumps up against the prosaic realities, both political and domestic, of everyday life in contemporary Athens.

By treading such well-worn ground, mythological comedies also set themselves on a collision course with those more 'serious' genres whose storytelling traditions are similarly grounded in myth. Epic will always lurk at the margins of any plot which touches on the Trojan War; a comic *Medea* will inevitably speak to its tragic analogues.[16] The parodic potential of this kind of storytelling has already been well explored by, for example, Emmanuela Bakola (2010: 118–79, with a focus on Cratinus) and Matthew Farmer (2017: 90–103, with a focus on Strattis). Plays such as Cratinus' *Dionysalexandros* and Aristophanes' *Aeolosicon* are, however, more than mere parody. Rather, by splicing together a series of discontinuous scripts at the level of the story concept, these plays make a joke of narrative structure itself.

In the opening sentence of the *Poetics*, Aristotle famously states that one of his central concerns will be 'how it is necessary to arrange the plot if the poetry is going to have excellence' (1447a2–3: πῶς δεῖ συνίστασθαι τοὺς μύθους εἰ μέλλει καλῶς ἕξειν ἡ ποίησις). There is a repeated emphasis in the *Poetics* on the importance of 'arrangement' (σύνθεσις), and Aristotle argues that an essential quality of successful poetic works is that their narratives are governed by what is 'probable or necessary' (1451b9: κατὰ τὸ εἰκὸς ἢ τὸ ἀναγκαῖον, 1451b35: εἰκὸς ... ἀνάγκη). This formulation is usually understood as emphasizing the importance of the causal relationship between events in a plot.[17] In particular, this emphasis on the 'probable or necessary', in combination with Aristotle's simultaneous emphasis on the importance of a beginning, middle and end (1450b26: ὅλον δέ ἐστιν τὸ ἔχον ἀρχὴν καὶ μέσον καὶ τελευτήν), suggests that a successful plot is one in which events are organized not only one after the other, in a temporal sequence, but *because* of one another (1452a4:

δι' ἄλληλα), in a causal sequence (Belfiore 1992: 113). Such tightly bound chains of cause and effect are, of course, highly artificial. In spite of this, storytelling traditions organized according to linear causality have since Aristotle been associated with realism,[18] while, by contrast, there is a tendency to ascribe comedy to a kind of anti-realist storytelling tradition,[19] at odds with more 'serious' mimetic genres such as epic and tragedy (which, let us remember, Aristotle claims to be more 'universally true' than even history (*Poetics* 1451b4-7)). However, as we have seen throughout this book, comedy is often at pains to undermine the representational qualities of the serious poetic tradition, and these kinds of 'domino effect' causal structures are, to put it mildly, low-hanging fruit.[20]

The first part of this chapter will look at Aristophanes' *Aeolosicon*. Premiered in 386 BC, this play seems to have centred on a protagonist who was simultaneously Aeolus, god of the winds, and the (apparently famous) chef Sicon (cf. Sosipater fr. 1). Like the non-human characters in the previous chapter whose dual identities allow them to occupy two competing scripts at once, the plot of this play therefore seems to be structured around a central joke-like incongruity. In addition to the central impossibility of the protagonist's double mythic/mortal identity, the play's conceit puts a series of further collisions in motion: as low-class cook meets divine king, the hyper-materiality of comedy, which is arguably best exemplified in its aesthetic attachment to food and the bodies that consume it, is spliced into a rather loftier story-world associated with epic (cf. *Od.* 10.1–79) and tragedy (cf. Euripides' *Aeolus*). By forcing these opposing narrative worlds into contact, the play therefore casts the comic storytelling tradition as one that represents the realism of everyday life, and the fantastical world of traditional mythic (and particularly tragic) storytelling is by contrast made to seem far-fetched and absurd.

Beyond Aristophanes, it seems not only the content, but also the narrative arrangement of tragic and epic stories came in for ridicule. In the 430s, Cratinus wrote a pair of plays which focused on the origins of the Trojan War. *Nemesis* told the story of Helen's conception, and the *Dionysalexandros* that of the judgement of Paris. Both plays appear to have contained an element of political satire, and to have used their comic aetiologies of the Trojan War to comment on more contemporary conflicts.[21] While *Nemesis* seems to have aimed its potshots primarily at Zeus and Pericles for their roles in stirring up trouble, the plot of the *Dionysalexandros* constitutes a more sustained aetiological joke.[22] The play, in which Dionysus attempts to disguise himself as Paris in order to steal Helen for himself, hinges on a disruption of the traditional myth, and the plot is therefore constructed around a 'near miss': what if Paris had not claimed Helen and taken her to Troy? In this way, the play draws attention to the 'domino effect' structures which underpin serious mythic storytelling, and the ease with which such structures can be brought crashing down. The play piles up farcical deviations from the 'correct' story, and the plot seems to be structured around a kind of running joke in which its hero desperately tries to divert the story away from its traditional (and inevitable) ending, apparently culminating in a visual gag where Dionysus changes himself into a sheep to avoid detection by the real Paris. While *Dionysalexandros* does eventually conclude with Helen accompanying Paris to Troy, the audience is left wondering what might have happened had the pieces not eventually fallen properly into place. Such 'near misses' are also an occasional feature of Aristophanes' plays: the final section of this chapter will turn to two narrow escapes in the *Acharnians* and *Peace*, and examine how these too are tied into questions about cause and effect both poetic and political.

As a whole, these plays demonstrate comedy's sustained interest in the gap between poetic and historical systems of causality. Linear chains of cause and effect are characterized as a system of signification whose conventionality blinds us to its unreality, and the serious storytelling tradition is presented as absurdly un-representational. In turn, the plays explore how jokes themselves can form an alternative narrative model. By building their plots around a joke-like incongruity which then plays out in the individual gags throughout the drama, comedy presents us with a form of narrative founded on the same insoluble, even at times incomprehensible, multiplicity which structures all joke-carrying texts. The results are cast as both more absurd and more naturalistic than the serious narrative tradition, paradoxically and incongruously suggesting that it is only in replicating the anti-representational impulses of the joke that stories can truly represent reality. The sheer impossibility of squaring these contradictory ideas is, of course, half the fun, and demonstrates that comedy's literary-philosophical propositions are always, at heart, a joke.

Aristophanes' *Aeolosicon* and the poetics of the everyday

The *Aeolosicon* of 386 BC was among Aristophanes' last plays, and was apparently produced under the oversight of his son Araros (see hypothesis IV to Ar., *Plut.*). The fragments of this play (or possibly plays) are fairly scanty, numbering only sixteen, of which none is more than five lines, and several just single words.[23] The title, as we have established, suggests that the play's conceit rested on a character who was simultaneously Aeolus, god of the winds, and a chef named Sicon; however, whether the chef impersonated the god or vice versa is difficult to say.[24] What is more certain is that the play parodied Euripides' *Aeolus*. Euripides' play was perhaps something of an easy target (and it was certainly a frequent target; Aristophanes parodies it in no fewer than four of his extant plays), since it contained a particularly provocative combination of sex and violence:[25] the fragments and hypothesis show that it focused on the fallout of Macareus' rape of his sister Canace, after which he persuaded his father, Aeolus, to marry his sons to his daughters; Macareus' ploy to gain Canace as his wife was, however, foiled when Aeolus had his children draw lots, and Canace was betrothed to another of her brothers.[26] *Aeolus* was used by Aristophanes as a classic example of Euripidean shamelessness and sophism, a combination typified in fragment 19, where the speaker (presumably Macareus) asks: 'What is disgraceful, if it doesn't seem so to its practitioners?' (τί δ' αἰσχρὸν, ἢν μὴ τοῖσι χρωμένοις δοκῇ;).[27]

Against this background, the fragments of Aristophanes' *Aeolosicon* are striking for their focus on quotidian objects. Cheese-graters (fr. 7 PCG: τυρόκνηστις), keys (fr. 15 PCG: κλειδίον), coal-pans (fr. 7 PCG: ἐσχάρα) and a soap dish (fr. 16 PCG: σμηματοφορεῖον) all make an appearance. Fragments 2 and 14 also focus on those grubbiest of everyday items, coins, suggesting that the rather more high-minded debate about the value of wealth which seems to have featured in the agon of Euripides' tragedy (cf. *Aeolus* frs. 20, 22) found its comic analogue.[28] These fragments hint at how *Aeolosicon*'s double-scripted plot conceit filtered down into its poetics. Comedy's mundane materiality is made to intrude constantly into the mythic universe, and the resultant collisions between high and low, tragic and comic, myth and reality cast Old Comedy as a naturalistic genre embedded in the fabric of everyday life, in contrast to the distant and fantastical realm of 'serious' mythological storytelling. In this way, the structural joke which underlies the play as a whole is embedded in its language and idiom.

This manoeuvre is encapsulated by the play's first remaining fragment:

ἥκω Θεαρίωνος ἀρτοπώλιον
λιπών, ἵν᾽ ἐστὶ κριβάνων ἑδώλια

I have come, leaving the bread shop of Thearion
Where is the bread oven's seat.

Ar., fr. 1 PCG

These lines are clearly tragic in register, especially their final word ἑδώλια ('dwelling place' or 'seat'). The first word in particular evokes the conventions of tragic prologues,[29] and the fragment in fact closely parodies the opening lines of Euripides' *Hecuba*, spoken by the ghost of Polydorus (1–2: **ἥκω** νεκρῶν κευθμῶνα καὶ σκότου πύλας / **λιπών, ἵν᾽** Ἅιδης χωρὶς ᾤκισται θεῶν, 'I have come, leaving the hollow vaults of the dead and shadowy gates, where Hades dwells apart from the other gods').[30] In this tragic context, the word κριβάνων ('bread oven') sticks out as distinctly comic. The insertion of a cooking utensil into the parody is funny in its own right, and more so to anyone who recognizes that this inert object has taken the place of Hades, god of the dead, in Euripides' lines (fr. 1: ἵν᾽ ἐστὶ κριβάνων, cf. *Hec.* 2: ἵν᾽ Ἅιδης χωρὶς). However, as so often with Aristophanes, there is more to the joke. As Hades' realm is transformed into Thearion's, the choice of the word κρίβανος to represent the low and everyday is a particularly clever touch, since the hollow earthenware vessel mirrors the hollow vaults of Euripides' (*Hec.* 1: νεκρῶν κευθμῶνα) underworld topography (and indeed elsewhere the word is used metaphorically to describe an underground vault or cavern).[31] Euripides' vaults of the dead have become Aristophanes' vaulted oven, and tragic grandeur falls into low comic bathos in a move which mirrors on a small scale the play's entire conceit.

Further fragments see other everyday objects undergoing their own metamorphoses. Fragment 3, for example, sees the speaker complain that his money is shrinking into less valuable denominations:

ὅπερ <δὲ> λοιπὸν μόνον <ἔτ᾽> ἦν ἐν τῇ γνάθῳ
διώβολον, γεγένητ᾽ ἐμοὶ δικόλλυβον

> The only two-obol bit I had left in my cheek
> Turned into a two-collybos on me!
>
> Ar., fr. 3 PCG

On the surface, this joke simply plays on the idea that the habit of transporting coins in your mouth can lead them to corrode and become smaller. However, the joke also relies on a collision between two different ways of conceptualizing the system of monetary valuation. Is the value of money 'real', determined by its weight in precious metal? Or is it rather more abstract, conjured into existence through our collective imagination? The answer (at least prior to the abolition of the gold standard) is, of course, both: an obol is worth more than a collybos because it is a larger coin, but it cannot simply *become* a collybos if it wears away into one. A corroded obol is still an obol.

On the other hand, when it comes to money, stability of category is no guarantee of value, and more abstract economic forces seem also to be evoked by the speaker. As Orth observes in his discussion of this fragment (2017: 49–50), inflation is not infrequently a topic of complaint in Aristophanes: in the *Assemblywomen*, for example, a speaker complains that in the time it takes to make a transaction, his copper coins are declared worthless (Ar., *Eccl.* 816–22). The joke here in *Aeolosicon* seems therefore to tap into familiar comic territory, as the speaker similarly complains that money cannot be trusted to retain its worth from one moment to the next. In sum, therefore, this joke confronts us with the uncomfortable paradox which underpins monetary transactions, whereby value is determined by both concrete physical form, and unstable, abstract and unpredictable economic systems. In creating a collision between these two apparently mutually exclusive but nevertheless simultaneously applicable frameworks, Aristophanes' joke insists on the absurdity of the entire enterprise.

There may additionally be a level of broad parodic engagement here. In Euripides' *Aeolus*, Macareus and his father appear to have argued about whether wealth truly has worth; here, perhaps, Euripides' moral and philosophical question becomes rather more literal, as well as more low-class, since where Euripides' characters debate the value of divine riches, Aristophanes' quibble about two-bit copper coins. In its focus on the possibility of transformation in both form and value, this one-liner also plays into the overall theme of the plot, in which the cook Sicon becomes the god Aeolus, or vice versa. A further fragment seems also to embed this theme of transformation into the comic texture of the play:

> τῶν δὲ γηθύων
> ῥίζας ἐχούσας σκοροδομίμητον φύσιν
>
> Roots of spring onion
> with a garlic-masquerading form.
>
> Ar., fr. 5 PCG

In this fragment, the speaker (perhaps the eponymous *Aeolosicon*, given the culinary topic) seems to be extolling the virtue of a relatively obscure species of allium (γηθύων),[32] which in turn has the form or character (φύσιν) of another allium. The tone here is oddly elevated for such workaday ingredients; Orth (2017: 59) detects tragic influences in both word choice and placement, with φύσις in particular suggesting a philosophical register (cf. e.g. *Clouds* 276). The humorous clash between high and low is encapsulated in the coinage σκοροδομίμητον ('garlic-masquerading'). The term *mimesis* elsewhere appears in Aristophanes at moments of heightened metatheatre (*Thesm.* 156, *Ran.* 109) where one character is taking on the disguise of another, and by the early fourth century was beginning to emerge as a specialist term of literary criticism.[33] In combining this word with σκόροδον ('garlic'), Aristophanes creates a joke-like collision between the poetic and the culinary. In its clash between the language of high art and the business of cookery, the word σκοροδομίμητον epitomizes the *Aeolosicon*'s overall premise, reducing the plot's two simultaneous scripts into this single, funny word.

The language of *mimesis* also keys into the play's storytelling premise. In both fragments 3 and 5, we see objects apparently changing form and passing themselves off as things they are not, mimicking the protagonist's double, unstable identity as both Aeolus and Sicon. By here couching this vegetal transformation in the metatheatrical terminology of disguise, cookery itself takes on a poetic significance. Perhaps this was a theme throughout the play. Indeed, cookery often has metapoetic overtones in comedy, and this seems to have become a more prominent trope in the fourth century. John Wilkins, in his book *The Boastful Chef*, has shown that not only is the language of food and eating a core element of comedy's poetics, but the role of food preparation became increasingly important as the stock character of the chef emerged in the so-called Middle period of comedy (Wilkins 2000b: 387–407). In particular, Wilkins argues that the 'boastful chefs' of the comic stage present the transformative potential of cookery as almost miraculous, their art rivalling even that of poetry. If the Sicon of Aristophanes' play fit this mould, then it is possible that throughout the play, poetic and culinary invention ran in parallel, with the chef's ability to transform food through cookery assimilated into the playwright's skill in transforming tragic myth into comic entertainment, and the god Aeolus into bumptious comic cook.[34]

Despite the highly fragmentary nature of our evidence, it is possible to sketch out how the *Aeolosicon* might have exploited the comic potential of its premise. As the tragic myth of Aeolus meets the more down-to-earth world of the comic cook, the plot itself constitutes a kind of joke which runs along two simultaneous scripts. These scripts are constantly in the background as the audience processes the action, and the clash between them can be activated in different ways to comic effect. As we have seen, several of the surviving fragments hint at how this might have played out. At the most basic level, as fragments 1 and 5 suggest, the *Aeolosicon*'s central incongruity creates the opportunity for some fun at tragedy's expense, as high-flown Euripidean language meets comic bathos.

There is, however, more to the play's comic texture than paratragedy alone. The preponderance of commonplace domestic objects in the fragments suggests that *Aeolosicon* used the clash between tragic myth and comic poetics to highlight comedy's connection to the materiality of everyday life; in turn, this sets tragedy up as a genre removed from ordinary life to the point of ridiculousness.[35] Finally, fragment 5 suggests that comedy's transformative potential, encapsulated in the play's refashioning of tragic god as comic everyman, was explored through a metatheatrical poetics of cookery: in the play, it seems, chef and comic poet in turn make the quotidian transcendent, and the transcendent quotidian. Whichever was the direction of the disguise, these competing tensions (between high and low, fantastical and realist, mythical and mundane) seem to have found their expression in the person of Aeolosicon himself.

Comic aetiologies and the Trojan War

Disguise and double identities are also central to a series of comic plots which treated the origins of the Trojan War. Aristophanes' *Daedalus* and Cratinus'

Nemesis both told the story of Helen's conception, and Cratinus' *Dionysalexandros*, whose title suggests a double-scripted plot structure similar to the *Aeolosicon*, focused on the judgement of Paris.[36] Each of these plots featured a central act of impersonation: in the *Daedalus* and *Nemesis*, Zeus was seen taking on the form of a bird, and in the *Dionysalexandros* the god Dionysus passed himself off as Paris. *Nemesis* and *Dionysalexandros* seem also to have had an element of political satire, as their protagonists were made intermittently to stand in for the politician Pericles.[37] Like the *Aeolosicon*, therefore, these three 'origin' plays built incongruous double scripts into the structure of their plots.

These plays are also notable for the way that they combine this kind of double scripting with a focus on cause and effect. In focusing on the origins of the Trojan War, the story content of these comedies alone means that issues of aetiology and causality are inescapable, and the plays appear to have capitalized on this to varying degrees, with the *Dionysalexandros* in particular gaining significant comic mileage from mucking around with the traditional chain of events. The issue of causality was certainly modish in the middle to late fifth century; perhaps most famously, Herodotus began his *Histories* with a promise to investigate the ultimate cause (αἰτίην, Hdt. 1.1) of the Persian Wars, and as Rosalind Thomas has shown, both Herodotus' intellectual preoccupations and his vocabulary reflect a wide-ranging engagement with contemporary philosophical thought.[38] Comedy was, of course, highly alert to contemporary intellectual fashions, and it is not therefore surprising to see that, against this background, both Cratinus' and Aristophanes' Trojan War plays seem to have something to say about cause and effect.

The birth of Helen in *Nemesis* and *Daedalus*

Cratinus' *Nemesis* (*c.* 431 BC)[39] and Aristophanes' *Daedalus* (*c.* 420 BC)[40] presented variations on the birth of Helen myth. In the *Nemesis*, as the title suggests, Cratinus focused on a version of the story found in the *Cypria* in which the goddess Nemesis was raped by Zeus and bore Helen as her daughter. The play seems to have integrated this with the now more well-known story of Leda and the Swan; fragments 114 and 115 suggest that in the play, Zeus raped

Nemesis in the form of a bird, and the resultant egg was passed to Leda for safekeeping.⁴¹ By contrast, *Daedalus* seems to have strayed more radically from the traditional myth(s): in the play, the inventor Daedalus apparently aided Zeus in his seductions by turning his engineering skills to the production of various animal disguises.⁴²

Although the fragments of *Nemesis* have little by way of political content, Plutarch (Plut., *Per.* 3.5) insisted that fragment 118 (μόλ' ὦ Ζεῦ ξένιε καὶ καραιέ, 'Come, oh Zeus, guest-god and head-god') attacked the politician Pericles, and this would fit with evidence from *Cheirones* (fr. 258 PCG) and *Thrattai* (fr. 74 PCG) which shows that Cratinus made something of a running joke of identifying Pericles with the king of the gods, alongside ridiculing the politician for his oversized head (Revermann 1997).⁴³ Given Pericles' reputation for womanizing, we can surmise that Cratinus likely used Zeus' exploits to lampoon him at least intermittently in the play.⁴⁴ Additionally, the mentions of Sparta in fragments 117 and 119 suggest that Helen's Spartan origins were used to link the Trojan War to the Peloponnesian War. The fragments of the *Daedalus* suggest that the mythical war was similarly used to evoke the contemporary one; in particular, fragment 199 refers ambiguously to a debate about ὁ πόλεμος ('the war'). In this regard, both comedies seem to play into something of a trend in fifth-century drama, since Athenian comedians and tragedians alike regularly used the Trojan War as a stand-in for the war with Sparta (Storey 2006a, Wright 2007). These plays' comic premise therefore has a number of competing and incongruous scripts inbuilt. In addition to a clash between the mythical and contemporary conflicts, Zeus in both the *Nemesis* and *Daedalus* occupies a double and even triple identity, as political satire collides with each play's central theme of disguise and trickery.

The fragments of *Nemesis* suggest that the characters' transformation into birds was the driving force behind not only the plot, but the comic poetics of the play. Fragment 114 sees a character (most likely Zeus) being instructed to transform himself into a big bird (ὄρνιθα ... μέγαν); 'little birds' appear in fragment 120; and a flamingo (fr. 121 PCG: φοινικόπτερον, cf. Ar., *Av.* 273) and cockerel (fr. 115 PCG: ἀλεκτρυόνος) also feature. These latter species are rather more bombastic and less elegant than the swan which features in the usual myth of Helen's conception,⁴⁵ and their insertion into the play creates a clash between the serious aesthetics of prior tragic and epic versions and the flamboyance of Cratinus' comic reimagining. This clash might well have been amplified through the use of costume; comparison with Aristophanes' *Birds* is suggestive of how this element might have added to the spectacle.[46]

Fragment 116 shows how the clash between the bird/human(oid) scripts which underscore the plot might have been exploited on the level of individual jokes.[47] The fragment seems to have been spoken by Zeus in the form of a bird, as he acclimatized himself to his new and unfamiliar form, and the herbaceous diet that came with it:

ὡς ἐσθίων τοῖς σιτίοισιν ἥδομαι·
ἅπαντα δ' εἶναί μοι δοκεῖ ῥοδωνιὰ
καὶ μῆλα καὶ σέλινα καὶ σισύμβρια

Oh I take great pleasure in this food I'm eating,
The whole lot seems to be rosebuds
And apples and celery and watermint.

Cratinus fr. 116 PCG

As we might expect given the god's intentions, this fragment is packed full of *double entendre*, and we encounter a metaphorical assimilation (familiar to us from Chapter 1) of sex and eating. On the basis of a gloss by the Byzantine scholar Photius in his *Lexicon*, which in turn most likely drew on the scholion to Theocritus 11 which preserved this fragment (Σ Theocritus 11.10),[48] all four of the foodstuffs listed here have sometimes been interpreted as euphemistic.[49] However, I think that this is to miss the joke, which is funny precisely because celery and watermint are *not* workable *double entendres*. Indeed it is worth noting that the scholiast who quotes these lines merely emphasizes the erotic overtones of roses and apples, both of which are similarly mentioned by Theocritus as typical symbols of erotic love (*Theoc.*, 11.10: ἤρατο δ' οὐ μάλοις οὐδὲ ῥόδῳ). The first two foods mentioned by the speaker therefore set up an erotic tone (with the roses alluding to female genitalia, and the apples to breasts);[50] but the celery and mint then intrude into this stock metaphor, thereby emphasizing the incompatibility of the two spheres of reference, and the ultimate ridiculousness of equating sex and food.

We might also consider how this line reads in the context of Zeus' avian disguise. The first two foods he consumes clearly superimpose the avian and human scripts whose clash underlies the play's entire comic conceit. However, as he moves into describing the joys of celery and watermint, neither of which recalls the sexual desire which was the impetus for his transformation, it seems almost like he is becoming wrapped up in his new birdlike identity and forgetting his prior concerns: Zeus the god wanted 'roses' and 'apples'. Zeus the bird is more interested in herbs.

Zeus' double identity in the play is complicated through the apparent introduction of political satire. Plutarch's suggestion that fragment 118 (μόλ' ὦ Ζεῦ ξένιε καὶ καραιὲ, 'Come, oh Zeus, guest-god and head-god') alluded to Pericles has led some scholars to interpret the play as political allegory; however, Bakola's in-depth reading of the *Nemesis* concludes (I think convincingly) that such allegorical readings 'are unsustainable, not only because the textual evidence is limited, but because even within themselves such allegories could not uphold the degree of correspondence often argued for'.[51] As Bakola's discussion shows, some of the correspondences are particularly problematic: in making Zeus stand for the womanizing Pericles, Nemesis takes on the role of Aspasia; however, this doesn't really work, since, as Bakola says, 'it is very difficult ... to read the mythic heroine being deceived and forced to copulate with Zeus as an allegory of Aspasia' (2010: 224). Instead, I would suggest that it is the very messiness of these correspondences which makes *Nemesis*' comic scenario so funny: as the characters take on different identities at different points, and bring different scripts into different incompatible combinations, the play's interpretative strands become tangled. If Matthew Wright (2007: 430) is correct to say that 'the comedians used the Trojan War as a means of exploring contemporary conflict, and that in particular they recurrently focused on the issue of causation in its own right', then this tangledness is significant. The story of Helen's birth is supposed to trace a single, causal line to the war with Troy. Cratinus' *Nemesis*, by contrast, presents us with nothing but interpretative disorder.

The fragments of *Daedalus* suggest a take on the birth of Helen that focused more explicitly on this issue of causality. The speaker of fragment 199 emphasizes the triviality of the war's origins:

περὶ τοῦ γὰρ ὑμῖν ὁ πόλεμος
νῦν ἐστι; περὶ ὄνου σκιᾶς

And what's this war about for you lot
now? About a donkey's shadow.

Ar., fr. 199 PCG

As a scholion on Aristophanes' *Wasps* 191 explains, 'to fight over a donkey's shadow' was a common proverbial expression meaning to fight over nothing (Biles and Olson 2015 ad loc.); the phrase was apparently derived from a story in which a man leases out his donkey, but claims that the privilege of resting in the animal's shade is not included in the fee. In the context of a plot about disguise and transformation, both the shadow's lack of materiality, and also its shapeshifting qualities seem significant. The war's origins, in other words, are not only trivial, but impossible to pin down, changing as they do from one moment to the next.[52]

Daedalus seems to have placed an overt emphasis on the metatheatrical qualities of its disguise plot. Fragment 192 features an address to the crane-operator much in the style of Aristophanes' *Peace* 173–6 and Strattis fragment 4 (both of which were discussed in the previous chapter):

ὁ μηχανοποιὸς ὁπότε βούλει τὸν τροχὸν
ἐᾶν κἀνεκάς λέγε, 'χαῖρε φέγγος ἡλίου'

Crane-operator, whenever you want the pivot-wheel
raised, say 'farewell ye lustre of the sun'.

Ar., fr. 192 PCG

If Daedalus in the play, as seems likely, was involved in inventing devices to aid Zeus in his amorous exploits (a conclusion strongly supported by the use in fragment 201 of the highly technical verb ἀρχιτεκτονεῖν, 'to be an architect'), then it seems inconceivable that some link was not made between Daedalus' machines and the *mechane*. And indeed, the speaker's concern for the specific components of the *mechane* in this fragment (τὸν τροχὸν, 'wheel' or 'pivot') suggests an engineer's interest in the technology's nuts and bolts. In such a scenario, Daedalus would become a kind of comic producer, contriving Zeus' performances in different animal roles, and directing the god's implementation of his theatrical machines. To have such a *comoididaskalos* figure literally pulling the strings behind the incident which, ultimately, causes the Trojan War is to suggest that comedy, and not tragedy or epic, is the genre best placed to put the most famous story of all time into motion.

Dionysalexandros and the causes of war

How this conceit filtered down into the *Daedalus*' comic texture is unclear; the fragments preserved are, unfortunately, not very funny, even if the plot as a whole seems to have made one big joke from its motifs of theatrical disguise and shifting identity. The evidence for Cratinus' play *Dionysalexandros* is somewhat better, since in 1904 a Hellenistic papyrus containing a lengthy hypothesis of the play was published (P.Oxy. 663, Grenfell and Hunt 1904). This play treats another potential starting point for the Trojan War, namely the judgement of Paris. Like *Nemesis* and *Daedalus*, the *Dionysalexandros* therefore has an inbuilt aetiological theme, and similarly seems to have combined this with some degree of political satire. Even more than the 'Zeus in disguise' plots of the *Nemesis* and *Daedalus*, this play also exploited the double script which results from a character with an ambiguous identity. In a manner similar to the *Aeolosicon* with which this chapter began, the *Dionysalexandros*' central conceit was to superimpose two characters on top of one another. The plot therefore combines its focus on the origins of the war with a rather disruptive double-scripting device whereby the god Dionysus, and not Paris, undertakes the judgement in the hope of stealing Helen for himself. The plot's very design therefore forces us to ask: what would have happened had this foundational moment gone a different way?

The precise details of how the plot played out are, of course, contentious. The hypothesis, though lengthy, is missing key parts from its left-hand column.[53] Even were it complete, the reliability of Hellenistic hypotheses is not a given; in particular, scholars of this period had a tendency to overemphasize the satirical elements of Old Comedy, which they saw primarily as a historical source on the politics of fifth-century Athens (Bakola 2010: 193–6). Several key points are disputed. Are the satyr chorus suggested by the hypothesist (42: οἱ σάτυ(ροι))[54] the same group who jeer at Dionysus earlier in the play (11–12: Διόνυσον ἐπισκώ(πτουσι) (καὶ) χλευάζου(σιν)), or is there a second chorus of Idaean shepherds who take Paris' side against the god?[55] What, precisely, was the play's relationship to satyr drama, and to what extent did it tread on its sister genre's toes?[56] And, perhaps most pertinently for the present discussion, what was the nature of the satire of Pericles described by the hypothesist, who claims that the politician was 'ridiculed in the drama most skillfully through innuendo for how he had brought war upon the Athenians' (44–7: κωμωιδεῖται δ' ἐν τῶι δράματι Περικλῆς μάλα πιθανῶς δι' ἐμφάσεως ὡς ἐπαγηοχὼς τοῖς Ἀθηνίοις τὸν πόλεμον)?[57]

Let us begin, then, with what we do know. In the play, Dionysus takes the role of Paris (Alexander) in judging the contest between the three goddesses Athena, Hera and Aphrodite, who each offer him the traditional bribes (hypothesis lines 12–18). After naming Aphrodite the victor, Dionysus then sails to Sparta to retrieve Helen, and brings her back to Mt Ida. The Greeks pursue him, as does the real Paris. To avoid detection, Dionysus hides Helen in a basket and changes himself into a ram (hypothesis lines 30–3, cf. fr. 45). Paris captures the errant pair, apparently intending to hand them both over to the Achaean army. However, at the last minute he chokes: though he surrenders Dionysus, Helen does not wish to go back to her husband, and so, taking pity on her, Paris marries her himself (34–9). The play therefore uses its double Dionysus-as-Paris script as an impetus to deviate further and further from the 'true' story, before finally putting the pieces back together again at the end so that the play concludes with Paris married to Helen and the Greeks seeking vengeance.

The incongruous double script which structures the *Dionysalexandros*, and the resultant gap which increasingly opens up between the traditional myth and the events of the play, is further complicated by a level of political satire. As with the *Nemesis*, discussed above, a sustained allegory seems unlikely, since comedy's rather anarchic poetics are not well-suited to this kind of hermeneutic continuity. However, it seems that at times Dionysus' womanizing exploits were used to attack Pericles, whose own susceptibilities to female charm were sometimes blamed for the war with Sparta (cf. *Acharnians* 527, where Pericles' consort Aspasia is cited as a key player in the war's origin). The comic protagonist therefore seems to accumulate identities as the play goes on; by the time he is apprehended, Dionysus has become Paris, Pericles, and a sheep.[58]

Every new role that Dionysus adopts takes us further from the mythohistorical origins of the war, and his accumulation of identities therefore generates the plot's parallel accumulation of mythical errata. In this way, the joke which underpins the entire plot is linked to its disruption of traditional causality, which is so extreme that at one point it appears that Paris is *almost* about to prevent the Trojan War instead of causing it! The *Dionysalexandros'* comic plot therefore looks two ways. On the one hand, the play's central joke serves to emphasize its distance from the mythic tradition of epic and tragedy, and the orderly aetiological progression of the 'true' story acts as a foil for the much more chaotic events of the play. On the other hand, the political satire (however intermittent) emphasizes comedy's role in analogizing and illuminating contemporary events. As a result, the play's ultimate joke is to suggest that it is not the serious historio-mythic tradition which can help us to understand how the present came to be, but rather the anarchic anti-aetiologies of comedy which are the best lens through which to view and interpret the modern world.

How this played out at a more granular level is less clear. The fragments of the play are few, and, like the *Daedalus*, disappointing in terms of actual jokes. It seems that much of the humour was derived from seeing characters in incongruous settings and situations. Fragments 42 and 43, for example, suggest a character more used to the finer things in life adjusting to the harsh realities of a shepherd's life on Mt Ida (Bianchi 2016: 260, 264):

παραστάδας καὶ πρόθυρα βούλει ποικίλα

Do you want doorposts and painted porticoes?

Cratinus fr. 42 PCG

οὔκ, ἀλλὰ βόλιτα χλωρὰ καὶ οἰσπώτην πατεῖν

No, but to tread green cowpatties and sheep filth underfoot.

Cratinus fr. 43 PCG

Ian Storey suggests that perhaps these fragments came from a scene in which Helen surveyed her new home after being captured by Dionysus, or otherwise that they relate to the god himself when he realizes that adopting the role of Paris has its disadvantages as well as its perks (2011: 287). Either way, the humour here is essentially character-based, as the audience laugh at the incongruity of either the glamorous Helen or the effete Dionysus forced into a life of rustic simplicity. It is tempting also to read a metatheatrical joke into fragment 42. The word παραστάδας has an elevated, tragic register, and is frequently used by Euripides to designate the grand architecture of palaces and temples;[59] and πρόθυρα is used with some regularity in the *Odyssey* to describe the palaces of Odysseus, Menelaus and Circe.[60] The joke therefore has the potential to be double-layered. The speaker finds themselves transplanted not only physically from their usual grandeur to this peasant backwater, but also generically from their traditional home in epic and tragic myth to this crude, comic landscape, complete with characteristic scatology (cf. βόλιτα fr. 43), and with stage scenery to match.

Fragment 40 may also have a metatheatrical edge, this time with a focus on costume:

A: στολὴν δὲ δὴ τίν᾽ εἶχε; τοῦτό μοι φράσον.
B: θύρσον, κροκωτόν, ποικίλον, καρχήσιον

A: What kind of clothes did he have? Tell me that.
B: A thyrsus, a saffron dress (a fancy one!) and a wine cup.

Cratinus fr. 40 PCG

The ensemble described here is clearly that of Dionysus. Given the first speaker's interrogative tone, it is possible that he is trying to ascertain the identity of the culprit who has absconded with Helen. If so, comparison with Dionysus' Herakles outfit in the *Frogs* would be productive; while his disguise in Aristophanes' play is not especially convincing, he does at least go to the effort of throwing a lion skin on top of his saffron gown (*Ran*. 46). Perhaps his Paris impersonation in the *Dionysalexandros* was even more transparent, allowing the audience to laugh at the stupidity of anyone taken in by it.

Fragment 45 would indeed suggest that the god of the theatre was not exactly a master of disguise in the play:

ὁ δ᾽ ἠλίθιος ὥσπερ πρόβατον βῆ βῆ λέγων βαδίζει

And then this pillock goes about saying 'baa baa' like a sheep.

Cratinus fr. 45 PCG

This must surely relate to Dionysus' transformation into a ram, as described by the hypothesist (32–3: ἑαυτὸν δ᾽ εἰς κριὸ[ν / μ(ε)τ(α)σκευάσας). The hypothesist's term μετασκευάσας suggests that costume and props (σκευή) were involved, and therefore hints at a scene with clear metatheatrical overtones. The fragment's speaker makes clear that the god is not an especially persuasive actor, however, and describes the performance in what are clearly disparaging terms (cf. ἠλίθιος). Together with fragment 40 above, this suggests the possibility at least that the god of the theatre's unexpectedly poor theatrical skills became something of a running joke as he took on multiple identities throughout the play.

The overt theatricality of the *Dionysalexandros*' central conceit may therefore have played out at the level of its individual jokes, with the plot's double-scripting device reflected in a parallel interest in the comic potential of disguise. Meanwhile, the play's repeated postponement of its inevitable ending takes it further and further from the neat, linear aetiologies of serious myth making and towards something more anarchic. In turn, the play's additional level of political satire presents its new and distinctly comic myth as an analogue for contemporary history. In the *Dionysalexandros*' telling, it is comedy, and not the traditional myths of tragedy or epic, which will help you understand the world as it falls to pieces under the pressure of the Peloponnesian War.

Aristophanes on the causes of war

Two of Aristophanes' extant plays, the *Acharnians* (425 BC) and *Peace* (421 BC), also embed a comic interest in aetiology in their plots. Although, unlike *Nemesis*, *Daedalus* and the *Dionysalexandros*, these plays are ostensibly set in contemporary Athens, it has been well established that both are underpinned by sustained episodes of paratragedy. Each therefore has a mythic substratum to its plot; the *Acharnians* sees its hero Dicaeopolis act the starring role in Euripides' *Telephus*, and *Peace* parodies the flight of Bellerophon in Euripides' tragedy of the same name.[61] Of these, the *Acharnians*' tragic model does relate peripherally to the early stages of the Trojan War, since the action of the *Telephus* took place during the Greeks' journey to Troy.[62] However, even this play does not focus particularly on the war's aetiologies. Rather, both *Acharnians* and *Peace* are in different ways concerned with creating new, comic mythologies of the causes of the war with Sparta.

The *Acharnians*' engagement with these narratives is concentrated in the famous speech made by Dicaeopolis to the chorus in lines 496–556. Made in self-defence before the irate chorus, these lines see Dicaeopolis justifying his decision to bypass the city's democratic institutions and make an individual peace treaty with the Spartans. In doing so, the hero concocts a new mythohistorical aetiology of the war which draws on a number of genres, including tragedy, epic, and even prose historiography. The scholarship on this speech is extensive, and I do not wish to crowd further what is already a crowded field. To this end, after setting out in brief some of the excellent existing interpretations of this passage, I will add only a few comments to suggest how this speech may illuminate by comparison some of the plays already discussed in this chapter.

Dicaeopolis' speech is underpinned by a complex and shifting set of scripts which in many ways parallel the double- and triple-scripting devices which we have seen to accompany comic protagonists in plays such as the *Aeolosicon* and *Dionysalexandros*. By the time he begins his address, Dicaeopolis has put on the ragged costume of Euripides' tragic hero Telephus (who is *himself* in disguise as a beggar) which he borrows directly from the tragedian (*Acharnians* 393–489); as Dicaeopolis puts it in lines 440–1: 'I must seem this day to be a beggar, and to be who I am, yet not appear to be' (δεῖ γάρ με δόξαι πτωχὸν εἶναι τήμερον, / εἶναι μὲν ὅσπερ εἰμί, φαίνεσθαι δὲ μή).[63] To the hero's triple-layered identity, signalled by his visible layers of costume, the speech then adds yet another voice. In lines 502–3, Dicaeopolis appears to speak as if he were the playwright Aristophanes himself (οὐ γάρ με νῦν γε διαβαλεῖ Κλέων ὅτι / ξένων παρόντων τὴν πόλιν κακῶς λέγω. 'Cleon won't be able to cast aspersions on me this time, saying that I've disparaged the city in front of foreigners').

The most successful analyses of this scene have for the most part taken one of two approaches. Scholars including Foley (1988), Slater (2002: 115–32), Compton-Engle (2015) and Sells (2019: 23–52) treat Dicaeopolis' multilayered identity through the lens of metatheatre and parody, and examine the role of Dicaeopolis' overtly theatrical performativity in creating shifts in voice and identity throughout the play. In parallel to this, Goldhill (1991: 167–222) and Platter (2007: 42–62) have used the framework of Bakhtinian dialogism to describe the destabilizing polyphony of Dicaeopolis' speech. To these excellent interpretations, I would only add that the scene might equally be understood as exploiting the incongruities created through the layering of multiple, incompatible scripts. Seen in another light, in other words, Dicaeopolis' speech is one big joke.

To this mix, Aristophanes adds an extended riff on the causes of the Peloponnesian War (515–37). Where the *Dionysalexandros* presents a mythical story of woman-stealing as an analogy for contemporary events, the *Acharnians* here reverses the joke: the lines describe a series of tit-for-tat thefts of prostitutes in suspiciously mytho-historical terms. It is here worth quoting the passage in full:

> ἡμῶν γὰρ ἄνδρες, κοὐχὶ τὴν πόλιν λέγω,
> μέμνησθε τοῦθ', ὅτι οὐχὶ τὴν πόλιν λέγω,
> ἀλλ' ἀνδράρια μοχθηρά, παρακεκομμένα,
> ἄτιμα καὶ παράσημα καὶ παράξενα,
> ἐσυκοφάντει Μεγαρέων τὰ χλανίσκια·
> κεἴ που σίκυον ἴδοιεν ἢ λαγῴδιον   520
> ἢ χοιρίδιον ἢ σκόροδον ἢ χόνδρους ἅλας,
> ταῦτ' ἦν Μεγαρικὰ κἀπέπρατ' αὐθημερόν.
> καὶ ταῦτα μὲν δὴ σμικρὰ κἀπιχώρια,
> πόρνην δὲ Σιμαίθαν ἰόντες Μεγαράδε
> νεανίαι 'κκλέπτουσι μεθυσοκότταβοι·   525
> κᾆθ' οἱ Μεγαρῆς ὀδύναις πεφυσιγγωμένοι
> ἀντεξέκλεψαν Ἀσπασίας πόρνα δύο·
> κἀντεῦθεν ἀρχὴ τοῦ πολέμου κατερράγη
> Ἕλλησι πᾶσιν ἐκ τριῶν λαικαστριῶν.
> ἐντεῦθεν ὀργῇ Περικλέης οὑλύμπιος   530
> ἤστραπτ', ἐβρόντα, ξυνεκύκα τὴν Ἑλλάδα,
> ἐτίθει νόμους ὥσπερ σκόλια γεγραμμένους,
> ὡς χρὴ Μεγαρέας μήτε γῇ μήτ' ἐν ἀγορᾷ
> μήτ' ἐν θαλάττῃ μήτ' ἐν ἠπείρῳ μένειν.
> ἐντεῦθεν οἱ Μεγαρῆς, ὅτε δὴ 'πείνων βάδην,   535
> Λακεδαιμονίων ἐδέοντο τὸ ψήφισμ' ὅπως
> μεταστραφείη τὸ διὰ τὰς λαικαστρίας·

For some of our own men, and I do not say the city,
Remember that, that I do not say the city,
But just some wretched little whippersnappers, counterfeits,
valueless and un-hallmarked and half-foreign,
Trumped up charges against those Megarian cloaklets.
And should anyone see so much as a cucumber or piglet,
Or hare-let, or garlic-let or a grain of salt,
it was denounced as Megarian and sold off at once.
But this was just a trifling domestic matter,
Until some drunk-cottabosing youths went Megarawards

and stole some whore, Simithea.
And the Megarans, garlic-primed and sore,
Stole in return two whores from Aspasia.
And from this cause the war broke out
For all the Greeks: from three cocksuckers!
And so Olympian Pericles hurled his thunderbolts
In anger and thundered and stirred up Greece,
And laid down laws written up like drinking songs,
So that it was decreed that no Megarian should remain
On land or marketplace or sea or shore.
And the Megarians, starving bit by bit,
Begged the Spartans to get the decree reversed,
This, on account of these cocksuckers.

Ar., *Ach.* 515–37

Like the *Dionysalexandros*, Dicaeopolis' tall tale splices together three incompatible scripts, so that the myth of Helen clashes with contemporary political satire (note the Zeus-like Pericles, familiar to us from Cratinus' play) and comic absurdity. The general thrust of the narrative is clearly modelled on Helen's kidnap by Paris. In turning this story into a grubby series of prostitute-thefts and escalating reprisals, Aristophanes most likely also builds in a parody of Herodotus, whose opening of the *Histories* (1.2–4) narrates a series of mythical abductions, including Io, Europa and Helen (see Olson 2002: liii–liv). Herodotus identifies these as the ultimate cause of enmity between Greece and Persia, and therefore of the Persian War (via the Greeks' original invasion of Asia in the Trojan War, 1.4.1). These underlying 'serious' scripts drawn from epic myth and historiography are therefore brought into collision with Dicaeopolis' absurd and obscene story of a war caused by, in his words 'the theft of three cocksuckers' (529, 537).

This comic triangulation of myth, history and political satire is made increasingly absurd by the addition of a number of smaller-scale jokes. First, we find a comic metaphor describing the men responsible for sparking the conflict as debased currency (517–18), so that moral worthlessness is expressed in pseudo-economic terms. The comparison itself is not especially funny on its own, and indeed, given its reappearance in *Frogs* (718–26), may be something of a stock metaphor. However, its configuration here is comically exaggerated, piling up four adjectives in a row which essentially repeat the metaphor over and over again (παρακεκομμένα, ἄτιμα καὶ παράσημα καὶ παράξενα, 'counterfeits, valueless and un-hallmarked and half-foreign').[64] The list includes a mildly amusing pun: ἄτιμα primarily refers to lack of moral value, but may also be used in an economic context to refer to the value of goods (cf. Xen., *Vect.* 4.10–11), and so the word nicely encompasses both the vehicle and tenor of the metaphor. The joke proper appears in the next line, when illegal tender collides with illegal goods: the men who have themselves been described as illegitimate currency are described as decrying (519: ἐσυκοφάντει) illegitimate imports, and the narrative therefore becomes ironic to the point of complete absurdity.

This absurd quality, which creates a clash between the speech's overtly comic poetics and its epic and historiographical narrative models, is amped up in the following lines. The squabble over Megarian imports is made to seem utterly trivial and ridiculous through Dicaeopolis' list of disputed goods (520–1: κεἴ που σίκυον ἴδοιεν ἢ λαγῴδιον / ἢ χοιρίδιον ἢ σκόροδον ἢ χόνδρους ἅλας). Not only does the list decrease in size from the small (σίκυον, 'cucumber') to the practically microscopic (χόνδρους ἅλας, 'grain of salt'), encompassing two diminutives along the way (λαγῴδιον, χοιρίδιον; these are followed by the word σκόροδον, 'garlic', which, while not itself diminutive, almost mirrors in its -οδον ending the -ῴδιον and -ίδιον of the two diminutives which precede it; I have tried to capture this in my translation, 'garlic-let'). The foods listed also have sexual overtones; cucumbers are, for obvious reasons, used as a phallic euphemism (Henderson 1991: 125), and the piglets here anticipate the highly obscene joke in the 'piglet' scene later in the play (729–835, discussed in Chapter 1, pp. 64–6). The combination here of the trivial and the sexual (cf. also 529: λαικαστριῶν, 537: λαικαστρίας, 'cocksuckers') exemplifies comedy's aesthetics, and creates an incongruous clash with the epic and historical narratives which underpin the speech.

The jokes here are more than mere decoration. By taking serious mythohistorical aetiologies of prior wars and repackaging them in absurd, trivial and random terms, the speech creates a contrast between the coherent narratives of past conflicts, and the anarchic messiness of the contemporary world. This passage, with its hints of authorial voice and pseudo-parabatic tone, therefore faces off against more traditionally educative and explanatory modes of literature, poking gentle(ish) fun at their serious aetiologies, while presenting a model of understanding the modern world which is distinctively comic. Tragedy might help you make sense of the Trojan War, history the Persian, but for this new and bleakly farcical chapter, only comedy will do.

Aristophanes' interest in disrupting traditional aetiologies resurfaces in his play of 421, *Peace*. The play premiered in a moment of optimism, following as it did hot on the heels of the (unfortunately short-lived) Peace of Nikias.[65] Despite this, the play is surprisingly combative, poetically if not politically; Hall (2006: 344–9) has drawn attention to Trygaeus' epic song contest in the play's second half, in which the hero banishes warlike Homeric verses in favour of epic motifs of feasting and celebration,[66] while the *Peace*'s oppositional relationship with tragedy has drawn attention from Dobrov (2001), Ruffell (2011: 314–60) and Sells (2019: 119–46). The play is also striking for its insistence on re-contesting the origins of a war which was apparently at this point over. This combination of literary and aetiological competition has many similarities with the *Dionysalexandros*, and like Cratinus' play, *Peace* also builds a number of jokes about causality into its plot. However, where the *Dionysalexandros* is constrained by the inevitability of ending in line with its mythic model, *Peace*'s looser relationship to its mythical paradigm allows for a rather different set of cause-and-effect jokes.

As we saw in the previous chapter, the opening of the *Peace* is structured around a comic set-piece, in which the protagonist Trygaeus transforms the grand ascent of Euripides' hero Bellerophon atop his winged horse into a bathetic, rickety flight on the back of a dung beetle. Trygaeus' double identity as a Bellerophonalike allows Aristophanes to state an allegiance to a mythic model, and so to present his own comic plot against this more serious narrative foil. The play's wider paratragic interactions, however, are not my interest here. Rather, I want to explore briefly how the play uses a single joke at tragedy's expense as the impetus for an investigation of the differing causal frameworks which underlie comedy in comparison to its more serious generic rivals.

The plot of the *Peace* in the first half of the play is propelled not only by the joke-like substitution of tragic horse with comic beetle, but also by a single act of comedic literalization. Euripides' *Bellerophon* seems to have been particularly bleak in its outlook. Fragment 285, which is almost universally taken to be a section of the play's prologue spoken by Bellerophon,[67] sees the hero insist that it is better first, never to have been born (285.2: κράτιστον εἶναί φημι 'μὴ φῦναι' βροτῷ.); and second, never to experience good things (285.18: ἄριστον μὴ πεπειρᾶσθαι καλῶν), since this only exacerbates life's later and inevitable sufferings. This seems to have been followed by the famous 'atheistic' fragment,[68] in which Bellerophon makes the radical claim that there are no gods in heaven:

φησίν τις εἶναι δῆτ' ἐν οὐρανῷ θεούς;
οὐκ εἰσίν, οὐκ εἴσ', εἴ τις ἀνθρώπων θέλει
μὴ τῷ παλαιῷ μῶρος ὢν χρῆσθαι λόγῳ.

Does someone say that there are in fact gods in heaven?
There are not, there are not, if any of mankind wishes
Not to be a fool and rely on legends of old.

Eur., fr. 286.1–3 TrGF

In a typically literalistic comic move, *Peace* turns Bellerophon's atheistic melancholy into a joke. Where the tragic hero believes there are no gods in heaven because they are the invention of storytellers (286.3: παλαιῷ ... λόγῳ), our comic hero Trygaeus finds that there are no gods in heaven only because they have just moved house. When he arrives on Olympus following his Bellerophon-inspired flight, Hermes (the sole inhabitant left behind to take care of the last pots and pans, *Pax* 201–2) informs him of his narrow miss:

Τρ: ἴθι νυν κάλεσόν μοι τὸν Δί'.
Ἑρμ: ἰηῦ ἰηῦ ἰηῦ,
       ὅτι οὐδὲ μέλλεις ἐγγὺς εἶναι τῶν θεῶν·
       φροῦδοι γάρ· ἐχθές εἰσιν ἐξῳκισμένοι.

Trygaeus: Come on then, call Zeus for me.
Hermes: Ha ha ha! Don't think you'll be getting anywhere *near* the gods!
           They've vanished, moved house just yesterday.

Ar., *Pax* 195–7

The joke here is more multilayered than it first appears. At a basic level, it relies on a collision between tragic and comic outlooks, the former philosophizing and profound, the latter trivial and absurd. As the scene unfolds, we find an additional comic reversal: where Euripides' Bellerophon despaired of the gods, Aristophanes' gods have instead despaired of mankind, deciding to up sticks rather than watch the Greeks forever at war with one another (*Pax* 204–9).

More than this, however, the joke asks us to compare the organization of tragic versus comic plots. Much like the narrative jokes in the *Dionysalexandros* (which derive comic force from their disorderly, random disruption of the orderly, linear patterns of cause and effect that structure the original story), the joke here in *Peace* creates a clash between the predictable cause-and-effect patterns of the tragic plot and the sheer haphazardness of events in comedy.

This sense of the haphazard is carried over into Hermes' explanations of the origins of the war. The god offers two incompatible models of causality. On the one hand, he presents the Peloponnesian War as the result of vast, theological factors: the Olympian gods have abandoned mankind to the god War (204–9), and he in turn has buried the goddess Peace deep in a pit (223). On the other, he represents the war as the outcome of a series of pettifogging quarrels, beginning with Pericles intentionally inciting hostility with the controversial Megarian decree to distract attention from potential corruption charges (605–9);[69] and ending with the farmers being stirred up by self-serving orators who exploit their love of figs and raisins to whip up disproportionate anger against the Spartan invasions of Attica (632–8). The resultant clash between the cosmic and the trivial makes the entire business seem ridiculous. Not only this, but these competing versions of events emphasize the sheer unpredictability of the course of history: whether the war is the result of divine intervention or random petty squabbling, these factors are beyond comprehension, either too big or too small to be truly understood, let alone predicted.

The fact that Hermes is, of course, talking complete nonsense is part of the joke. Trygaeus and the chorus both express surprise at Hermes' version of events, wryly stating that 'I never learned this from anybody before' (615: 'γὼ 'πυσμην οὐδενός), and 'there's much that's been concealed from us' (618: πολλά γ' ἡμᾶς λανθάνει). The reason for this is that the entire narrative is comic invention from start to finish. However, by allowing the audience to laugh at Trygaeus' and the chorus' apparent epiphany, this joke also pokes fun at the idea that any single narrative can truly explain why things happen as they do. When (as with Trygaeus' arrival on Olympus) any tiny coincidence can alter the course of history, do stories really help us at all? Or is the narrative convention of cause and effect so artificial and removed from reality as to be, like Hermes' story of the war, utter nonsense?

Conclusions

We are a long way here from Aristotle's 'probable and necessary' (*Poetics* 1451b9). Throughout this chapter, we have seen comedies whose plots are deliberately disruptive to just the kinds of linear chains of causality which Aristotle suggests are essential for storytelling. Jokes have been essential to these disruptions. Plays like the *Dionysalexandros* and *Aeolosicon* are founded on a single, joke-like incongruity, and use this conceit to splice together multiple incompatible scripts at the level of their plots. While the *Dionysalexandros* and *Aeolosicon* are perhaps more overt in their deployment of this mechanism, other plays, like the *Nemesis*, *Daedalus*, *Acharnians* and *Peace*, are similarly founded on the incongruities which result from disrupting a standard mythic model. Such models are, of course, particularly pleasing to disrupt; not only do they allow comedians to throw a relatively stable narrative tradition into chaos, but, given their association with more 'serious' storytelling traditions, revisiting these myths sets comedy on a direct collision course with epic and tragedy. Fun, as we have seen throughout this chapter, can always be had at the expense of such cultural titans as Homer and Euripides. Aristotle, of course, knows this. His image of Orestes and Aegisthus departing the stage hand in hand as friends (Arist., *Poetics* 1453a35) acknowledges precisely these dynamics.

These plays are more than just superficial fun at myth's expense, however. Embedded in their joking disruptions of traditional storylines is a sustained interest in how narrative is put together, and how (or perhaps if) it represents reality. To this end, a number of comedies also train their gaze on issues of aetiology. Plots cluster around the origin stories of the Trojan War in particular. Cratinus' *Nemesis* and Aristophanes' *Daedalus* each appear to have played around with questions of causality, and to have used jokes about the causes of the Trojan War to adumbrate more contemporary conflicts and their origins; and the *Dionysalexandros*, whose plot is overtly founded on an incongruous double script, seems to have pushed this analogy between mythic and contemporary aetiologies even more into the foreground. Such plays were, however, far from allegorical. Indeed, looking at their multiple layers of representation through the lens of joke theory allows us to appreciate that shifting discontinuities and interpretative impossibilities are central to the conceit. The multiple identities which cluster around the *Dionysalexandros'* protagonist, and the multiple narrative and interpretative scripts that this activates in turn, are not there to be solved and made congruent through a single allegorical reading. The joke relies precisely on the impossibility of resolving these clashes. In their very multiplicity, these plays' comedic structures present a messy way of understanding the world, and one which stands in stark contrast to the neat chains of causality which characterize the Greek world's foundational stories.

Aristophanes' *Acharnians* and *Peace*, although they have a mythic substratum to their plots, bring these joke causalities fully into the contemporary world. These plays' divergent aetiologies of the Peloponnesian War literally make a nonsense of more traditional accounts. In splicing together multiple, incongruous strands drawn from myth, history, tragedy and epic, and representing them in new, comic form, these plays vie, however insincerely, for their own position in public and political discourse. As Dicaeopolis himself says, 'comedy *too* knows what's right' (Ar., *Ach.* 500: τὸ γὰρ δίκαιον οἶδε καὶ τρυγῳδία). *Peace* and *Acharnians* each show how easily the narrative arcs of the apparently serious, realist storytelling tradition can be disrupted by mere happenstance and in doing so, they also expose the precarity of these structures. A missed encounter, a last-minute substitution, a political ruse with unintended consequences: these, in Aristophanes' telling, are the things that make history.

As comedians expose neat, linear chains of cause and effect as ultimately artificial, a product not of truthful mimetic representation but of poetic convention, comedy in turn undermines the truth-value of the 'serious' storytelling tradition, and its utility as a means to negotiate political reality. Jokes sit at the heart of this proposition. By suggesting that the systems of causality which shape history are based on the same erratic and insoluble multiplicity which structures all joke-carrying texts, comedy presents not only its plots, but its very poetics as a model of how best to perceive and represent the world.

Conclusions: Comedy and the Avant-Garde in the Fifth Century and Beyond

ἄλλα δ' ἄλλαν θραῦεν σύρτις
μακραυχενό-
πλους, χειρῶν δ' ἔγβαλλον ὀρείους πόδας ναός, στόματος
δ' ἐξήλλοντο μαρμαροφεγ-
γεῖς παῖδες συγκρουόμενοι·

And all about, the shoal splintered
the long neck-voyagers,
and from their hands they cast
the ship's mountain-feet, and from their mouths leapt
their shining children of crystalline rock, crashing together.

Timotheus fr. 791.88–93 PMG

This peculiar little passage comes not from a comedy, but from a fragment of the dithyrambic poet Timotheus. A proponent of the so-called 'New Music', readers may in fact recall Timotheus' name from Chapter 2 of this book, where he featured alongside Melanippides and Cinesias in a catalogue of Music's abusive lovers (Pherecrates *Chiron*, fr. 155 PCG). This is usually how we envisage comedy's relationship with the avant-garde artists of the late fifth and early fourth centuries: as Timotheus and co. were shaping the innovative poetics of the post-Classical age, comedy's more conservative instincts provoked it to snipe from the sidelines, and to lampoon the New Music as obscure to the point of absurdity.[1] At most, as Gregory Dobrov has argued, comedy was not entirely immune to the literary revolution happening around it, and eventually came to incorporate those same poetic qualities it had once reviled; dithyramb was, in Dobrov's words, 'absorbed into the comic arsenal as an odd sort of poetry, a style comprising a rather narrow inventory of techniques: bold metaphors, an abundance of descriptive participles, new and complex adjectives, asyndetic relatives and appositives, and odd periphrases for the ordinary' (1997: 69). Comedy was, in other words, not a driving force of poetic innovation, but rather a critic and ultimately a consumer of novelty. In turn, Dobrov suggests that these apparently dithyrambic qualities – over-the-top metaphors, complex neologisms, a piling-up of descriptors – are fundamentally external to comedy's poetics; the term 'arsenal' in particular implies that even once incorporated, these qualities retain an element of parodic force to be weaponized against other modes of speech with loftier pretensions. This fairly dominant view of comedy's poetics as essentially acquisitive, while not incorrect, seems to me to underplay the extent to which comedy actively shaped the poetic climate of its era. In other words, while the genre is certainly omnivorous, the traffic of influence surely does not only go one way, nor does it run only downstream from 'higher' genres to 'lower' ones.

As we have seen throughout this book, comedy's poetics are often experimental to the point of eccentricity. I've argued that comedy regularly exploits the contiguities between poetry and jokes as part of a literary project which pushes the representational possibilities of language to their absolute limits. Of course, poetic jokes in comedy frequently carry a degree of parodic force, and comedy takes a particular interest in the mechanics of 'serious' literature. Jokes targeting the ridiculous potential of key poetic tropes such as ekphrasis and metaphor, and (given the way that comedy's paradigm of seriousness is often shaped around tragedy in particular) the conventions of dramatic *mimesis*, are a stalwart of the genre. But I hope that the examples in this book have shown that jokes in comedy are also a site of extraordinary creative energy in their own right. Indeed, the experimental qualities of dithyramb listed by Dobrov above seem to me to be no less characteristic of comedy's poetics.

As this book draws to a close, I want to place comedy's experimentalism within the wider context of the late fifth and early fourth centuries, and to suggest that the genre should be central to our understanding of the poetic radicalism of this era. This was certainly a period marked by innovation. As Armand D'Angour has argued, the increasingly professionalized nature of performance culture in this period allowed for the development of more complex musical and poetic styles, and most notably the flourishing of the

'New Music' which centred around dithyrambic poets such as Timotheus (D'Angour 2006: 270).[2] While the precise nature of the New Music's newness is still subject to vigorous debate, there is a consensus that the 420s onwards saw the development of a markedly different form of composition in which overall effect was privileged over and above clarity of meaning, and in which ornate and even obscure language was accompanied by complex and highly melismatic music which often spread a single syllable out over a number of notes.[3] As Eric Csapo has argued, it may have been precisely this subordination of sense to sound which attracted so much hostility in a culture which venerated the art of *logos* (2004b).

Comedy was, of course, a key witness to these developments, and provided a sharp commentary on the New Music's innovations;[4] Pherecrates' satire of the New Music's practitioners in his *Chiron* has already been discussed in detail earlier in this book, but other examples include Aristophanes' repeated targeting of Cinesias, and the famous frog chorus of the *Frogs*.[5] However, comedy is more than just an observer, and I'd like to suggest that the genre was in fact an active participant in the creative environment that nurtured the experimentalism of the New Music. While its aims and aesthetics may be different, we've seen throughout this book how jokes in comedy stretch the possibilities of language and literature to breaking point. Pherecrates' Music may complain bitterly about how the artistic contortions of Timotheus and his associates have bent her out of shape, but, as so often, comedy saves its sharpest satire for those genres closest to its own poetic activities, projecting onto others the criticisms which might in fact most obviously apply to itself. We should not, in other words, allow comedy's attacks on others' novelty to distract us from its own, but rather treat these attacks as testament to the genre's investment in artistic radicalism. To truly understand this era of innovation requires us to place comedy back at the cultural centre as a genre which, in pushing language to its most extreme and anti-representational possibilities, can be seen as anticipating the avant-garde poetics of the New Music.

The comic qualities of the New Music were not in fact lost on early-twentieth-century commentators. The fragment of Timotheus' *Persians* with which this chapter began was first published in 1903 in an *editio princeps* edited by Wilamowitz, and was met with no little excitement. In an early reaction to this publication, Basil Gildersleeve lamented that '[t]hree months hence it will be impossible to make the slightest observation about Timotheos, without consulting all the dreary literature, all the journals, all the programmes. The air will be filled with the shouts of scholars ... and there will be no room for my obviousness' (1903: 222). In spite of these wryly self-effacing comments, Gildersleeve's discussion is insightful, and his comments on the relationship between Timotheus' poetry and Old Comedy are particularly illuminating. Gildersleeve describes how his first impression of Timotheus' text is that it contains 'a series of γρῖφοι [riddles] such as Greek comedy delights in' (226),[6] and his discussion goes on to compare the quality of Timotheus' verse to Aristophanes, stating that 'the first impression made ... on my irreverent mind was comic rather than otherwise' (229–30).

While Gildersleeve chides himself for his inability to take Timotheus entirely seriously, the comparison here bears careful consideration. With this in mind, let us return to the passage with which this conclusion opened:

ἄλλα δ᾽ ἄλλαν θραῦεν σύρτις
μακραυχενό-
πλους, χειρῶν δ᾽ ἔγβαλλον ὀρείους πόδας ναός, στόματος
δ᾽ ἐξήλλοντο μαρμαροφεγ-
γεῖς παῖδες συγκρουόμενοι·

And all about, the shoal splintered
the long neck-voyagers,
and from their hands they cast
the ship's mountain-feet, and from their mouths leapt
their shining children of crystalline rock, crashing together.

Timotheus fr. 791.88–93 PMG

Timotheus' descriptions of the ships at Salamis in these lines are to my mind more than reminiscent of some of the metaphor-jokes discussed in Chapter 1 of this book. Although he does not foreground them to the extent that a poet such as Cratinus might, the passage exploits a series of joke-like clashes whereby landscape, bodies and vessels are mapped onto one another in an almost absurd series of images. As in comedy, these metaphors are often condensed into single compound coinages, which the listener must unpack. To Timotheus' μακραυχενόπλους ('those sailing along the long-neck [of the sea]', lines 89–90) we might easily compare Cratinus' βαλανειομφάλους ('acorn-shaped navels', fr. 54, discussed in Chapter 1, p. 34), or, as Gildersleeve does, Aristophanes' ἱππαλεκτρυών ('horse-cock', Ar., *Ran.* 932).[7]

The nexus of bodies/ships/landscape in Timotheus' lines is at points extremely difficult to unravel.[8] The verse often omits key nouns, relying only on adjectival descriptors from which the objects themselves must be inferred; the compound μακραυχενόπλους, which I translate above as 'long neck-voyagers', implies both ships (to do the sailing) and a body of water (shaped into a narrow passage like a long neck), but neither is named explicitly. The metaphor then shifts, so that the vessels and not the sea become body-like, as the oars are described as the 'ships' feet' (91: πόδας ναός); these body parts are in turn assimilated back into the landscape, as the feet are described as 'mountainous' (90–1: ὀρείους,). The metaphor is ringed with an almost comic contrast, whereby the sailors cast from their hands (90: χειρῶν) the feet (91: πόδας) of the ships, and this tangle of body parts adds to the chaos of the scene. The final metaphor of the passage contains another landscape/body metaphor, only this time it is reversed. Whereas in lines 89–90 the sea took on the characteristics of a body, in lines 92–3 the sailors' bodies are incorporated into the landscape as their teeth become 'shining rocks' (μαρμαροφεγγεῖς) which are disgorged into the ocean. The clash here is made more jarring by the juxtaposition of the words ἐξήλλοντο ('they leapt', line 92) and παῖδες ('children', line 93); this personification reinforces the passage's sense of metaphorical disjunct as the teeth become both embodied humans and inert rocks simultaneously. Given the earlier metaphor of ships-as-bodies, there is also a pleasing visual symmetry as the bodies of the sailors are smashed up in much the same manner as the ships that contained them (θραῦεν, line 88, 'splintered').

In an analysis of what he terms a 'dithyrambic' passage of Euripides' *Electra*, Eric Csapo suggests that a central quality of New Musical verse is that it is essentially imagistic rather than narrative in quality. Comparing the first stasimon of the *Electra* to the series of images on a *metope*, Csapo argues that '[i]nstead of building events up into a story, or propositions up into an argument, Euripides' verse offers us an almost purely paratactic sequence, a gallery of images. Each image is not so much meaningful as highly suggestive, emotionally charged, and in many cases ambiguous' (2009: 108). In Csapo's reading, the listener is heavily involved in supplying information based on their knowledge of the world and of this mode of art. The radical interpretative openness of this kind of poetry, and the 'reception work' it presupposes on the part of the audience, is also commented on by LeVen (2013: 55), who considers this key to Timotheus' 'riddling' quality. According to LeVen, 'the diction can appropriately be qualified as "riddling", since it is often unclear to what object ... the poet refers in such an indirect way, and its exact identification is left up to the audience's interpretation' (48).

I suggested in the Introduction to this book that this high degree of interpretative openness is one of the features which unites jokes and poetry. Like the passages of comedy which have been the subject of subsequent chapters, Timotheus' riddling verse makes an exaggerated feature of language's ability to stretch far beyond simple, denotive representation, and instead exploits its potential for almost endlessly recursive polyvalence. In a discussion of humour in Greek comedy, Nick Lowe comments on 'the absence of clearly defined limits to the audience's or reader's imaginative work' (2008: 12). The same description might easily apply to Timotheus' account of the Battle of Salamis, which, as Csapo and LeVen so clearly show, is one of impressionistic, imagistic effect rather than clear narrative rendition. Csapo even goes so far as to suggest that 'New Musical verse appeals directly to the senses, the subconscious, and the emotions' (2009: 108). For all their myriad intellectual and poetic complexities, jokes in comedy also seek to elicit an instinctive, bodily response from their audience in the form of emotion – in their case laughter.

Like the comic playwrights, poets such as Timotheus also seem interested in the potential gap between our perception of the world and its representation in language. It is perhaps worth returning here to Schopenhauer's comments on the incongruity that exists between our sensuous knowledge of the world and our understanding of it in rational thought, and on the role this incongruity plays in humour (1844: I §13). In the Introduction, I suggested that Schopenhauer's understanding of jokes is particularly pertinent for our reading of Greek comedy, which as a genre is interested in interrogating the limitations of linguistic, and particularly poetic, representation. The experimentalism of the New Music also betrays its practitioners' concern with the limitations of established poetic practice. However, where comedy seeks to prise apart the gap between, in Schopenhauer's terms, 'concepts and real objects', the New Music, with its dedication to sensual immediacy, attempts to close it.

While these approaches differ, reading a poet such as Timotheus side by side with the jokes of Old Comedy I hope goes some way towards showing that comedy deserves to be seen as a key player in the artistic environment which engendered the radical poetics of the late fifth and early fourth centuries. We have seen throughout this book that Greek comedy is both an astute critic of, and an active participant in, the linguistic and poetic innovation that defined this period. I have argued that, far from being mere surface phenomena, jokes in Greek comedy are a critical site of engagement with the language and convention of poetic representation. More than this, I have suggested that it is jokes' very closeness to poetic language which enables them to take such a role. Their similarities as two modes of speech which are inherently rule-bending and even rule-breaking, and which to a greater or lesser degree prioritize form over meaning, enable us to see jokes and poetic language on a continuum.

One criticism that might be levelled at this book is that it takes jokes rather too seriously. However, I'd like to suggest that while jokes in comedy are certainly artistically important, and even philosophically consequential, these attributes are not inevitably synonymous with seriousness. Certainly, comedy at times claims seriousness for itself, most famously in the *Acharnians*, where Dicaeopolis asserts that the audience should not be indignant to hear political advice in a comedy, since 'comedy *too* knows what's right' (Ar., *Ach*. 500: τὸ γὰρ δίκαιον οἶδε καὶ τρυγῳδία). However, we need not take these protestations of seriousness entirely seriously, nor is it necessary to find some truly serious message encoded in jokes for them to be worthy of our attention. Rather, I would suggest that for all the poetic experimentalism of comedy's jokes, there is an inescapable and indeed enjoyable flippancy to the deconstruction of the relationship between language and meaning which I have argued is a central component of the genre's humour. Such playfulness should not, however, count against jokes in our assessment of their importance to and influence on the artistic environment of this period. Indeed, its very lack of seriousness arguably liberates comedy to push at the boundaries of poetic possibility, and to pave the way for other, more earnest genres to follow in its wake. After all, if comedy's poetic experiments overreach and end up missing the mark, the comedian can fall back on the eternal defence that it's 'only a joke'.

Notes

Introduction

1 Aristotle's anticipation of incongruity-based models of the joke was commented on initially by Morreall (1987: 14), but see also Attardo (1994: 19–22). Aristotle's theory of jokes as a kind of utterance where two ideas are linked in a way which is unexpected or 'opposite' (1412a21: παρὰ τὸ ἐναντίως) and yet on some level intelligible does indeed seem to anticipate models of opposition, as per Raskin (1985) and Attardo (1994), or, perhaps more so, 'appropriate incongruity', as per Oring (1992, 2003). Incongruity theories of humour are discussed in greater detail below.

2 Freud's suggestion ([1905] 2002: 76) that jokes, like metaphors and riddles, are a form of 'indirect' representation is likely to have been influenced by Aristotle's discussion. See also Oring (2003: 5) for some brief but useful comments on the overlap between metaphors and jokes. Scott 2019b explores this issue in depth.

3 The -ικός suffix is modish in tone, and perhaps suggestive of new-fangled poetic practice. On -ικός suffixes, see Chantraine (1933: 384–96), and on such suffixes in Aristophanes' comic language, see Willi (1996: 139–45).

4 Attardo (1994: 21): 'Whether or not these passages anticipate modern developments is, after all, unimportant, when one assesses Aristotle's influence. The importance of Aristotle's influence on the theory of humor cannot be exaggerated.' Pages 21–45 set out the nature of this influence in detail, and Attardo concludes that Aristotle (along with Cicero and Horace) set the paradigm for all later discussions of the topic. *Poetics* 1449a is also discussed by Attardo (1994: 19–20), though this passage has otherwise proved less popular amongst proponents of incongruity theory.

5 Oring 1992: ch. 1, 2003: ch. 1. Oring suggests that Raskin's claim that, for example, the scripts LOVE and GOING TO THE DOCTOR are 'opposite' is not true in any meaningful sense. While some jokes clearly do rely on an opposition between, e.g., the abstract and concrete, Oring argues that it is reductive to claim that only opposition may underpin jokes, and he is surely correct to suggest that LOVE and GOING TO THE DOCTOR are incongruous rather than opposite.

6 Oring 2003: 2–3 argues that the failure to make the link, however spurious, 'appropriate' in some way leads to nonsense and not an actual joke. So, for example, if for the above joke, the answer given was 'because camels live in the desert', it would not be funny, since there has been no attempt to force a mapping of scripts through some appropriate linking device. Oring notes that small children who have developed an awareness of the question–answer joke format, but have not yet fully understood the structural rules which govern such jokes, often make unsuccessful jokes in this nonsense-riddle manner. Children's jokes are also discussed by Freud ([1905] 2002: 122–3).

7 See especially 1987: 43, where Palmer suggests that jokes may run two simultaneous but incompatible logics at once, so that 'the gag is characterized by the simultaneous presence of both modes of reasoning, which are maintained in tension, or balance with each other'. This model has obvious similarities with Oring's 'appropriate incongruity' theory.

8 For a discussion of *peripeteia* and its role in Aristotle's understanding of *mythos*, see Belfiore 1988.

9 See especially Attardo 1994: 25–45, which sets out Aristotle's influence on later theories of humour.

10 Kant 1790: § 54.332: 'Das Lachen ist ein Affekt aus der plötzlichen Verwandlung einer gespannten Erwartung in nichts.' ('Laughter is an affect arising from a strained expectation being suddenly reduced to nothing.' ([1790] 2007: § 54.332))

11 See Palmer 1987: 69–70, Oring 2003: 5. For a detailed analysis, and refutation, of these arguments, see Scott 2019b.

12 See Shklovsky [1917] 2004 for the origins of this term.

13 [1905] 2002: 70–6; while Freud names only metaphor, poetic language in general might also be included in his comparison. Freud's emphasis on the importance of brevity in humour seems also to suggest that there must be space for the listener to interpret; to spell too much out, in Freud's reading, kills the joke.

14 See also Lowe 2008: 12 who notes the potentially complex 'aperture' of jokes which he describes as 'the absence of clearly defined limits to the audience's or reader's imaginative work.'

15 Morreall 1987: 51–82 includes Schopenhauer in his collection of sources on the philosophy of humour, and he is discussed briefly also by Raskin 1985: 31–2 and Attardo 1994: 47–8.

16 Schopenhauer's original German text reads as follows: 'Das Lachen entsteht jedesmal aus nichts Anderm, als aus der plötzlich wahrgenommenen Inkongruenz zwischen einem Begriff und den realen Objekten, die durch ihn, in irgend einer Beziehung, gedacht worden waren, und es ist selbst eben nur der Ausdruck dieser Inkongruenz' (1844: I §13).

17 The wide range of comedy's intergeneric interactions is set out in Bakola, Telò and Prauscello 2013.
18 Key works on this topic include Rau 1967, Foley 1988, Silk 1993, Dobrov 2001, Platter 2007, Ruffell 2011: ch. 8, Nelson 2016.
19 Bakola (2010) focuses on Cratinus, and demonstrates that Aristophanes' predecessor also engaged deeply with tragic models. Farmer (2017) takes in a wide range of comic poets, and argues persuasively that paratragedy was a key feature of the comic genre.
20 See also Hall 2006: 341–4, Carey 2013a, Rawls 2013.
21 Cf. for example *Ach.* 496–555, in which Dicaeopolis' speech to the chorus appears to also contain an element of 'authorial voice', a problem which has been discussed at length, most notably by Goldhill (1991), Hubbard (1991) and Biles (2011); or Praxagora's speech at *Eccl.* 583–5, where she directly addresses the audience on the subject of her radical ideas.
22 See e.g. Storey 2003, Bakola 2010, Kidd 2014, Farmer 2017.
23 See also Brock 2004 on 'constellations' of jokes.
24 I use the term contemporaries rather broadly, and this book includes some poets such as Antiphanes who date from the so-called Middle period of comedy. The distinction between Old and Middle comedy is increasingly collapsing. Sutton (1990: 95) argues that '[s]ome of the characteristic features of Middle Comedy are already foreshadowed in Old Comedy and, contrariwise, some features that we are accustomed to consider characteristic of Old Comedy were slow to disappear from the comedy of the next century'. Csapo (2000) and Henderson (2014) similarly argue that there was no clear-cut process of evolution from 'political' Old Comedy to 'domestic' Middle; Sidwell (2000) suggests abandoning the term Middle Comedy altogether, in favour of a model which treats New Comedy as the product not of linear evolution (Old to Middle to New) but rather of generic cross-fertilization via tragedy.
25 On this line of *Acharnians*, see e.g. Goldhill 1991: 194–5, Biles 2011: 71–80, Sells 2019: 42–50.
26 See e.g. Slater 2002 on metatheatre, and Farmer 2017 on paratragedy. A fuller discussion of these topics can be found in Chapter 2.
27 Silk 2000: 98–159 analyses Aristophanic metaphors alongside other elements of the poet's language and style. Aristophanes' poetic style is also analysed by Taillardat, who at points uses the language of 'opposition' to describe the poet's imagery, e.g. 1965: 5, 'Mille images opposées se heurtent dans un désordre magique.' Taillardat frequently offers useful analyses of Aristophanes' metaphors; however, his approach is not so rigorously theorized as Silk's, and he is at points somewhat dismissive of 'modern' (i.e. post-Classical) theories of metaphor (cf. 1965: 7–8).

28 The gendered dynamics of Aristophanic metatheatre are also discussed by Zeitlin 1985.

1 Playing with Words: Jokes and Poetic Language

1 For some discussion of this play, see Arnott 1960, Pöhlmann 1971, Rosen 1999, Ruijgh 2001, Smith 2003, Boschi 2016.
2 On the obscene if obscure joke in these lines, cf. Rosen 1999: 156.
3 As will become clear, I use the term ekphrasis in this chapter to denote a passage of vivid description. The definition of the term ekphrasis, and its relative utility in application to literature of the fifth and fourth centuries BC, will be discussed further below, but for a thorough overview of the term and its definition see Webb 2009, who convincingly shows that the more narrow definition of ekphrasis as the description of an artwork is a twentieth-century phenomenon.
4 The vast bibliographies on each of these topics will be addressed individually later in this chapter, but as a starting point, on comic metaphor see Newiger 1957, Silk 2000: ch. 3, Ruffell 2014: 60–85, Scott 2019b, and on metaphor in Greek poetry more generally, Stanford 1936, Silk 1974, Boys-Stones 2003. On ekphrasis, and especially the description of landscape, see Parry 1957, Elliger 1975, Haß 1998, and on ekphrasis more generally, Fowler 1991, Goldhill 2007, Webb 2009.
5 It is interesting to note the relative dearth of similes as a subject of comic jokes. This may simply be the result of dealing with a fragmentary corpus which clearly constitutes only a very partial reflection of the genre's original trends. That said, there are some possible explanations for a preference for metaphors over similes in comic discourse. First, a trope which asserts only that something is *like* something else has less potential for absurdity than one which asserts that something *is* something else (cf. Oring 2003: 5). Secondly, similes are associated in particular with epic poetry, which is less often a target of comic mockery than e.g. tragedy.
6 Schopenhauer's comments are discussed in more detail in the Introduction, pp. 9–10.
7 Arist., *Poet.* 1455a22–5: δεῖ δὲ τοὺς μύθους συνιστάναι καὶ τῇ λέξει συναπεργάζεσθαι ὅτι μάλιστα πρὸ ὀμμάτων τιθέμενον· οὕτω γὰρ ἂν ἐναργέστατα [ὁ] ὁρῶν ὥσπερ παρ' αὐτοῖς γιγνόμενος τοῖς πραττομένοις ... ('it is necessary to arrange the plot (*mythos*) and to finish it in poetic style (*lexis*) so that it is placed before the eyes, so that thus seeing it most vividly (*enargestata*) as if actually present as things are happening'). For a discussion of this passage in relation to *enargeia*, see Zanker 1981: 307.
8 See Zanker 1981, Webb 2009 for more detailed discussions of the role of *enargeia* in ekphrasis.

9 See Peponi 2016: 2, 'The juxtaposition of, or osmosis between, these two visual modalities, vision and visualization, is of paramount importance for our understanding of Greek visuality. Lyric poets played a key role in promoting ways of bringing them together.' The role of visuality in lyric poetry is also discussed extensively by Fearn 2017 *passim*, who suggests that 'oscillations between presence and absence' (272) are key to lyric's negotiation between verbal and visual representation.

10 On assertions of 'seriousness' in comic poetry, see Silk 2000: ch. 7, Sells 2018: ch. 1.

11 For a more detailed discussion of the close structural relationship between metaphors and jokes, see Scott 2019b.

12 I here follow the standard capitalization conventions of conceptual metaphor theory, as established by Lakoff and Johnson in their book *Metaphors We Live By* (1980).

13 Cf. Raskin 1985, Oring 1992: ch. 1, Oring 2003: ch. 1.

14 See also Palmer 1987 and Brock 2004, who have further challenged theories of the joke which rely on models of binary opposition, and suggested that we should instead see 'constellations' (Brock 2004: 359) of multiple oppositions working simultaneously alongside one another.

15 See also Arist., *Rh.* 1406b7, where Aristotle again acknowledges the comic potential of metaphorical language (χρῶνται γὰρ καὶ οἱ κωμῳδοποιοὶ μεταφοραῖς).

16 Cicero's suggestion that jokes can be split into two categories, those which play on words (*dictu*) and those which play on ideas (*re*), seems to have been particularly influential on Freud's thinking. For a more detailed discussion of Cicero's remarks and their influence on Freud, cf. Attardo 1994: 26–9, 54–5.

17 Note also that Freud's argument that 'in a joke when the use of the same or a similar word takes us from one sphere of ideas to another, remote, one . . . [t]he re-discovery of what is familiar . . . is pleasurable' (Freud [1905] 2002: 118) overlaps in interesting ways with Ricoeur's theory of metaphor's 'power to "redescribe" reality' (Ricoeur 2003: 5).

18 For a full discussion of absurdity in jokes, see Oring 2003: chs 1, 2.

19 Oring 2003: 5, 'It seems to me that the reason riddles and jokes are humorous while definitions and metaphors are not is that in jokes the engagement of the incongruity and the search for its appropriateness is *spurious* rather than *genuine*.'

20 A slightly more balanced viewpoint can be found in Arist., *Rh.* 1410b, in which he suggests that metaphorical comparisons must be neither too obvious nor too obscure. In other words, Aristotle appears to suggest that a successful poetic metaphor must be sufficiently, but not excessively, defamiliarizing.

21 See Taillardat 1965: 5, 'Mille images opposées se heurtent dans un désordre magique.' Taillardat compares the violence of Aristophanes' metaphorical collisions to the ancient sport of quail-tapping ('Il fait battre les mots, comme les jeunes Athéniens de son temps faisaient battre les coqs et les cailles').

22 On the plot of *Pytine*, see Rosen 2000, Biles 2002, Ruffell 2002, Bakola 2010: 60–4. There is some disagreement about the play's ending, and particularly whether the poet was ultimately reformed (which Biles in particular regards as unnecessary); however, there is broad agreement on the overall shape of the plot.

23 The overall plot of the *Knights* is often referred to as 'allegorical' (e.g. Hubbard 1991: 66: 'The whole play operates as an allegory'; Slater 2002: 70 describes the play's opening as preparing the audience for an 'exposition of the political allegory'; Dover 2004: 239: 'At least one play of Aristophanes is allegorical: *Knights*'); however, for a discussion of why this term is problematic with reference to Old Comedy, see Kidd 2014: 69–71. The metaphorical plot structure of *Knights* is discussed extensively by Newiger 1957: ch. 1 and Ruffell 2011: chs 3, 5. Newiger's discussion, in common with the rest of his study of metaphors in Aristophanes, focuses primarily on the phenomenon of personification, while Ruffell's significantly broader analysis suggests that the play is based around a series of metaphorical 'networks', such as *polis*-as-*oikos*, politicians-as-sellers, politicians-as-lovers, etc.

24 Compare Ar. *Eq.* 517, where comedy is imagined as a hetaira-like figure granting 'favours' to poets. On female metapoetic personifications in Old Comedy, including *Pytine*, see Hall 2000.

25 Aristophanes' skill in re-animating stock (even clichéd) metaphors and presenting them in a new and interesting way is noted by Taillardat 1965: 498.

26 See also Silk 2000: 143 for an analysis of this passage; Silk points out especially the switches between abstract and concrete, and the intrusion of the tenor into the vehicle, both of which he argues are characteristic of Aristophanic metaphor. Similarly, Taillardat 1965: 499 argues that Aristophanes' ability to transform abstract metaphors into concrete imagery is one of his great poetic skills.

27 See LSJ, s.v. ἀφελής. The adjective form itself is derived from φελλεύς, meaning stony ground, plus an alpha privative; however, it appears to be used more commonly in its non-literal sense.

28 Whether Cleon or his family really were involved in the tanning industry is unclear. Sommerstein 1981 ad loc. notes that Edward Heath was nicknamed 'the Grocer' by contemporary political satirists, despite having no links to greengrocery.

29 On this phenomenon of accumulation and lists in Aristophanes, see Spyropoulos 1974; and Silk 2000: ch. 3, especially 144–59, on accumulations which also contain disjunctions (including collisions between abstract and concrete).
30 On the phenomenon of 'embodiment' in metaphors, whereby abstract concepts are given embodied physicality, see Kövecses 2010: ch. 8.
31 Storey 2011 ad loc. See also Bakola 2010: 48–9, who argues in favour of a metapoetic theme in this play; Bianchi 2016 ad loc. for a further discussion of the play's title. Bakola proposes on the basis of the feminine participle ἀναρύτουσ᾿ that the addressee may have been some kind of female poetic personification (e.g. Cratinus' Muse), which would suggest further similarities between this play and *Pytine*.
32 See Bianchi 2016 ad loc. on the Dionysiac implications of the term *thriamboi*.
33 This compound is otherwise only attested in Plutarch *De Primo Frigido* 949f.
34 A detailed discussion of this play, and particularly its *agon*, can be found in Bakola 2010: 70–9. Bakola suggests that the reference in fr. 6 to a blind man (fr. 6.3: ὁ τυφλός) may indicate that Archilochus' opponent was Homer; however, there is also some evidence (cf. Diogenes Laertius 1.12) for Hesiod being present on stage. Bianchi 2016: 15–18 argues that fr. 2 strongly suggests that Hesiod was in fact a character in the play.
35 See Bakola 2010: 71, who concludes that the fragment is probably from the *antode*. Bianchi 2016: 66–7 discusses the hexameter metre of this fragment in more detail.
36 Cf. e.g. Ath., 3.121e: ἁλμυροὺς λόγους. Compare the Latin use of *sal* to mean witty language and (potentially invective, if only jestingly so) banter in e.g. Catull., 13.5: *et sale et omnibus cachinnis*.
37 E.g. Dion. Hal., *Comp*. 22: ἡ λέξις … πολὺ τὸ ἀντίτυπον καὶ τραχὺ καὶ στρυφνὸν ἐμφαίνει.
38 E.g. Ar., *Vesp*. 1515, Ar., fr. 432, Antiph., fr. 221.
39 See particularly *Vesp*. 903. For βαΰζω used of human speech see e.g. Ar., *Thesm*. 173, Aesch., *Ag*. 449; of dogs barking Heraclitus fr. 97.
40 On the aggressive qualities of obscenity in Old Comedy, see Henderson 1991: 10–13. Robson 2006: 78–87 offers a more detailed analysis of the element of aggression in comic obscenity, arguing that obscene language may be inclusive, as well as aggressive and exclusive.
41 As I have argued elsewhere (see Scott 2019b: 246), the poetic style of this fragment, and especially the structure of the metaphor, seems to be more characteristic of Cratinus than of Eupolis. However, Olson and Seaberg 2018 ad loc. suggest that Athenaeus' attribution of the fragment to Eupolis is more reliable than the attribution to Cratinus found in the *Et. Gen.*

42 Shaw 2014: 563, 'Comic poets play on the red color and generally phallic shape of crustaceans' bodies and claws to allude to male genitalia.'
43 Oring 2003: 5, discussed above p. 20.
44 See Olson 2007: 82–3.
45 See Farioli 2001: 109 n. 202, who points out some similarities between the fragments of the *Nomoi* and Pherecrates' *Persians*, which leaned heavily into Golden Age themes. The role of food in the comic Golden Age is discussed by Farioli at length (2001: 27–127). On the possible role of Solon in the *Nomoi*, see Martin 2015.
46 Storey 2011: 333. The similarity between 'cheese' and 'Tyro' is incidental; however, Minthe was turned into a mint plant by a jealous Persephone in an aetiological story explaining the plant's name. For this story, see Strab., 8.3.14. On female personifications in Old Comedy, see Hall 2000, Kidd 2014: 77–83.
47 Cf. Kidd 2014: 77–83 on 'having sex with abstractions'. Kidd discusses the inherent impossibilities created by the embodied abstractions which are a common feature of the Comic stage (e.g. Theoria and Opora in Aristophanes' *Peace*).
48 See for example *Acharnians* 1064–6, where Dicaeopolis instructs a bridesmaid to instruct the bride in turn to anoint her husband's penis with oil in preparation for sex.
49 See Wilkins 2000b: 36–7 for a discussion of the overlap between food and sex in comedy. Henderson 1991: 117–20, 134–7, 166–9 also gives an overview of the use of agricultural terminology in comic obscenity.
50 For a similar metaphorical usage in modern English, cf. the use of 'bugger' to denote someone or something difficult (e.g. 'he's a real bugger to work with'). As with the Greek εὐρύπρωκτος, this obscenity has in certain contexts been stripped of its literal meaning, and the act of buggery simply stands metaphorically for any difficult or awkward person or object.
51 There is considerable disagreement among scholars as to whether 'the radish treatment', whereby an adulterous male citizen was punished by having a radish inserted into his anus, was actually performed in Athens. For an overview of the arguments against, see Cohen 1985, and for the opposite view, Carey 1993.
52 How this fragment fits into the overall plot or themes of the play is entirely unclear. The title, which translates as 'female runaways', suggests a chorus of runaway slaves and the fragments suggest there may also have been an element of tragic parody in the play. See Bianchi ad loc. for a discussion.
53 As LSJ, s.v. βαλανειόμφαλος suggests.
54 'Acorn-navelled' is suggested by Storey 2011: 297 in his translation of this fragment. Bianchi 2016 ad loc. favours a derivation from βαλανεῖον.

55 On the phenomenon of excesses of meaning leading to nonsense, see Kidd 2014: 6–7, who notes that, often, '[u]tterances which are generally called "nonsense" do not "mean nothing" but rather mean too much'.
56 E.g. Ar., *Lys.* 413.
57 E.g. Gal., 10.381, Poll., 2.171; the term in fact survives in modern medical English (e.g. balanitis). The euphemistic meaning of βάλανος is discussed by Henderson 1991: 119.
58 On some of the uncertainties surrounding the early career of Plato Comicus, see Sutton 1980, Rosen 1989, Pirrotta 2009: 21–6, Hartwig 2010; on the comedian's possible rivalry with Aristophanes in particular, see Sommerstein 2000: 439, Pirrotta 2009: 27–31.
59 On this play's double title, see Pirrotta 2009: 86–7.
60 See also Sommerstein 2000, which suggests that, like Aristophanes and Eupolis, Plato also wrote 'demagogue comedy'.
61 For a discussion of this rather obscure line, see Biles and Olson 2015 ad loc. (though note that Borthwick 1968a suggests an emendation of this word to σφάλαξ ('mole'), and this is accepted by MacDowell 1971 ad loc.). The alternate form φάλαγξ also appears at Ar., *Ran.* 1314.
62 See Olson 2002 ad loc., who notes that pitch made from tree resin might also be used to add body to cheap wine.
63 On this phenomenon of what Silk helpfully terms 'switching' in Aristophanes, see Silk 2000: 137–59; ibid. 122 also briefly discusses the above passage of *Acharnians*.
64 A further potential double meaning is also folded into this passage. When Dicaeopolis tastes the first of the three treaties, he expresses his displeasure with the words οὐκ ἀρέσκουσίν μ' (189), 'it doesn't please me/isn't acceptable to me'. However, the verb also has religious connotations, particularly when used in the context of libation-pouring or other kinds of sacrificial practice (e.g. Theognis 762: σπονδὰς θεοῖς ἀρέσασθαι, 'to propitiate the gods with libations'). Read in this way, the passage therefore sets Dicaeopolis up as simultaneously peace-seeking libation-pourer, discerning wine-consumer, and propitiated god accepting, and rejecting, the offerings poured to him.
65 On the title of this play, see Olson 2022: 85–6.
66 On fish-sellers in comedy, see Wilkins 2000b: 167–9, Paulas 2010.
67 I here paraphrase the description given by Theon in the *Progymnasmata* (Theon *Prog.*, 11: ἔκφρασις ἐστὶ λόγος περιηγηματικὸς ἐναργῶς ὑφ' ὄψιν ἄγων τὸ δηλούμενον). As Webb 1999 has comprehensively shown, the narrow definition of ekphrasis as specifically a description of a work of art is a product of twentieth-century scholarship, and would not be recognized by an ancient audience.

68 As Zanker 1981 in particular has shown, the term *enargeia* is closely associated with ekphrasis from the outset of the latter's use as a rhetorical descriptor. For a further discussion of the role of *enargeia* in the definition and practice of ekphrasis, see among others Fowler 1991, Elsner 2002, Goldhill 2007, Webb 2009: ch. 4.

69 I borrow this unusual yet precise terminology of 'thereness' from Cunningham 2007.

70 I do not claim, of course, that such ambivalence is unique to comic poetry. The ambivalent oscillations between absence and presence in lyric ekphrases are discussed for example by Fearn 2017, who suggests (5) that Pindar's ekphrastic poetry in particular 'makes an issue out of literary referentiality'; note, however, that Fearn's discussion relates specifically to the description of artistic objects, and not to the act of vivid description more generally. With regard to tragedy, Zeitlin argues that Euripides in particular mobilizes ekphrastic language in 'thematizing the implications both of vision and of the interplay between illusion and reality' (1994: 142). On the intertextual poetics of ekphrasis in Euripides, see also Torrance 2013: ch. 2. The central role in tragedy of what he terms 'reported space' is also discussed by Carter 2006.

71 On the structural role of entrances and exits in Aristophanic comedy, see Poe 1999.

72 See Worman 2015 for the most recent and detailed examination of this phenomenon. Worman argues that the very earliest examples of Greek poetry employ metaphorical landscapes in their metapoetic discourse, and that rural landscapes especially take on a key metapoetic role from Hesiod onwards. Worman suggests that such metapoetic landscapes in (for example) Hesiod and Pindar lay the groundwork for later, more explicitly literary-critical discourses, including that found in comedies such as Aristophanes' *Frogs*.

73 pp. 9–10.

74 The bibliography on the shield of Achilles is unsurprisingly extensive, but see for example Atchity 1978, Taplin 1980, Byrne 1992, Becker 1995, Francis 2009.

75 See e.g. Lauxtermann 1998, Platt 2002, Männlein-Robert 2007, Zanker 2004, Goldhill 2007, Squire 2013b.

76 Of particular note are Fowler 1991, Elsner 1996, Putnam 1998.

77 On Philostratus' famously ekphrastic *Imagines* in particular see Pasquariello 2004, Newby 2009, Squire 2013a. Such disobedient ekphrases are also a notable feature of the Greek novel; see Holzmeister 2014 for a summary.

78 On utopianism and the comic Golden Age in Aristophanes, see for example Konstan 1997, Zeitlin 1999. Ruffell 2000, Farioli 2001 and Ruffell 2014 provide a broader exploration of the theme in comedy beyond Aristophanes.

79 Fowler 1991.
80 See for comparison Elliger 1975: 243–74, who argues that Euripidean landscapes also have this quality of past/future, in contrast to the squalid realities of the tragic stage.
81 Bram 2006: 373, 'Ekphrasis presents the mimetic illusion as able to do what Plato had feared: it can delude us.' See also Goldhill 2009: 5, who points out that later rhetorical handbooks are suspicious of these qualities, and of the way that through ekphrasis the listener is 'dragged by force away from proof, away from demonstration towards passive experience'. On the experiential quality of ekphrasis, see also Zanker 1981 on *enargeia*.
82 It is worth reiterating that the ancient stage had nothing akin to, for example, the rotating stage in the Olivier Theatre in London. At most, there might be a single painted backdrop, but the evidence for *skenographia* is limited; see Small 2013 for a discussion. Lowe 2006 suggests that scene changes in comedy were essentially conceptual, rather than involving the actual physical alteration of the stage space through e.g. changes of backdrops. Poe 1999 suggests that 'acts' in Aristophanes were largely marked through entrances and exits, and that these (in addition to formal, metrical divisions) took the place of what might in the modern theatre be scene changes.
83 On this fragment, see Franchini 2020 ad loc. The *Miners* is also discussed by Urios-Aparisi 1996: 80–1. For the unusual role of slaves in the play's utopian plot, see Sells 2013: 104–6.
84 This group of plays is discussed by both Farioli 2001: 27–115 and Ruffell 2014: 207–8.
85 Aristophanes often derides this as a cheap stunt. See for example Ar., *Wealth* 797–9: οὐ γὰρ πρεπῶδές ἐστι τῷ διδασκάλῳ / ἰσχάδια καὶ τρωγάλια τοῖς θεωμένοις / προβαλόντ' ἐπὶ τούτοις εἶτ' ἀναγκάζειν γελᾶν. ('It's not right for the producer to chuck dried figs and nibbles at the spectators just to get a laugh.') On the Golden Age themes in *Nomoi*, see n. 45 above.
86 See also Franchini 2020: 94–5 for some suggestions as to the plot of the play. Franchini proposes that the miners who made up the play's chorus may have been slaves (like those who worked in the Laurion mines in Attica), and that the speaker of fr. 113 is a messenger from the underworld whose utopian vision of the afterlife contrasts with the misery of life as a slave miner, perhaps leading the characters and chorus of the play to attempt to dig down into the underworld as a means of escape.
87 As Farioli 2001: 94 points out, since Pherecrates' utopia is located in the underworld, the prominence of rivers in this fragment is comically apt, since rivers are, of course, a key geographical feature of the Tartarean landscape.

88 The noun μυστίλη refers literally to a piece of bread hollowed out so that it can be used as a spoon for soup; I substitute the English 'crouton' for its similar soup-specific associations.
89 On the plot and dating of this play, see Pellegrino 2016: 280–1, Bagordo 2020: 182–4.
90 Bagordo 2020 ad loc. suggests that the conversation may be between two divine figures, the first representing the new gods and the second the old gods whom they have displaced.
91 See Crates fr. 19, where the speakers discuss this new vegetarian (or at least pescetarian; as in fr. 16, fish is not forbidden) regime. The *Wild Beasts*' theme of vegetarianism may have had an element of philosophical satire. See Perrone 2019: 99–100.
92 In addition to Crates fr. 16, fr. 17 of *Wild Beasts* is automatist in nature, presenting a self-operating bathhouse where the bath runs itself, the scented oil appears of its own accord, and so on. See Ruffell 2000: 481–6 for a discussion of automatist utopias which includes Crates fr. 16. A more extended discussion of this fragment can be found in Farioli 2001: 58–66. On the role (or rather absence) of slaves in the automatist utopia of the play, see Konstan 2012; on the chorus, Wilkins 2000a.
93 See Slater 2002: 119–20; Slater cites a similarly metatheatrical passage in Aristophanes' *Peace* where Hermes claims that the other gods have moved house, leaving him behind alone to look after their σκευάρια (*Pax* 201).
94 See Dunbar 1995: 145–6 on ἐς κόρακας, and ibid. 192–4 on the πόλος/πόλις pun.
95 For a discussion of this creation of (as it were) something from nothing in the *Birds*, see Konstan 1997: 10, who writes, of the πόλος/πόλις pun, '[w]hat hitherto was by its nature mobile and permeable is now perceived as a fixed place and potential barrier'. The transformation of the playing space from what he terms an *outopia* into the world of Nephelokokkygia is discussed in detail by Slater 2002: 132. See also Lowe 2006: 57–9 for the use of space in the play.
96 See Rusten 2013, who argues convincingly that these choral passages mimic the language of 'fabulous ethnography' (307).
97 Orestes the mugger also appears in Ar., *Ach.* 1166.
98 This is the subject of a similarly extended joke in Ar., *Vesp.* 15–19. See also *Eq.* 1369–72, *Nub.* 353, *Pax* 444–6, 670–8, 1295–304, *Av.* 290 for jokes about Cleonymus' cowardice. For a discussion, see Moulton 1979, Sommerstein 1996.
99 This is a stock joke in comedy; see Taillardat 1965: 423–4.
100 See Dunbar ad loc. for a detailed discussion of each of these puns.
101 Again, see Dunbar ad loc. for detailed discussion of each pun.

102 The adjective ὀπτός is indeed attested, albeit considerably later, in Lucian and Athenaeus. See LSJ, s.v. ὀπτός.
103 Peisetairos' role as a kind of comic producer in the *Birds* is explored by Slater 2002: ch. 7.

2 Playing with Theatre: Jokes and Dramatic Performance

1 *Blackadder the Third*, episode 4 'Sense and Senility' (1987), [TV Programme] BBC1, 8 October.
2 Farmer's 2017 monograph *Tragedy on the Comic Stage* is the most recent, and to my mind some of the best, work on this topic. See also Silk 1993, Nelson 2016. Bakola 2010: ch. 3 explores the topic with relation to Cratinus in particular.
3 In addition to Slater's work, see Ruffell 2011, Marshall 2014. Metapoetry (as opposed to metatheatre) is also discussed by Hall 2000.
4 This is Slater's argument *passim*. See also e.g. Foley 1988, Zeitlin 1981, Ruffell 2011, Sells 2018.
5 On the difficulties of the term 'illusion' with relation to ancient theatre, however, see e.g. Taplin 1986, Slater 2002: 3.
6 The language of 'opposition' favoured by Raskin is critiqued by Oring 1992, 2003. Oring's critique is discussed in the Introduction, pp. 4–7.
7 That metatheatre and parody are part of the anti-realist fictional world of Old Comedy has been argued in depth by Ruffell 2011. In contrast to Slater's 2002 study of metatheatre, Ruffell focuses on those moments of overt 'illusion-breaking' which she argues add to the fantastical aesthetic of comic poetics.
8 For the dates of Archippus' career, see Storey 2012, Miccolis 2017: 12–13. Sifakis 1971: 76 dates the *Fishes* to 401–400 BC.
9 On Crates' *Wild Beasts*, see Rothwell 2007: 123–6, Perrone 2019: 98–121. Rothwell also suggests (2007: 126–8) that Archippus' *Fishes* may have been influenced by Aristophanes' *Birds*, given the apparent similarities in plot between the two plays. See also Sifakis 1971: 102 on plot similarities between *Fishes* and *Wild Beasts* and Aristophanes' 'animal chorus' plays; Wilkins 2000 on the topic of 'edible choruses' such as those in *Fishes* and *Wild Beasts*.
10 The attribution of the substantial papyrus fragment known as the *Comoedia Dukiana* to Archippus' *Fishes* is much contested. See Willis 1991 [1993], Luppe 1993, Csapo 1994, Farioli 2001: 161, Rothwell 2007: 128–30, 194–7, Storey 2012: 9–12, Miccolis 2017: 100–5. Since this fragment is not of particular relevance to the present discussion, I will refrain from stating an opinion on its attribution.

11 If Sifakis 1971: 102 is correct in his assertion that most animal choruses engaged in some kind of conflict with the human characters of the play, then a fish takeover is perhaps the more likely of these two suggestions. Farioli 2001: 156–74 agrees that a war between men and fishes formed the basis of the plot, though she concludes that it is difficult to ascertain whether the conflict took place before or during the action of the play. See also Miccolis 2017: 95–7, who suggests that the peace treaty may have fallen at either the beginning or the end of the play.
12 See Farioli 2001: 162–3 on the identification of the sea bream with Aphrodite in Archippus fr. 18 PCG. Farioli suggests that the bream is appointed as the goddess' priest on account of its golden beauty, and not because of any prior association between Aphrodite and the bream.
13 Where in the *Fishes* this comic set-piece fell is unclear. It seems that the glutton Melanthius was bound, gagged, and fed to the fishes as part of some kind of mythic parody of the myth of Hesione (Archippus fr. 28 PCG). It is not clear whether this took place as part of the initial hostilities between the fishes and the Athenians, or as part of the peace settlement described in fr. 27. Farioli 2001: 164–71 suggests (based on an analogy with Aristophanes' *Birds*) that the fish may also have punished fishermen, fishmongers and gluttons. Farioli argues that, as in the *Birds* (and in contrast to Crates' *Wild Beasts*, where abstention from meat is apparently tied to the play's Golden Age theme), 'il nutrimento sembra caratterizzarsi soprattutto come strumento di controllo sociale' (2001: 166), and that the fish-state was imperialist in nature rather than straightforwardly utopian.
14 On Archippan wordplay, see Rothwell 2007: 127 and Storey 2012: 7, who describes the puns in *Fishes* in particular as 'not very inspired'.
15 Storey 2012: 7 suggests an English version of the pun as follows: 'There are doctors in the sea? Yes, the very best plastic sturgeons!' The formulation is rather brilliant, and very much in keeping with the groan-inducing qualities of the original Greek.
16 See Thompson 1947: 39–42 for the identification of the Greek γαλεός as a shark or dogfish. Miccolis 2017 ad loc. notes that the precise species is unclear.
17 See Parke 1967: 178–9 on the mythical origins of the Galeotai.
18 On 'coldness' as a literary-critical term in Greek comedy, see Wright 2012: 108–12.
19 See Parke 1967: 178, who suggests that this lizard was considered to have prophetic properties of some kind, and that perhaps the Galeotai were so named for their use of these lizards in divination.
20 See for example Andrews 1948 on 'mouse-fishes' and 'pig-fishes' in Greek. This naming pattern was much more widespread in Greek than it is in English, where (despite a 2009 campaign by the animal rights group PETA to rebrand fish as 'sea-kittens') only comparatively few marine species are in fact named after land animals (e.g. dogfish, seahorse).

21 The frog's loud and ugly singing voice was to the Greeks practically proverbial, and is often a feature of Aesopic fables containing frogs. See e.g. p. 90. On the potential resonances of Aristophanes' frog chorus as a parody of the New Music, see D'Angour 2020.
22 Ants, for example, appear to form the chorus of plays by Pherecrates (*Ant-men*), Plato Comicus (*Ants*), and Cantharus (*Ants*).
23 See Storey 2012 for a more detailed discussion of the *hetaira* puns in these fragments.
24 It is interesting to consider whether the male fish characters in the *Fishes* wore comic phalluses. The Getty Birds Vase, on which see Green 1985, clearly depicts men dressed in bird costumes with comic phalluses attached, showing that it is possible for animal characters in comedy to be phallic. As discussed below in this chapter, Aristophanes' *Wasps* in fact makes a feature of the wasp-men's phallic stingers. However, the image of phallic fish is particularly peculiar to my eye, given that (unlike at least some birds) fish conspicuously lack this equipment. If Archippus' fish were indeed wearing phalluses, this would have increased the incongruous clash between their fishy and human identities; however, I remain agnostic on this point.
25 See Compton-Engle 2015: ch. 5 on animal costumes in Comedy, and especially 127–8 on the difficulties of creating elaborate choral costumes which do not impede the dance movements of the choreuts. Farioli 2001: 159 suggests that the chorus' fish costumes may have focused on the upper halves of their bodies, leaving the legs free to dance. While practical, this of course would have made the choreuts' legs even more prominent.
26 One exception to this seems to be Eupolis' *Nanny-Goats*. The identification of this chorus as female rests on two feminine participles, in fr. 13 and fr. 24. See Storey 2003: 68.
27 The *Acharnians*' version of events (cf. *Ach.* 497–556) is, of course, likely to be an exaggeration of the historical reality. See De Ste. Croix 1972: 225–46 on the Megarian decree; Olson 2004: 205 on the relationship between the *Acharnians* and other historical sources for the Megarian decree and its contents.
28 On the cod-Megarian dialect in these lines, see Colvin 1999: 127–9.
29 See Compton-Engle 2015: 93–4, who argues that Dicaeopolis' control over costume and disguise is a central theme of the *Acharnians*.
30 Henderson 1991: 131. Olson 2004: 261, however, finds insufficient evidence for Henderson's claim.
31 Ar., *Lys.* 1158: ἐγὼ δὲ κύσθον γ' οὐδέπω καλλίονα. Ar., *Ran.* 432–4: καὶ Καλλίαν γέ φασι / τοῦτον τὸν Ἱπποκίνου / κύσθῳ λεοντῆν ναυμαχεῖν ἐνημμένον. The usage in Eup., fr. 247 will be discussed in more detail later in this chapter. See also Ar.,

Thesm. 1114; however, the text is disputed, since the Scythian archer's pidgin is hard to decipher.

32 The word is punningly hinted at by Lysistrata at *Lys.* 1184. On women's obscene language in comedy, see McClure 1999: ch. 6; on women's speech in comedy more generally, Sommerstein 1995, Willi 2003: ch. 6.

33 Hall 2000 discusses the metapoetic potential of the female body in Old Comedy, and Kidd 2014: 77–83 the nonsensical possibilities of 'having sex with abstractions'. On personification in Old Comedy more generally, with a particular focus on Aristophanic comedy, see Newiger 1957. Female personification in the *Cities* in particular is discussed by Rosen 1997, who suggests that the political relationship between Athens and her allies is in the play likened to that between men and women, i.e. mutually beneficial, but with one party clearly and rightfully in charge. One interesting exception to this trend seems to be Eupolis' *Demes*, which, given the gender of the noun, must surely have had a male chorus, but unfortunately the fragments give little clue as to its particulars. See Storey 2003: 124–9, Telò 2007: 37–44 on the chorus in *Demes*.

34 See A. M. Wilson 1977 on the individuated chorus in Old Comedy.

35 It is not clear from the relevant fragments of *Cities* (Eup., fr. 245, 246, 247 PCG) who is introducing each city, since unfortunately there is no indication of speaker. A comparison with the *Birds* might suggest a conversation between one character who is familiar with the fantastical world of the play (as the Hoopoe in *Birds*), and one who is a newcomer from the 'real' world (of Athens, perhaps?). However, since the City Dionysia festival itself saw the allies visiting Athens, we might similarly expect the chorus to be visiting the city from abroad, making the identification of their introducer more difficult still. On the identification of the cities of the chorus, see A. M. Wilson 1977, Storey 2003: 217–21.

36 Storey 2003: 218 rightly points out that to introduce each and every chorus member in detail would take 75–100 lines, and would probably become repetitive. A. M. Wilson's solution (1977: 282) of having only the final entrants in the sequence introduced in detail is, I think, persuasive, and mirrors the *Birds*, where only some of the individuated chorus are given a full introduction in this manner, with the rest simply called out each by name.

37 Although ψιλός is more usually a reference to a man's baldness, women in Old Comedy frequently refer to depilating their pubic hair in preparation for sex. See for example Ar., *Lys.* 89, 151, 824–8, *Eccl.* 13. The portrayal of depilation in Aristophanes is discussed by Robson 2013. Olson 2016 ad loc. is, I think, incorrect in his reluctance to accept an obscene meaning here.

38 I here follow Storey 2003: 219 and Olson 2016: 296 in splitting the text between two speakers.

39 On military metaphors for sex in Old Comedy, see Henderson 1991: 170–3. Such military metaphors are a stock feature of Latin elegiac poetry, for which see e.g. Cahoon 1988.
40 See Norwood 1931: 193, Whittaker 1935: 183, A. M. Wilson 1977: 282, Storey 2003: 218. As each of these one-page references makes clear, costume is not discussed in any great detail.
41 See Sansone 2011 on the particular difficulties of interpreting this fragment.
42 Compton-Engle's suggestions here (2015: 125) are rooted in her overall approach to costume in Old Comedy, whereby she suggests, in a modification of Taplin's 'significant action hypothesis', that comedians would use the spoken text to comment on those most significant visual effects on stage (2015: 7).
43 Compare for example the Getty Birds Vase, on which the two bird-men are clearly depicted wearing leggings decorated with a kind of feather pattern. This vase, and its possible relationship to Aristophanes, is discussed by Green 1985, Taplin 1987, 1993: 101–4. See also London BM 509, by the Gela Painter, *c.* 480 BC, which similarly depicts men in bird costumes decorated with a feather pattern.
44 Although usually translated into English as 'Reconciliation', the Greek διαλλαγή implies a process of exchange or bartering which is not adequately conveyed by this English term. While the verb διαλλάσω (from which διαλλαγή is derived) can be used to mean 'reconcile' (e.g. Ar., *Lys.* 900, *Thesm.* 2.95), its primary meaning has to do with interchange, and it can for example be used of exchanging money. Cf. LSJ, s.v. διαλλάσω. The entire scene does indeed show a process whereby peace is achieved through land exchanges, with each side agreeing to cede certain territories, and the body of Reconciliation throughout the scene acts as a proxy for these negotiations.
45 This passage is discussed in detail by Newiger 1957: 106–8. Newiger's analysis focuses primarily on the question of whether Reconciliation should be considered a symbol or an allegory (with Newiger strongly concluding that the former is the more appropriate term), but the discussion also profitably compares this scene to the personification of War in *Ach.* 971–99 in order to demonstrate the particular effect of a staged personification in comparison to one which is only a figure of speech. See also Taaffe 1993: 69–71. There has been some contention as to whether naked female figures such as Diallage were played by real women, or by male actors in drag, for which see Holzinger 1928, Vaio 1973, Henderson 1987: 195, Zweig 1992, Compton-Engle 2015: 35–45, 56–7. The consensus in more recent scholarship favours a male actor, and I think rightly so.
46 I follow Sommerstein 1985, Olson 1998, and N. G. Wilson 2007 in removing line 896b (πλαγίαν καταβάλλειν, εἰς γόνατα κῦβδ' ἱστάναι) as a probable interpolation; it is very repetitious, and interrupts the flow of the passage.

47 (Whitman 1964: 114). Newiger (1957: 10–98) similarly opts to ignore this passage in his consequently brief discussion of Theoria's personification; Taillardat declines to include it in his catalogue of sporting metaphors in Aristophanes.
48 The force of this plural is lost in translations which render it along with παίειν, ὀρύττειν etc. as an infinitive (see Sommerstein 1985, Henderson 1998 ad loc.), instead of more literally as a dative following ἐξέσται; however, I accept that Sommerstein and Henderson's choice of an infinitive may be preferable in some ways, since the more grammatically literal translation is achieved only at the expense of the passage's flow.
49 There is a substantial body of scholarship addressing this fragment. See Süß 1967, Borthwick 1968b, Restani 1983, Anderson 1994: 127–34, Dobrov and Urios-Aparisi 1995, Dobrov 1997, De Simone 2004, Olson 2007: 182–6, Fongoni 2009, Pöhlmann 2011. The majority of scholarship approaches this fragment as evidence for dithyramb, and particularly the stylistic innovations of the New Music. On Pherecrates' comic style in particular, see Urios-Aparisi 1996, Henderson 2000.
50 Plutarch *De Musica* (*Moralia* 1141d–42a) says only that Music was brought on in the form of a woman (ἐν γυναικείῳ σχέματι). Dobrov and Urios-Aparisi 1995 make a persuasive case for the identification of Music as a courtesan, arguing that the female speaker adopts a tone of professional resignation rather than full outrage at her treatment. See also Restani 1983 on the tone and language used by the speaker.
51 A detailed analysis of Cinesias' representation in Old Comedy can be found in Kidd 2016: ch. 3. See also Zimmermann 1997.
52 See Schönewolf 1938: 67, Byrne 1994, Pöhlmann 2011.
53 Cf. Dobrov and Urios-Aparisi 1995: 155, '[Music's] body becomes a lyre'.
54 The characterization of New Music as 'twisting', and the particular use of the term καμπή, is discussed by Restani 1983: 156–66, Zimmermann 1992: 122, Franklin 2013: 226–31. The erotic overtones of musical performance, and the potential semantic overlap between musical and sexual performance, is discussed by Prauscello 2004.
55 See Olson 2007: 183, who takes this as a dative of measure of distance.
56 Henderson 1991: 170 reaches a similar conclusion regarding this line, and Franchini 2020 ad loc. also accepts that the meaning here is obscene.
57 There is also some evidence for pine nuts being used as an aphrodisiac, for which see *PGM* VII.185; however, it is unclear whether such a use was widespread.
58 On the pun here, see Franchini 2020 ad loc.
59 The repetitive nature of the puns also serves another purpose, keeping Music's abstract identity focused: she is not just music in general but, despite the obvious sexual potential of aulos puns, a stringed instrument, and I would suggest that it is

highly likely that this was reflected through the actor's costume. Whether Music was actually costumed *as* a lyre, or merely came on stage carrying one, is hard to say, though the former option is rather appealing, and certainly no more difficult than for example the cheese-grater costume apparently required in the trial scene of Aristophanes' *Wasps*. (Cf. Ar., *Vesp*. 963; the instruction to the cheese-grater to 'take the stand' (ἀνάβηθι, τυρόκνηστι) to me implies an actor in a costume, rather than a prop, and this would be in keeping with the rather anarchic nature of this scene, which sees the stage populated with dogs, puppies, and a whole series of kitchen utensils.)

60 Torchio 2021: 57 also suggests that the play may have had a peasant protagonist akin to Dicaeopolis or Trygaeus.

61 An alternative name for the *parodos*. The fragment is reported by a scholiast commenting on *Birds* 296, in which Euelpides comments that the flurry of wings which accompanies the chorus' entrance to the stage obscures the *eisodos* (295–6: ὦναξ Ἄπολλον, τοῦ νέφους. ἰοὺ ἰού, / οὐδ' ἰδεῖν ἔτ' ἔσθ' ὑπ' αὐτῶν πετομένων τὴν εἴσοδον.). See Torchio 2021: 67.

62 On this fragment's probable role in the *parodos*, see Torchio 2021: 83.

63 The metaphorical usage of this verb to refer to a downcast expression is also attested in Eur., *El*. 1078, Eur., *Phoen*. 1308; the word perhaps has a paratragic flavour.

64 On the proxemics of the chorus' entry in Aristophanes' *Clouds*, see Revermann 2006, who notes that their introduction is unusually lengthy.

65 Cf. Ar., *Thesm*. 574–81, *Ran*. 52–7 for jokes about Cleisthenes effeminacy; *Eccl*. 167–8 contains a very similar joke aimed at Epigonos, and the effeminacy of political speakers in general is commented on in *Eccl*. 111–14. A full list of jokes about Cleisthenes in Old Comedy can be found in Sommerstein 1996: 353.

66 On the episodic structure of comedy, see Park Poe 1999, Park Poe 2000, Lowe 2000: 86–8, Ruffell 2011: ch. 4.

67 Note, however, that Telò 2016: ch. 5 has argued that there is a paratragic undercurrent in the *Clouds*.

68 Whether this type of animal chorus appeared elsewhere in Old Comedy is impossible to say. Certainly, none of the fragmentary evidence suggests another chorus of theriomorphized men, as opposed to anthropomorphized animals. However, this explicit awareness of performativity is clearly emphasized on several of the vases which appear to show animal choruses, and in which the human actors are depicted under the animal costume, as for example in the Berlin 'Knights' vase (Berlin Staatliche Museen F 1697. Antikensammlung, Staatliche Museen zu Berlin; cf. Green 1985), in which the 'horses' are clearly shown as men in horse costumes. This might lead us to expect that such explicit metatheatrical awareness was a feature built into choral animal-performance from its beginnings.

69 Both Sifakis 1971 and Rothwell 2007 in their studies of animal choruses in comedy class the *Wasps*' chorus as an animal chorus.
70 Compare Cratinus fr. 6 (discussed in the previous chapter), which plays on the metaphorical meaning of ἁλμυρός to denote harsh poetic language.
71 Compare the English expression 'a sting in the tail'.
72 The conflation of bees and wasps in this play is discussed at some length by Corbel-Morana 2012: 164–7.
73 On choral disrobing, see Compton-Engle 2015: 126–8. Biles and Olson 2015 ad loc. suggest that the removal of one's cloak was standard preparation for a fight.
74 The chorus' later description of themselves as 'wasp-waisted' (1072: μέσον διεσφηκωμένον) suggests a costume which mimicked the shape (and presumably also the colouring) of wasps' bodies. There has been some debate as to the chorus' stingers, specifically with regard to the relationship between the stinger and the comic phallus. For a full discussion, cf. Rothwell 2007: 256–7. While there is a strong argument for some symbolic equivalence between the wasp sting and the phallus, given the way in which the wasp sting is equated with virile masculinity (for which cf. Reckford 1987: 236–8, Hubbard 1989: 100), it seems unlikely that (as Newiger 1957: 79–80 argues) the stings were in fact visually represented only metaphorically through the use of the choruses' phalloi, especially given the doubt surrounding the evidence for comic choruses wearing phalloi (cf. Rothwell 2007: 25–7).
75 Biles and Olson 2015 ad loc. note that swearing an oath by Heracles often denotes shock or surprise.
76 Corbel-Morana 2012: 157 suggests that the association between wasps and being earth-born may be based on the fact that hornets build their nests on the ground and that the image evokes the belief that cicadas were born out of the earth. However, this rationalization of the argument that wasp stings are a sign of the chorus' status as Athenian men seems to somewhat miss the joke.
77 The impression that the military feats described by the chorus are archetypes or emblems is increased by the fact that the narrative seems to amalgamate several different historical events, including the Persian assault on Athens (*Vesp.* 1079: τῷ καπνῷ τύφων ἅπασαν τὴν πόλιν καὶ πυρπολῶν) described in Hdt. 8.50, Marathon (*Vesp.* 1078–88, which clearly describes a land battle), and possibly also Thermopylae (*Vesp.* 1084, which seems to recall events similar to those related by Hdt. 7.226). For a further discussion of the assimilation of various battles in these lines, cf. MacDowell 1971: 271–2, and Carey 2013, who argues that the passage here also absorbs the naval countermeasures against Persia into its composite description. Compare the rather straighter rendition in Ar., *Ach.* 692–702.

78 For the association between birds and nets, cf. e.g. Ar., *Av.* 194, 528. Nets seem to have been used in hunting songbirds.
79 A detailed analysis of the use of the *mechane* in this scene can be found in Scott 2019a. On the symbolism of the beetle, and particularly its scatological associations, see Moulton 1981, Hubbard 1991, Tordoff 2011. On the *Peace*'s paratragic engagement with Euripides' *Bellerophon*, cf. Ruffell 2011, Zogg 2014, Sells 2018; on the play's broader paratragic and parodic qualities, Slater 2002: ch. 6, Hall 2006: ch. 11.
80 On the use of the *mechane* in tragedy, see Mastronarde 1990, Newiger 1990. The device's mechanics are also discussed in detail by Robkin 1975 and Lendle 1995.
81 See Farmer 2017: 94 for the suggestion of paratragedy in Strattis' *Atalantus*. The interest in theatrical convention in fr. 4 could certainly fit comfortably in a play with paragtragic themes. Orth 2009: 59–62, however, suggests that the plot was more mythological in character, and that fr. 3 in particular implies an emphasis on hunting which would fit with a play focused on Atalanta the huntress. Alternatively, Orth suggests that the play may have focused on a male character and his metaphorical 'hunt' for *hetairai*. The lack of clarity with regard to the play's title (variously preserved as *Atalantus*, *Atalantai* and *Atalante*) is unhelpful, and makes any effort to reconstruct the plot exceedingly difficult; see Orth 2009: 59.
82 On the mechanics of such a dismount, see Mastronarde 1990: 270, who suggests that the actor might have needed to be released from a harness in order to dismount.
83 See Aristophanes' *Gerytades* fr. 160 PCG, which uses the words μηχανοποιός and κράδη in close succession, and cf. Pollux 4.128. Metaphorical descriptions of the *mechane* are discussed by Perrone 2008, who notes that fig metaphors and nautical metaphors are particularly common.
84 Collard, Cropp and Lee 1995: 110 place this fragment in the play's final scene. See also Dobrov 2001, Dixon 2014 on the plot of the *Bellerophon*.
85 Cf. Slater 2002: 17–18, who notes that appearances of the *ekkyklema* in Aristophanes are often marked by verbs of wheeling, as in Ar., *Ach.* 408 and *Thesm.* 96, 265. A further paratragic use of the verb ἐκκυκλέω may be found at *Vesp.* 1474, for which see Biles and Olson 2015 ad loc. The paratragic overtones of this line are also discussed by Wright 2013: 221–2.
86 The association between tragic stage technology and the endings of plays seems to have been widespread. See Arist., *Poetics* 1454a37–b8, which states that the ending of a play should follow logically from the plot, and should not appear ἀπὸ μηχανῆς as in the Medea; and Plato's *Cratylus* 425d, where Socrates jokes about the *mechane* coming to the rescue of tragedians who have written themselves into a tight spot.

87 This fragment, and its role in the paratragic plot of the *Phoenician Women*, is discussed in detail by Farmer 2017: 99.
88 Note, however, that the authorship of this fragment is disputed by some; see Olson 2022: 336–7 for a discussion.
89 The language of poetic novelty in comedy is discussed in Wright 2012.
90 In reality, tragedy is, of course, far from naturalistic. From comedy's perspective, however, it matters less whether tragedy is in fact naturalistic, or even illusionistic, and only whether it can plausibly be characterized as such. On the vexed question of whether Greek drama can be described as in any way illusionistic, cf. Sifakis 1971: 7–14, Taplin 1986, Slater 2002: ch. 1.
91 I here follow the text of Henderson 2002 and not N. G. Wilson's 2007 OCT.
92 See P. Wilson and Taplin 1994, who argue that by this point in the early fourth century, the image of a torch-bearing Fury, while in all likelihood deriving originally from the finale of the Oresteia, had become something of a general cliché of tragic theatre. Plays featuring Orestes were commonplace; such plays were written by Euripides' nephew, also named Euripides (TrGF 1.17 T1); Philocles (TrGF 1.24 T9, cf. Wright 2016: 98); Theodectas (TrGF 1.72 F5); Aphareus (TrGF 1.73 F1); Carcinus the Younger (TrGF 1.70 F 1g); and Cleophon (TrGF 1.77 F). Cf. Wright 2016: 83–4 on the House of Atreus in the fragments of fifth- and fourth-century tragedy. For Furies as an image of tragicness in fourth-century iconography, see Taplin 2007: 22–6. The Erinyes' association with torches in both literature and iconography is discussed by Aguirre 2010. Note also *Against Timarchus* 190–1, in which the audience is warned not to expect that wicked men will be punished by torch-bearing Furies as they are in tragedy.

3 Playing with Plot: Jokes and Storytelling

1 See also *Poetics* 1453a13–15, where Aristotle suggests that a good tragic plot should progress from fortune to misfortune rather than the opposite (μεταβάλλειν οὐκ εἰς εὐτυχίαν ἐκ δυστυχίας ἀλλὰ τοὐναντίον ἐξ εὐτυχίας εἰς δυστυχίαν). Sommerstein 2005 argues that while in practice tragedy had considerably more flexibility with regard to its treatment of myth than this statement of Aristotle's might suggest, tragic endings in particular were more tightly bound by mythic convention.
2 On mythic plots in non-Aristophanic comedy, and for a list of plays which seem to have had such plots, cf. Bowie 2000.

3 Nesselrath 1995 discusses the 'Birth of Gods' plays which proliferated in fourth-century comedy, though note that Hermippus' career dates to the fifth century, showing that such plays were not the preserve of later poets.
4 On the categorization of comedy into Old, Middle and New, see Sutton 1990, Nesselrath 1990, Csapo 2000, Sidwell 2000, Konstantakos 2014, Henderson 2014, all of whom problematize the category of Middle Comedy to varying degrees, with Sidwell going so far as to suggest the term should be abandoned.
5 On mythological burlesque in Cratinus, see Bakola 2010: 180–230.
6 On Aristophanes' *Daedalus* and its apparent similarities with Cratinus' *Nemesis*, see Wright 2007. And on *Lemnian Women*, see Farmer 2017: 88–90, who examines the play and its mythological plot from the standpoint of tragic parody.
7 See Chapter 1, pp. 21–8. Chapter 2, pp. 75–80. also showed how in the *Wasps* a single joke can be deployed in a more sustained way across an entire play.
8 See for example Ruffell 2011: 179–213 on networks of jokes in Aristophanes' *Knights*. Most recently, Lowe 2020 has analysed *Acharnians* 98–108 to demonstrate how 'a whole web of comic strands that have been threaded into the scene as it unfolds are woven together to deliver not a single payoff but a firecracker string of them' (2020: 21).
9 The title, in its use of the name Alexandros, arguably also evokes Homer, since in the *Iliad* (in contrast to later sources), Paris is more usually referred to as Alexandros (45 times, as opposed to 11 occurrences of Paris). See De Jong 1987.
10 Grenfell and Hunt 1904. This hypothesis has been the subject of a great deal of scholarly debate; see most notably Körte 1904, Croiset 1904, Norwood 1931, Luppe 1966, Ebert 1978, Lerza 1982, Storey 2006b, Bakola 2010: 180–208.
11 The surviving fragments of *Anthroporestes* unfortunately do not give much clue as to plot. See Farmer 2017: 33–4, Orth 2009: 43–9.
12 The overall plot of the *Knights* is often referred to as allegorical (e.g. Hubbard 1991, Slater 2002: 70, Dover 2004: 239). For a discussion of why this term is problematic with reference to Old Comedy, see Kidd 2014: 69–71.
13 Raskin 1985: 81. While Raskin's focus here is on single words, it is easy to see how invoking a familiar, traditional story ('the judgement of Paris'; 'the rape of Europa'; or indeed, 'Beauty and the beast') may similarly function to activate our 'knowledge of a small part of the world', in Raskin's terms.
14 See also Robson 2006: 16–17 for the similar concept of 'frame abuse' (with frame here roughly equivalent to Raskin's scripts). Robson gives the example of 'buying a train ticket' to show how any given scenario triggers the audience's associations and expectations, which can then be subverted or otherwise abused to create humour; again, we might easily substitute the 'frame' of 'the judgement of Paris', etc.

15 Antiphanes here claims that tragedy alone is able to draw on the advantages of this pre-existing tradition, while comedy must invent its plots from scratch; however, the existence of mythological comedies demonstrates that this isn't strictly true. On Antiphanes fr. 189 and the comic plot, see Lowe 2000b, and on the fragment more generally, Olson 2022: 336–48.
16 Two comedies titled *Medea* are known to us, of which one was by Cantharus and the other Strattis, the latter of whom was well known for extensive tragic parodies, as Farmer 2017: 95–103 has shown; see also Orth 2009: 23–8 on Strattis' parallel use of tragedy and myth. Note that, in addition to Euripides' play, Neophron and Carcinus are known to have written *Medea* tragedies.
17 Cf. e.g. Halliwell 1986: 105–6 on Aristotle's emphasis on the 'causal intelligibility of the tragic plot structure'; Halliwell suggests that Aristotle understands 'necessity' as '[representing] a degree of causal and logical cohesion which, even if human action can rarely if ever achieve this, would constitute a perfect embodiment of dramatic meaning' (106).
18 Cf. Belfiore 1992: 120–1, who suggests that Aristotle's term εἰκός may mean not just 'probable' but also 'plausible'. This sense that causality is 'plausible' or 'believable' (πιθανόν, *Poetics* 1451b) implies some degree of mimetic realism.
19 See for example Ruffell 2011, whose title includes the term 'anti-realism'. Lowe 2000a: 87 argues that Old Comedy 'respects no consistency of space, time, causal logic, dramatic illusion, or human psychology', and places it outside the mainstream tradition of what he terms the 'Classical' plot. Silk 2000: 280 argues that, in contrast to the causal unity prioritized by Aristotle, Aristophanes is instead characterized by thematic unity.
20 On the 'domino effect' in tragedy, see Lowe 2000a: 185; see Wohl 2015: 20 on Aristotle's preference for 'logical enchainment' as the organizing principle of tragic plotting.
21 Storey 2006b unusually suggests that *Dionysalexandros* might be dated as early as 437, and might comment not on the Peloponnesian War, but on the earlier conflict with Samos. However, the majority of commentators agree that the play, along with *Nemesis*, satirized the war with Sparta. See Bakola 2010: 180–207 for an overview of this topic; the disagreements in the scholarship are discussed further below, n. 57.
22 On the plot of the *Dionysalexandros*, see Bakola 2010: 180–207, Bianchi 2016: 203–7; this topic is discussed further below, pp. 102–3. While there are some uncertainties about the details, since the Hellenistic hypothesis is quite fragmentary (and of course such a hypothesis would not be entirely reliable even were it intact), the broad shape of the plot is clear.

23 There is some confusion about whether this *Aeolosicon* was Aristophanes' second version; however, it seems at least possible (*pace* Orth 2017: 21) that later commentators were aware of two manuscripts, one of which lacked the choral songs and which they therefore assumed to be a second, later version in the style of Middle Comedy (which was erroneously thought to lack choral songs). See Jackson 2019: ch. 4 on the chorus in the manuscripts of fourth-century comedy. Sommerstein 2009 discusses the particular difficulties of interpreting Platonius' testimony regarding the two versions of *Aeolosicon*.
24 The majority of scholars believe that Sicon took on the role of Aeolus in the play; see Orth 2017: 14–20 for a detailed discussion. Ornaghi 2007 argues for the reverse, however, and this possibility is also explored by Zagari 2018.
25 Euripides' *Aeolus* is explicitly parodied in *Peace* (114–19), *Women at the Thesmophoria* (177–8) and *Frogs* (850, 1081, 1475), and the myth is mentioned in *Clouds* (1370–3) as an example of incest.
26 Compare *Odyssey* 10.1–12; the siblings are similarly married to one another, but there are no tragic overtones and they are instead described as one big happy family.
27 Compare *Frogs* 1475, τί δ' αἰσχρόν, ἢν μὴ τοῖς θεωμένοις δοκῇ; ('What is disgraceful, if it doesn't seem so to the audience?').
28 On the plot and themes of Euripides' *Aeolus*, see Xanthaki-Karamanou and Mimidou 2014.
29 Cf. Euripides *Hecuba*, *Bacchae*, and *Trojan Women*, each of which begins with the opening word ἥκω. Orth 2017: 41 notes that the word ἥκω is associated with tragic entrances as early as Aeschylus, and is regularly used by comedians to signal paratragic register.
30 See Pellegrino 2015: 40, Orth 2017: 40–1.
31 See LSJ, s.v. κρίβανος, Montanari, s.v. κρίβανος.
32 See Orth 2017: 59. The word γήθυον is subject to discussion by lexicographers, who associate it with the γηθυλλίς (spring onion), and indeed this fragment is preserved by Athenaeus in a discussion about different kinds of leeks. The form γήθυον seems to be a variant on the more common (but still less common than the standard onion κρόμμυα) γήτειον. This fragment of Aristophanes is its earliest attestation.
33 See Else 1958 for a useful history of the word *mimesis* and its verbal cognates in the fifth and early fourth centuries. However, Else does not emphasize sufficiently the difference between the verb forms and the noun μίμησις; Handley 1953 shows that nouns ending in -σις in Aristophanes have a poetic register and are associated with abstraction.

34 Such metatheatrical identification between comic protagonist and *comoididaskalos* would be characteristic of Aristophanes, as Slater 2002 *passim* has argued.
35 The contrast between comic realism and tragic fantasy is slightly counterintuitive given Aristophanes' own frequent turns towards the fantastical (as for example in *Peace* and *Birds*), and the ekphrases discussed in Chapter 1 of this book show the role of fantasy in comedy. However, the genre is nothing if not inconsistent, and the presence of the fantastical elsewhere does not preclude the presentation of comedy as anti-fantastical here in the *Aeolosicon*.
36 On the plot of *Daedalus*, see Wright 2007: 427–8, Pellegrino 2015: 130; on *Nemesis*, see Henderson 2012: 1–12, Bakola 2010: 220–5. The scholarship on the *Dionysalexandros* is extensive, and the plot contentious; a good summary is given in Storey 2006b, and see also Körte 1904, Croiset 1904, Norwood 1931, Luppe 1966, Bakola 2010: 80–112, 180–207, Bianchi 2016: 203–7.
37 The extent of the political satire in the *Dionysalexandros* is subject to some debate. Körte 1904 and Norwood 1931 argued against extensive political satire, while Revermann 1997 suggests that costume might have been used to create a sustained element of satire throughout the play. The most nuanced and persuasive analysis, however, is that of Bakola 2010: 180–207, who argues that while sustained political allegory is not in keeping with comedy's discontinuous aesthetics, the allegory might function as one of several different 'strands' in the play; these strands, Bakola argues, 'are potentially functional at any given time, so although they do not always achieve prominence to the same degree, they are probably never dropped altogether' (206). Bianchi 2016: 206 follows Bakola, and argues that the political elements of the plot should not be overstated.
38 Thomas 2000 *passim*. See also Lloyd 1987 on the intellectual climate of this period.
39 Two relatively recent studies by Bakola (2010: 223) and Henderson (2012: 1) are agreed that *Nemesis* can be dated with some certainty to 431.
40 On the dating of the *Daedalus*, see Pellegrino 2015: 130, who suggests the 420s; however, the date of this production is highly uncertain.
41 For a detailed discussion of the different mythical strands combined in Cratinus' play, see Henderson 2012.
42 See Kock 1880: 435, who suggests that in the play Daedalus made devices similar to the mechanical bull which he invented for Pasiphae.
43 It appears that the large size and unusual shape of Pericles' head was a regular target of comic satire. Note that the fragments of *Cheirones* and *Thrattai* also use the Pericles-as-Zeus trope in combination with taking a potshot at Pericles' large head.

44 See Bakola 2010: 224, who argues convincingly that while the evidence does not support an interpretation of *Nemesis* as sustained allegory, 'Zeus' lust in this play could have been made to evoke the Athenian statesman'.
45 The chicken, or 'Persian bird', as it is called in Aristophanes' *Birds* 483–4, was associated primarily with the sport of cockfighting in this period. See Dunbar 1995: 330.
46 On costume in the *Birds*, see Compton-Engle 2015: 129–43.
47 I use human(oid) in recognition of the fact that Zeus is not human per se, but the gods are, of course, presented as if they were human in poetry from Homer onwards.
48 Photius glosses σέλιονον as τὸ γυναικεῖον αἰδοῖν, but gives no source for this definition, though, given his extensive knowledge of Greek comedy, he might well have had these lines from *Nemesis* in mind.
49 PCG ad loc., Henderson 1991: 135, 136, 149, 151, Bakola 2010.
50 Henderson 1991: 149 notes that the metaphor of breasts as apples is common throughout Greek erotic literature, and ibid. 135 lists a number of transparent uses of ῥόδον as a metaphor. These words are therefore quite different from the celery and watermint that follow, neither of which is attested in an obscene context beyond this fragment.
51 Bakola 2010: 224, arguing against Schwarze (1971: 24–40), Rosen (1988: 55–7) and Casolari (2003: 79–97, 109–12).
52 Wright 2007: 427–8 also discusses fragment 199 and its links to causality and the Trojan War.
53 A photograph of the papyrus can be found in Bakola 2010 (plate 3).
54 I follow the standard text of PCG; for an alternative version, see Bakola 2010: 322–3, who suggests some minor emendations.
55 Schmidd (1946) was the first to suggest a chorus of shepherds, and this line of argument was also taken up by Luppe (1966), Lerza (1982), Rosen (1988) and Casolari (2003). Bakola 2010: 82–8, in her extensive and persuasive analysis of this play, however, follows Körte (1904: 483), Croiset (1904: 299), Norwood (1931: 118), and, more recently, Storey (2005, 2006a) in suggesting a single chorus of satyrs; Bianchi 2016: 203–4 concurs that there was only a single chorus in the play. The issue of the formal differences between comedy and satyr drama has most recently been addressed by Marsh (2020).
56 For a discussion, see Storey 2005 and Bakola 2010: 81–112.
57 Croiset (1904), Schwartze (1971) and Revermann (1997) have argued in favour of a sustained political allegory in the play; Körte (1904) and Norwood (1931) argued that the play was primarily mythical burlesque. Bowie (2000), Ruffell

(2002) and Bakola (2010: 180–208) take what I think is the most persuasive middle ground, arguing that political satire was an important feature of the play, but that it did not take the form of sustained allegory.
58 Bakola 2010: 207 argues that the play 'is composed of multiple plot-strands which achieve prominence and then 'sink', only to reappear later,' and that the resulting discontinuity is a central feature of the play's comic texture.
59 Eur., *Phoen.* 415, *IT* 1159, *Andr.* 1121
60 *Od.* 1.103, 3.493, 4.20 10.220, 18.10, 101, 386, 21.299
61 There is an extensive bibliography on paratragedy in both plays, but see for starters, on *Acharnians*: Rau 1967: 19–41, Foley 1988, Slater 2002: 42–67, Platter 2007: 42–62, Sells 2019: 23–52; on *Peace*: Rau 1967: 115–36, Slater 2002: 115–32, Hall 2006: 321–52, Zogg 2014, Scott 2019a, Sells 2019: 23–52.
62 The play apparently told the story of Telephus' wounding by Achilles when the Greeks sacked his city of Mysia on the way to Troy. The action focused on Telephus' attempts to heal his suppurating wound by obtaining Achilles' spear, which the Delphic oracle promised would cure him. In the play, Telephus took the infant Orestes hostage in order to negotiate with the Greeks. On the plot of *Telephus*, see Heath 1987, Collard, Cropp and Lee 1995: 17–52.
63 On this scene, in addition to the scholarship cited in n. 61 above, see Harriott 1982, Compton-Engle 2015: 88–94.
64 On lists and accumulation in Aristophanes, see Silk 2000: 131–6. A catalogue of examples may also be found in Spyropoulos 1974, who argues that verbal accumulation is a central tool of verbal humour in Aristophanes.
65 See Thuc., 5.14–20, who relates that peace negotiations followed swiftly from the Battle of Amphipolis in 422 BC. Whitman (1962: 104) goes so far as to suggest that Aristophanes (re)wrote the entire play following the signing of the treaty; however, if Thucydides' timeline is correct, just the ongoing negotiations alone would arguably provide an atmosphere conducive to a play on the subject of peace.
66 On *Peace*'s interactions with epic, see also Telò 2013, who argues that that the *Peace*'s anti-Iliadic stance is variously Odyssean, Hesiodic and Archilochean in character.
67 See Dobrov 2001: 92–4 and Collard, Cropp and Lee 1995: 105, all of whom also assign fragment 285 to the play's prologue, in which they suggest that the hero Bellerophon, wandering on the Aleian plain, raged against his misfortune and the unfairness of the world, and denied the existence of the gods. Only Dixon (2014) diverges from the consensus, and suggests that this fragment should be assigned to Stheneboea, who he (again in contrast to all other reconstructions, which presume the action to take place after her death) suggests was a character in the *Bellerophon*. Dixon's suggestion is based on the appearance of the name

Stheneboea in the highly fragmentary first hypothesis of the *Bellerophon*. However, since hypotheses often begin by giving backstory to the play's events, the appearance of Stheneboea's name is not, in my opinion, sufficient reason to diverge from the majority consensus on this play.

68 Again, Dixon (2014) is the only scholar to demur from the consensus here.
69 See Olson 1998 ad loc. for details of the accusations against Pheidias and his ultimate exile.

Conclusions: Comedy and the Avant-Garde in the Fifth Century and Beyond

1 On comedy's frequent anti-novelty stance, see Wright 2012: 86–90, though, as Wright notes, this stance is far from unequivocal, given that comedians also regularly trumpet their own novelty and trash their competitors' jokes as derivative and repetitive.
2 D'Angour in particular argues that the New Music increasingly uncoupled accent pitch and musical pitch, and that this innovation was heavily dependent on an increasingly professional class of performers. On the professionalization of music in this period, see also for example Easterling and Hall 2002, Csapo 2004a, Stewart 2020; on the role of professionalization in shaping dithyramb in particular, Kowalzig and Wilson 2013.
3 On the relationship between text and melody in Greek music, see D'Angour 2018. Euripides' adoption of melismatic melodies in the style of the New Music is discussed by D'Angour 2016.
4 In addition to Dobrov 1997, see Zimmermann 1993, Wright 2012: 73–85.
5 On Cinesias in Aristophanes, see Kidd 2014: 87–117; on the musical satire of *Frogs*, see D'Angour 2020, who suggests that the frogs' puffed throats mimic the puffed cheeks of the aulos players who dominated the New Music.
6 These comments are also quoted in LeVen 2013, who discusses Gildersleeve's analysis in detail in her examination of the role of riddles in dithyramb and the New Music.
7 'Again we breathe the atmosphere of the mock lyrics of the *Birds*, of the *Frogs*; and the triple compounds ... remind us of the cockinesses, the "horse-cockinesses" of Aristophanes' comic fabrications.' Gildersleeve 1903: 230.
8 For a detailed analysis of the metaphors in the *Persians*, see Budelmann and LeVen 2014, who use the theory of 'blending' to analyse Timotheus' metaphorical language. For a discussion of the shortcomings of blending as a theory of

metaphor, however, see Scott 2019b. The complexity of Timotheus' verse here is not helped by some uncertainties as to the text. The meaning of σύρτις in line 88 is particularly contested. Janssen 1984 ad loc. reads it as a reference to the Syrtis (a pair of shallow gulfs off the coast of Libya, cf. Hdt. 2.32) and as therefore standing for a sandbank in general. Campbell 1993 ad loc. and Lambin 2013: 151 also follow this interpretation. By contrast, Horden 2002 ad loc. and Sevieri 2011 ad loc. suggest that the word is derived from σύρτης, meaning a line or cord, and therefore refers to the line of enemy ships rather than a geographical feature.

Bibliography

Aguirre, M. (2010), 'Erinyes as Creatures of Darkness', in Christopoulos, M., Karakantza, E. D. and Levaniouk, O. (eds), *Light and Darkness in Ancient Greek Myth and Religion*, 133–41, Plymouth: Lexington.

Anderson, W. D. (1994), *Music and Musicians in Ancient Greece*, Ithaca: Cornell University Press.

Andrews, A. C. (1948), 'Greek and Latin Mouse-Fishes and Pig-Fishes', *TAPA*, 79: 232–53.

Arnott, P. D. (1960), 'The Alphabet Tragedy of Callias', *CPhil.*, 55 (3): 178–80.

Atchity, K. J. (1978), *Homer's Iliad: The Shield of Memory*, Carbondale: Southern Illinois University Press.

Attardo, S. (1994), *Linguistic Theories of Humor*, Berlin: De Gruyter Mouton.

Bagordo, A. (2020), *Aristophanes* Skenas katalambanousi – Horai *(fr. 487–589): Übersetzung und Kommentar*, Göttingen: Verlag Antike.

Bakola, E. (2010), *Cratinus and the Art of Comedy*, Oxford: Oxford University Press.

Bakola, E., Prauscello, L. and Telò, M., eds (2013), *Greek Comedy and the Discourse of Genres*, Cambridge: Cambridge University Press.

Becker, A. S. (1995), *The Shield of Achilles and the Poetics of Ekphrasis*, Lanham, MD: Rowman & Littlefield.

Belfiore, E. (1988), 'ΠΕΡΙΠΕΤΕΙΑ as Discontinuous Action: Aristotle "Poetics" 11. 1452a22–29', *CPhil.*, 83 (3): 183–94.

Belfiore, E. (1992), *Tragic Pleasures: Aristotle on Plot and Emotion*, Princeton: Princeton University Press.

Bianchi, F. P. (2016), *Kratinos* Archilochoi – Empipramenoi *(frr. 1–68): Introduzione, Traduzione, Commento*, Heidelberg: Verlag Antike.

Biles, Z. P. (2002), 'Intertextual Biography in the Rivalry of Cratinus and Aristophanes', *AJPhil.*, 123 (2): 169–204.

Biles, Z. P. (2011), *Aristophanes and the Poetics of Competition*, Cambridge: Cambridge University Press.

Biles, Z. P. and Olson, S. D. (2015), *Aristophanes:* Wasps, *Edited with Introduction and Commentary*, Oxford: Oxford University Press.

Borthwick, E. K. (1968a), 'The Dances of Philocleon and the Sons of Carcinus in Aristophanes' *Wasps*', *CQ*, 18 (1): 44–51.

Borthwick, E. K. (1968b), 'Notes on the Plutarch de Musica and the Cheiron of Pherecrates', *Hermes*, 96: 60–73.

Boschi, A. (2016), 'La *Commedia delle lettere* e l'*Edipo re*: un confronto "grammaticale" tra il re e l'indovino', *Studi Italiani di Filologia Classica*, 14 (2): 169–79.

Bowie, A. (2000), 'Myth and Ritual in the Rivals of Aristophanes', in Harvey, D. and Wilkins, J. (eds), *The Rivals of Aristophanes: Studies in Athenian Old Comedy*, 317–39, London: Duckworth.

Boys-Stones, G. R., ed. (2003), *Metaphor, Allegory, and the Classical Tradition: Ancient Thought and Modern Revisions*, Oxford: Oxford University Press.

Bram, S. (2006), 'Ekphrasis as a Shield: Ekphrasis and the Mimetic Tradition', *Word & Image*, 22 (4): 372–8.

Brock, A. (2004), 'Analyzing Scripts in Humorous Communication', *Humor*, 17 (4): 353–60.

Budelmann, F. and LeVen, P. (2014), 'Timotheus' Poetics of Blending: A Cognitive Approach to the Language of the New Music', *CPhil.*, 109 (3): 191–210.

Byre, C. S. (1992), 'Narration, Description, and Theme in the Shield of Achilles', *CJ*, 88 (1): 33–42.

Byrne, M. (1994), 'The Invention of Tuning Pegs and Pins', in *Proc. Fourth Intern. Colloquium Study Group on Music Archaeology of the ICTM (Saint-Germain-en-Laye, October 1990)*, 59–61, Paris: Éditions de la Maison des sciences de l'homme.

Cahoon, L. (1988), 'The Bed as Battlefield: Erotic Conquest and Military Metaphor in Ovid's *Amores*', *TAPA*, 118: 293–307.

Campbell, D. A. (1993), *Greek Lyric V: The New School of Poetry and Anonymous Songs and Hymns*, Cambridge, MA: Harvard University Press.

Carey, C. (1993), 'Return of the Radish or Just When You Thought It Was Safe to Go Back into the Kitchen', *LCM*, 18 (4): 53–5.

Carey, C. (2013a), 'Comedy and the Civic Chorus', in Bakola, E., Prauscello, L. and Telò, M. (eds), *Greek Comedy and the Discourse of Genres*, 155–74, Cambridge: Cambridge University Press.

Carey, C. (2013b), 'Marathon and the Construction of the Comic Past', in Carey, C. and Edwards, M. (eds), *Marathon – 2500 Years*, 123–42, London: Institute of Classical Studies.

Carter, D. M. (2006), 'At Home, Round Here, Out There: The City and Tragic Space', in Rosen, R. M. and Sluiter, I. (eds), *City, Countryside, and the Spatial Organization of Value in Classical Antiquity*, 139–72, Leiden: Brill.

Casolari, F. (2003), *Die Mythentravestie in der griechischen Komödie*, Münster: Aschendorff Verlag.

Chantraine, P. (1933), *La Formation des Noms en Grec Ancien*, Paris: Champion.

Cohen, D. (1985), 'A Note on Aristophanes and the Punishment of Adultery in Athenian Law', *Zeitschrift der Savigny-Stiftung für Rechtsgeschichte: Romanistische Abteilung*, 102 (1): 385–7.

Collard, C., Cropp, M. J. and Lee, K. H. (1995), *Euripides: Selected Fragmentary Plays*, Vol. I, Warminster: Aris & Phillips.

Colvin, S. (1999), *Dialect in Aristophanes and the Politics of Language in Ancient Greek Literature*, Oxford: Clarendon Press.

Compton-Engle, G. (2015), *Costume in the Comedies of Aristophanes*, Cambridge: Cambridge University Press.

Corbel-Morana, C. (2012), *Le Bestiaire d'Aristophane*, Paris: Les Belles Lettres.

Croiset, M. (1904), 'Le *Dionysalexandros* de Cratinos', *Rev. Ét. Grec.*, 17 (76–77): 297–310.

Csapo, E. (1994), 'The Authorship of the Comoedia Dukiana', *ZPE*, 100: 39–44.

Csapo, E. (2000), 'From Aristophanes to Menander? Genre Transformation in Greek Comedy', in Depew, M. and Obbink, D. (eds), *Matrices of Genre: Authors, Canons, and Society*, 115–33, Cambridge, MA: Harvard University Press.

Csapo, E. (2004a), 'Some Social and Economic Conditions Behind the Rise of the Acting Profession in the Fifth and Fourth Centuries BC', in Hugoniot, C., Hurlet, F. and Milanezi, S. (eds), *Le statut de l'acteur dans l'Antiquité grecque et romaine*, 53–76, Tours: Presses universitaires François-Rabelais.

Csapo, E. (2004b), 'The Politics of the New Music', in Murray, P. and Wilson, P. (eds), *Music and the Muses: The Culture of Mousike in the Classical Athenian City*, 207–48, Oxford: Oxford University Press.

Csapo, E. (2009), 'New Music's Gallery of Images: the "Dithyrambic" First Stasimon of Euripides' *Electra*', in Cousland, J. R. C. and Hume, J. R. (eds), *The Play of Texts and Fragments: Essays in Honour of Martin Cropp*, 95–109, Leiden: Brill.

Cunningham, V. (2007), 'Why Ekphrasis?', *CPhil.*, 102 (1): 57–71.

D'Angour, A. (2006), 'The New Music – so What's New?', in Goldhill, S. and Osborne, R. (eds), *Rethinking Revolutions through Ancient Greece*, 264–83, Cambridge: Cambridge University Press.

D'Angour, A. (2016), 'Euripides and the Sound of Music', in McClure, L. K. (ed.), *A Companion to Euripides*, 428–43, Chichester: Wiley-Blackwell.

D'Angour, A. (2018), 'The Musical Setting of Ancient Greek Texts', in Phillips, T. and D'Angour, A. (eds), *Music, Text, and Culture in Ancient Greece*, 47–72, Oxford: Oxford University Press.

D'Angour, A. (2020), 'The Musical Frogs in *Frogs*', in Fries, A. and Kanellakis, D. (eds), *Ancient Greek Comedy: Genre – Texts – Reception*, 187–98, Berlin: De Gruyter.

De Jong, I. J. F. (1987), 'Paris/Alexandros in the *Iliad*', *Mnemosyne*, 40 (1–2): 124–8.

De Ste. Croix, G. E. M. (1972), *The Origins of the Peloponnesian War*, London: Duckworth.

De Simone, M. (2004), 'Nota a Pherecr. fr. 155, 25 K.-A.', in Medaglia, S. M. (ed.), *Miscellanea in ricordo di Angelo Raffaele Sodano*, 119–37, Naples: Guida.

Dixon, D. W. (2014), 'Reconsidering Euripides' *Bellerophon*', *CQ*, 64 (2): 493–506.

Dobrov, G. W. (1997), 'From Criticism to Mimesis: Comedy and the New Music', in Zimmermann, B. (ed.), *Griechisch-römische Komödie und Tragödie II*, 49–74, Stuttgart: M&P Verlag für Wissenschaft und Forschung.

Dobrov, G. W. (2001), *Figures of Play: Greek Drama and Metafictional Poetics*, Oxford: Oxford University Press.

Dobrov, G. W. and Urios-Aparisi, E. (1995), 'The Maculate Muse: Gender, Genre, and the *Chiron* of Pherecrates', in Dobrov, G. W. (ed.), *Beyond Aristophanes: Transition and Diversity in Greek Comedy*, 139–74, Atlanta: Scholars Press.

Dover, K. (2004), 'The Limits of Allegory and Allusion in Aristophanes', in Cairns, D. L. and Knox, R. A. (eds), *Law, Rhetoric, and Comedy in Classical Athens: Essays in Honour of Douglas M. MacDowell*, 239–49, Swansea: Classical Press of Wales.

Dunbar, N. (1995), *Aristophanes:* Birds, *Edited with Introduction and Commentary*, Oxford: Clarendon Press.

Easterling, P. and Hall, E., eds (2002), *Greek and Roman Actors: Aspects of an Ancient Profession*, Cambridge: Cambridge University Press.

Ebert, J. (1978), 'Das "Parisurteil" in der Hypothesis zum Dionysalexandros des Kratinos', *Philologus*, 122 (1): 177–82.

Elliger, W. (1975), *Die Darstellung der Landschaft in der griechischen Dichtung*, Berlin: De Gruyter.

Else, G. F. (1958), '"Imitation" in the Fifth Century', *CPhil.*, 53 (2): 73–90.

Elsner, J. (2002), 'Introduction: The Genres of Ekphrasis', *Ramus*, 31 (1–2): 1–18.

Elsner, J., ed. (1996), *Art and Text in Roman Culture*, Cambridge: Cambridge University Press.

Farioli, M. (2001), *Mundus Alter: Utopie e Distopie nella Commedia Greca Antica*, Milan: Vita e Pensiero.

Farmer, M. C. (2017), *Tragedy on the Comic Stage*, New York: Oxford University Press.

Fearn, D. (2017), *Pindar's Eyes: Visual and Material Culture in Epinician Poetry*, Oxford: Oxford University Press.

Foley, H. P. (1988), 'Tragedy and politics in Aristophanes' *Acharnians*', *JHS*, 108: 33–47.

Fongoni, A. (2009), 'Innovazione Ditirambiche e Terminologia Musicale nel *Chirone* di Ferecrate (Ps. Plut. *Mus.* 30, 1142a = Aristoph. fr. 953 K.-A. et Pherecr. fr. 155, 26–8 K.-A.)', in Castaldo, D., Restani, D. and Tassi, C. (eds), *Il sapere musicale e i suoi contesti da Teofrasto a Claudio Tolomeo*, 171–83, Ravenna: Longo Editore.

Fowler, D. P. (1991), 'Narrate and Describe: The Problem of Ekphrasis', *JRS*, 81: 25–35.

Franchini, E. (2020), *Ferecrate* Krapataloi *- Pseudherakles (frr. 85–163): Introduzione, Traduzione, Commento*, Göttingen: Verlag Antike.

Francis, J. A. (2009), 'Metal Maidens, Achilles' Shield, and Pandora: The Beginnings of "Ekphrasis"', *AJPhil.*, 130 (1): 1–23.

Franklin, J. C. (2013), '"Songbenders of Circular Choruses": Dithyramb and the "Demise of Music"', in Kowalzig, B. and Wilson, P. (eds), *Dithyramb in Context*, 213–36, Oxford: Oxford University Press.

Freud, S. ([1905] 2002), *The Joke and Its Relation to the Unconscious*, trans. J. Crick, London: Penguin.

Gildersleeve, B. L. (1903), 'Brief Mention', *AJPhil.*, 24 (2): 222–38.

Goldhill, S. (1991), *The Poet's Voice: Essays on Poetics and Greek Literature*, Cambridge: Cambridge University Press.

Goldhill, S. (2007), 'What Is Ekphrasis For?', *CPhil.*, 102 (1): 1–19.

Green, J. R. (1985), 'A Representation of the *Birds* of Aristophanes', in Frel, J. and Morgan, S. K. (eds), *Greek Vases In The J. Paul Getty Museum*, Vol. II, 95–118, Malibu: The J. Paul Getty Museum.

Grenfell, B. P. and Hunt, A. S. (1904), '663. Argument of Cratinus' ΔΙΟΝΥΣΑΛΕΧΑΝΔΡΟΣ', in *The Oxyrhynchus Papyri*, Part 4, 69–72, London: Egypt Exploration Fund.

Hall, E. (2000), 'Female Figures and Metapoetry in Old Comedy', in Harvey, D. and Wilkins, J. (eds), *The Rivals of Aristophanes: Studies in Athenian Old Comedy*, 407–18, London: Duckworth.

Hall, E. (2006), *The Theatrical Cast of Athens: Interactions between Ancient Greek Drama and Society*, Oxford: Oxford University Press.

Halliwell, S. (1987), *The Poetics of Aristotle: Translation and Commentary*, London: Duckworth.

Handley, E. W. (1953), '-σις nouns in Aristophanes', *Eranos*, 51: 129–42

Harriott, R. M. (1982), 'The Function of the Euripides Scene in Aristophanes' *Acharnians*', *G&R*, 29 (1): 35–41.

Hartwig, A. (2010), 'The Date of the *Rhabdouchoi* and the Early Career of Plato Comicus', *ZPE*, 174: 19–31.

Harvey, D. and Wilkins, J., eds (2000), *The Rivals of Aristophanes: Studies in Athenian Old Comedy*, London: Duckworth.

Haß, P. (1998), *Der locus amoenus in der antiken Literatur: Zu Theorie und Geschichte eines literarischen Motivs*, Bamberg: Wissenschaftlicher Verlag.

Heath, M. (1987), 'Euripides' *Telephus*', *CQ*, 37 (2): 272–80.

Henderson, J. (1990), *Aristophanes:* Lysistrata, *Edited with Introduction and Commentary*, Oxford: Clarendon Press.

Henderson, J. (1991), *The Maculate Muse: Obscene Language in Attic Comedy*, 2nd edn, New York: Oxford University Press.

Henderson, J. (2000), 'Pherekrates and the Women of Old Comedy', in Harvey, D. and Wilkins, J. (eds), *The Rivals of Aristophanes: Studies in Athenian Old Comedy*, 135–50, London: Duckworth.

Henderson, J. (2002), *Aristophanes*, Vol. IV: Frogs, Assemblywomen, Wealth, Cambridge, MA: Harvard University Press.

Henderson, J. (2012), 'Pursuing Nemesis: Cratinus and Mythological Comedy', in Marshall, C. W. and Kovacs, G. (eds), *No Laughing Matter: Studies in Athenian Comedy*, 1–12, London: Bristol Classical Press.

Henderson, J. (2014), 'Comedy in the Fourth Century II: Politics and Domesticity', in Fontaine, M. and Scafuro, A. C. (eds), *The Oxford Handbook of Greek and Roman Comedy*, 181–98, Oxford: Oxford University Press.

Holzinger, K. (1928), 'Erklärungen umstrittener Stellen des Aristophanes', *Sitz. Wien*, 208 (5): 37–41.

Holzmeister, A. (2014), '*Ekphrasis* in the Ancient Novel', in Cueva, E. P. and Byrne, S. N. (eds), *A Companion to the Ancient Novel*, 411–23, Chichester: Wiley-Blackwell.

Hordern, J. H. (2002), *The Fragments of Timotheus of Miletus, Edited with an Introduction and Commentary*, Oxford: Oxford University Press.

Hubbard, T. K. (1989), 'Old Men in the Youthful Plays of Aristophanes', in Falkner, T. M. and De Luce, J. (eds), *Old Age in Greek and Latin Literature*, 90–113, Albany: State University of New York Press.

Hubbard, T. K. (1991), *The Mask of Comedy: Aristophanes and the Intertextual Parabasis*, Ithaca: Cornell University Press.

Jackson, L. C. M. M. (2019), *The Chorus of Drama in the Fourth Century BCE: Presence and Representation*, Oxford: Oxford University Press.

Janssen, T. H. (1984), *Timotheus: Persae, A Commentary*, Amsterdam: Hakkert.

Kant, I. (1790), *Kritik der Urteilskraft*, Berlin: Lagarde und Friedrich.

Kant, I. ([1790] 2007), *Critique of Judgement*, trans. J. C. Meredith, rev. and ed. N. Walker, Oxford: Oxford University Press.

Kidd, S. E. (2014), *Nonsense and Meaning in Ancient Greek Comedy*, Cambridge: Cambridge University Press.

Kidd, S. E. (2019), *Play and Aesthetics in Ancient Greece*, Cambridge: Cambridge University Press.

Kock, T. (1880), *Comicorum Atticorum Fragmenta*, Vol. I, Leipzig: B. G. Teubner.

Konstan, D. (1997), 'The Greek Polis and Its Negations: Versions of Utopia in Aristophanes' *Birds*', in Dobrov, G. W. (ed.), *The City as Comedy: Society and Representation in Athenian Drama*, 3–22, Chapel Hill: University of North Carolina Press.

Konstan, D. (2012), 'A World without Slaves: Crates' *Thêria*', in Marshall, C. W. and Kovacs, G. (eds), *No Laughing Matter: Studies in Athenian Comedy*, 13–18, London: Bristol Classical Press.

Konstantakos, I. M. (2014), 'Comedy in the Fourth Centrury I: Mythological Burlesques', in Fontaine, M. and Scafuro, A. C. (eds), *The Oxford Handbook of Greek and Roman Comedy*, 160–80, Oxford: Oxford University Press.

Körte, A. (1904), 'Die Hypothesis zu Kratinos' Dionysalexandros', *Hermes*, 39 (4): 481–98.

Kövecses, Z. (2010), *Metaphor: A Practical Introduction*, 2nd edn, Oxford: Oxford University Press.

Kowalzig, B. and Wilson, P. (2013), 'Introduction: The World of Dithyramb', in Kowalzig, B. and Wilson, P. (eds), *Dithyramb in Context*, 1–27, Oxford: Oxford University Press.

Laird, A. (1993), 'Sounding out Ecphrasis: Art and Text in Catullus 64', *JRS*, 83: 18–30.

Lakoff, G. and Johnson, M. (1980), *Metaphors We Live By*, Chicago: University of Chicago Press.

Lambin, G. (2013), *Timothée de Milet: Le Poète et le Musicien*, Rennes: Presses universitaires de Rennes.

Lauxtermann, M. D. (1998), 'What Is an Epideictic Epigram?', *Mnemosyne*, 51 (5): 525–37.

Lendle, O. (1995), 'Überlegungen zum Bühnenkran', in Pöhlmann, E. (ed.), *Studien zur Bühnendichtung und zum Theaterbau der Antike*, 165–72, Frankfurt: Peter Lang.

Lerza, P. (1982), 'Alcune proposte per il "Dionysalexandros" di Cratino', *SIFC*, 54 (1–2): 186–93.

LeVen, P. A. (2013), '"You Make Less Sense than a (New) Dithyramb": Sociology of a Riddling Style', in Kwapisz, J., Petrain, D. and Szymanski, M. (eds), *The Muse at Play: Riddles and Wordplay in Greek and Latin Poetry*, 44–64, Berlin: De Gruyter.

Lloyd, G. E. R. (1987), *The Revolutions of Wisdom: Studies in the Claims and Practice of Ancient Greek Science*, Berkeley: University of California Press.

Lowe, N. J. (2000a), *The Classical Plot and the Invention of Western Narrative*, Cambridge: Cambridge University Press.

Lowe, N. J. (2000b), 'Comic Plots and the Invention of Fiction', in Harvey, D. and Wilkins, J. (eds), *The Rivals of Aristophanes: Studies in Athenian Old Comedy*, 259–72, London: Duckworth.

Lowe, N. J. (2006), 'Aristophanic Spacecraft', in Kozak, L. and Rich, J. (eds), *Playing Around Aristophanes: Essays in Honour of Alan Sommerstein*, 48–64, Oxford: Aris & Phillips.

Lowe, N. J. (2008), *Comedy* (Greece & Rome: New Surveys in the Classics), Cambridge: Cambridge University Press.

Lowe, N. J. (2020), 'Beyond a Joke: Making Humour Theory Work with Aristophanes', in Swallow, P. and Hall, E. (eds), *Aristophanic Humour: Theory and Practice*, 13–22, London: Bloomsbury.

Luppe, W. (1966), 'Die Hypothesis zu Kratinos' Dionysalexandros', *Philologus*, 110 (1–2): 169–93.
Luppe, W. (1993), 'Überlegungen zur "Comoedia Dukiana"', *ZPE*, 98: 39–41.
McClure, L. (1999), *Spoken Like a Woman: Speech and Gender in Athenian Drama*, Princeton: Princeton University Press.
MacDowell, D. M. (1971), *Aristophanes:* Wasps, *Edited with Introduction and Commentary*, Oxford: Clarendon Press.
Männlein-Robert, I. (2007), *Stimme, Schrift und Bild: Zum Verhältnis der Künste in der hellenistischen Dichtung*, Heidelberg: Universitätsverlag Winter.
Marsh, L. D. (2020), 'The Structure of Mythological Old Comedy', *Philologus*, 164 (1): 14–38.
Marshall, C. W. (2014), 'Dramatic Technique and Athenian Comedy', in Revermann, M. (ed.), *The Cambridge Companion to Greek Comedy*, 131–46, Cambridge: Cambridge University Press.
Martin, R. P. (2015), 'Solon in Comedy', *Trends in Classics*, 7 (1): 66–84.
Mastronarde, D. J. (1990), 'Actors on High: The Skene Roof, the Crane, and the Gods in Attic Drama', *Classical Antiquity*, 9 (2): 247–94.
Miccolis, E. R. (2017), *Archippos: Einleitung, Übersetzung, Kommentar*, Heidelberg: Verlag Antike.
Morreall, J., ed. (1987), *The Philosophy of Laughter and Humor*, Albany: State University of New York Press.
Moulton, C. (1979), 'The Lyric of Insult and Abuse in Aristophanes', *Museum Helveticum*, 36 (1): 23–47.
Moulton, C. (1981), *Aristophanic Poetry*, Göttingen: Vandenhoeck & Ruprecht.
Nelson, S. (2016), *Aristophanes and His Tragic Muse: Comedy, Tragedy and the Polis in 5th Century Athens*, Leiden: Brill.
Nesselrath, H.-G. (1990), *Die attische Mittlere Komödie: Ihre Stellung in der antiken Literaturkritik und Literaturgeschichte*, Berlin: De Gruyter.
Newby, Z. (2009), 'Absorption and Erudition in Philostratus' *Imagines*', in Bowie, E. and Elsner, J. (eds), *Philostratus*, 322–42, Cambridge: Cambridge University Press.
Newiger, H.-J. (1957), *Metapher und Allegorie: Studien zu Aristophanes*, Munich: Beck.
Newiger, H.-J. (1990), 'Ekkyklema und Mechané in der Inszenierung des griechischen Dramas', *Würzburger Jahrbücher für die Altertumswissenschaft*, 16: 33–42.
Norwood, G. (1931), *Greek Comedy*, London: Methuen & Co.
Olson, S.D. (1998), *Aristophanes:* Peace, Oxford: Clarendon Press.
Olson, S. D. (2002), *Aristophanes:* Acharnians, *Edited with Introduction and Commentary*, Oxford: Oxford University Press.
Olson, S. D. (2007), *Broken Laughter: Select Fragments of Greek Comedy*, Oxford: Oxford University Press.

Olson, S. D. (2016), *Eupolis* Heilotes – Chrysoun genos *(frr. 147–325): Translation and Commentary*, Heidelberg: Verlag Antike.
Olson, S. D. (2022), *Antiphanes* Zakynthios – Progonoi *(frr. 101–193): Translation and Commentary*, Göttingen: Verlag Antike.
Olson, S. D. and Seaberg, R. (2018), *Kratinos frr. 299–514: Translation and Commentary*, Göttingen: Verlag Antike.
Oring, E. (1992), *Jokes and Their Relations*, Lexington: University Press of Kentucky.
Oring, E. (2003), *Engaging Humor*, Urbana: University of Illinois Press.
Oring, E. (2016), *Joking Asides: The Theory, Analysis, and Aesthetics of Humor*, Logan: Utah State University Press.
Ornaghi, M. (2007), 'Note di Onomastica Comica (II): Aristofane e i Poeti Comici del V Secolo', *Quaderni del Dipartimento di Filologia Linguistica e Tradizione Classica 'Augusto Rostagni'*, N.S. 6: 23–60.
Orth, C. (2009), *Strattis: Die Fragmente, Ein Kommentar*, Berlin: Verlag Antike.
Orth, C. (2017), *Aristophanes* Aiolosikon – Babylonioi *(fr. 1–100): Übersetzung und Kommentar*, Heidelberg: Verlag Antike.
Palmer, J. (1987), *The Logic of the Absurd: On Film and Television Comedy*, London: BFI Publishing.
Palmer, J. (1994), *Taking Humour Seriously*, London: Routledge.
Parke, H. W. (1967), *The Oracles of Zeus: Dodona, Olympia, Ammon*, Cambridge, MA: Harvard University Press.
Parry, M. (1957), 'Landscape in Greek Poetry', *Yale Classical Studies*, 15: 3–29.
Pasquariello, C. (2004), 'Pirro o i Misii', in Ghedini, F., Colpo, I. and Novello, M. (eds), *Le Immagini di Filostrato Minore: La prospettiva dello storico dell'arte*, 105–15, Rome: Edizione Quasar.
Paulas, J. (2010), 'The Bazaar Fish Market in Fourth-Century Greek Comedy', *Arethusa*, 43 (3): 403–28.
Pellegrino, M. (2016), 'Le Commedie Perdute di Aristofane', *Studia Philologica Valentina*, 18 (15): 275–88.
Peponi, A.-E. (2016), 'Lyric Vision: An Introduction', in Cazzato, V. and Lardinois, A. (eds), *The Look of Lyric: Greek Song and the Visual*, 1–15, Leiden: Brill.
Perrone, S. (2008), 'Effetti Comici a Bordo di un Ramo di Fico: a Proposito di P.Oxy. XXXV 2742', *Paideia*, 63: 209–25.
Perrone, S. (2019), *Cratete: Introduzione, Traduzione e Commento*, Göttingen: Verlag Antike.
Pirrotta, S. (2009), *Plato comicus: Die fragmentarischen Komödien, Ein Kommentar*, Berlin: Verlag Antike.
Platt, V. (2002), 'Evasive Epiphanies in Ekphrastic Epigram', *Ramus*, 31 (1–2): 33–50.

Platter, C. (2007), *Aristophanes and the Carnival of Genres*, Baltimore: Johns Hopkins University Press.
Poe, J. P. (1999), 'Entrances, Exits, and the Structure of Aristophanic Comedy', *Hermes*, 127 (2): 189–207.
Poe, J. P. (2000), 'Multiplicity, Discontinuity, and Visual Meaning in Aristophanic Comedy', *Rh. Mus.*, 143 (3–4): 256–95.
Pöhlmann, E. (1971), 'Die ABC-Komödie des Kallias', *Rh. Mus.*, 114 (3): 230–40.
Pöhlmann, E. (2011), 'Twelve Chordai and the Strobilos of Phrynis in the *Chiron* of Pherecrates (*PCG* fr. 155)', *Quaderni Urbinati di Cultura Classica*, 99 (3): 117–33.
Putnam, M. C. J. (1998), *Virgil's Epic Designs: Ekphrasis in the* Aeneid, New Haven: Yale University Press.
Raskin, V. (1985), *Semantic Mechanisms of Humor*, Dordrecht: D. Reidel.
Raskin, V. and Attardo, S. (1991), 'Script theory revis(it)ed: joke similarity and joke representation model', *Humor*, 4 (3–4): 293–348.
Rau, P. (1967), *Paratragodia: Untersuchung einer komischen Form des Aristophanes*, Munich: Beck.
Rawls, R. (2013), 'Aristophanes' Simonides: Lyric Models for Praise and Blame', in Bakola, E., Prauscello, L. and Telò, M. (eds), *Greek Comedy and the Discourse of Genres*, 175–201, Cambridge: Cambridge University Press.
Reckford, K. J. (1987), *Aristophanes' Old-and-New Comedy*, Vol. I: *Six Essays in Perspective*, Chapel Hill: University of North Carolina Press.
Rehm, R. (2002), *The Play of Space: Spatial Transformation in Greek Tragedy*, Princeton: Princeton University Press.
Restani, D. (1983), 'Il *Chirone* di Ferecrate e la "Nuova" Musica Greca. Ricerca sul Lessico Retorico-Musicale', *Rivista Italiana di Musicologia*, 18 (2): 139–92.
Revermann, M. (1997), 'Cratinus' Διονυσαλέξανδρος and the Head of Pericles', *JHS*, 117: 197–200.
Revermann, M. (2006), *Comic Business: Theatricality, Dramatic Technique, and Performance Contexts of Aristophanic Comedy*, Oxford: Oxford University Press.
Ricoeur, P. (2003), *The Rule of Metaphor: The Creation of Meaning in Language*, trans. R. Czerny, K. McLaughlin and J. Costello, SJ, London: Routledge.
Robkin, A. L. H. (1979), 'That Magnificent Flying Machine: On the Nature of the *Mechane* of the Theatre of Dionysos at Athens', *Archaeological News*, 8: 1–6.
Robson, J. (2006), *Humour, Obscenity and Aristophanes*, Tübingen: Gunter Narr Verlag.
Rosen, R. M. (1988), *Old Comedy and the Iambographic Tradition*, Atlanta: Scholars Press.
Rosen, R. M. (1989), 'Trouble in the Early Career of Plato Comicus: Another Look at P.Oxy. 2737.44–51 (PCG III 2, 590)', *ZPE*, 76: 223–8.

Rosen, R. M. (1997), 'The Gendered Polis in Eupolis' *Cities*', in Dobrov, G. W. (ed.), *The City as Comedy: Society and Representation in Athenian Drama*, 149–76, Chapel Hill: University of North Carolina Press.

Rosen, R. M. (1999), 'Comedy and Confusion in Callias' *Letter Tragedy*', *CPhil.*, 94 (2): 147–67.

Rosen, R. M. (2000), 'Cratinus' *Pytine* and the Construction of the Comic Self', in Harvey, D. and Wilkins, J. (eds), *The Rivals of Aristophanes: Studies in Athenian Old Comedy*, 23–40, London: Duckworth.

Rothwell, K. S., Jr (2007), *Nature, Culture, and the Origins of Greek Comedy: A Study of Animal Choruses*, Cambridge: Cambridge University Press.

Ruffell, I. (2000), 'The World Turned Upside Down: Utopia and Utopianism in the Fragments of Old Comedy', in Harvey, D. and Wilkins, J. (eds), *The Rivals of Aristophanes: Studies in Athenian Old Comedy*, 473–506, London: Duckworth.

Ruffell, I. (2002), 'A Total Write-Off: Aristophanes, Cratinus, and the Rhetoric of Comic Competition', *CQ*, 52 (1): 138–63.

Ruffell, I. (2011), *Politics and Anti-Realism in Athenian Old Comedy: The Art of the Impossible*, Oxford: Oxford University Press.

Ruffell, I. (2014), 'Utopianism', in Revermann, M. (ed.), *The Cambridge Companion to Greek Comedy*, 206–21, Cambridge: Cambridge University Press.

Ruijgh, C. J. (2001), 'Le *Spectacle des lettres*, comédie de Callias (Athénée X 453c–455b), avec un *excursus* sur les rapports entre la mélodie du chant et les contours mélodiques du langage parlé', *Mnemosyne*, 54 (3): 257–335.

Rusten, J. (2013), 'The mirror of Aristophanes: The winged ethnographers of *Birds* (1470–93, 1553–64, 1694–1705)', in Bakola, E., Prauscello, L. and Telò, M. (eds), *Greek Comedy and the Discourse of Genres*, 298–315, Cambridge: Cambridge University Press.

Schmid, W. (1946), *Geschichte der griechischen Literatur*, Part 1, Vol. IV, Munich: Beck.

Schönewolf, H. (1938), 'Der jungattische Dithyrambos: Wesen, Wirkung, Gegenwirkung', dissertation, Giessen.

Schopenhauer, A. (1844), *Die Welt als Wille und Vorstellung*, 2nd edn, Leipzig: Brockhaus.

Schopenhauer, A. ([1844] 1907–9), *The World As Will And Idea*, 6th edn, 3 vols, trans. R. B. Haldane and J. Kemp, London: Kegan Paul, Trench, Trübner & Co., repr. 2012, Charleston: Nabu Press.

Schwarze, J. (1971), *Die Beurteilung des Perikles durch die attische Komödie und ihre historische und historiographische Bedeutung*, Munich: Beck.

Scott, N. (2019a), 'Flying too Close to the Sun: Dramatic Illusion and Theatrical Failure in Aristophanes' *Peace*', *Phoenix*, 73 (1–2): 1–14.

Scott, N. (2019b), 'Metaphors and Jokes in the Fragments of Cratinus', *Arethusa*, 52 (3): 231–51.
Sells, D. (2013), 'Slaves in the Fragments of Old Comedy', in Akrigg, B. and Tordoff, R. (eds), *Slaves and Slavery in Ancient Greek Comic Drama*, 91–110, Cambridge: Cambridge University Press.
Sells, D. (2018), *Parody, Politics and the Populace in Greek Old Comedy*, London: Bloomsbury.
Sevieri, R. (2011), *Timoteo: I Persiani*, Milan: La Vita Felice.
Shaw, C. A. (2014), '"Genitalia of the Sea": Seafood and Sexuality in Greek Comedy', *Mnemosyne*, 67 (4): 554–76.
Shklovsky, V. ([1917] 2004), 'Art as Technique', in Rivkin, J. and Ryan, M. (eds), *Literary Theory: An Anthology*, 2nd edn, 15–21, Oxford: Blackwell.
Sidwell, K. (2000), 'From Old to Middle to New? Aristotle's *Poetics* and the History of Athenian Comedy', in Harvey, D. and Wilkins, J. (eds), *The Rivals of Aristophanes: Studies in Athenian Old Comedy*, 247–58, London: Duckworth.
Sifakis, G. M. (1971), *Parabasis and Animal Choruses: A Contribution to the History of Attic Comedy*, London: Athlone Press.
Silk, M. S. (1974), *Interaction in Poetic Imagery: with Special Reference to Early Greek Poetry*, Cambridge: Cambridge University Press.
Silk, M. S. (1993), 'Aristophanic Paratragedy', in Sommerstein, A. H., Halliwell, S., Henderson, J. and Zimmerman, B. (eds), *Tragedy, Comedy and the Polis: Papers from the Greek Drama Conference, Nottingham, 18–20 July 1990*, 477–504, Bari: Levante Editori.
Silk, M. S. (2000), *Aristophanes and the Definition of Comedy*, Oxford: Oxford University Press.
Slater, N. W. (2002), *Spectator Politics: Metatheatre and Performance in Aristophanes*, Philadelphia: University of Pennsylvania Press.
Small, J. P. (2013), 'Skenographia in Brief', in Harrison, G. W. M. and Liapis, V. (eds), *Performance in Greek and Roman Theatre*, 111–28, Leiden: Brill.
Smith, J. A. (2003), 'Clearing Up Some Confusion in Callias' *Alphabet Tragedy*: How to Read Sophocles' *Oedipus Tyrannus* 332–33 et al.', *CPhil.*, 98 (4): 313–29.
Sommerstein, A. H. (1981), *The Comedies of Aristophanes*, Vol. II: Knights, Warminster: Aris & Phillips.
Sommerstein, A. H. (1985), *The Comedies of Aristophanes*, Vol. V: Peace, Warminster: Aris & Phillips.
Sommerstein, A. H. (1995), 'The Language of Athenian Women', in De Martino, F. and Sommerstein, A. H. (eds), *Lo Spettacolo delle Voci*, Part 2, 61–85, Bari: Levante Editori.
Sommerstein, A. H. (1996), 'How to Avoid Being a *Komodoumenos*', *CQ*, 46 (2): 327–56.

Sommerstein, A. H. (2000), 'Platon, Eupolis and the Demagogue-Comedy', in Harvey, D. and Wilkins, J. (eds), *The Rivals of Aristophanes: Studies in Athenian Old Comedy*, 437–51, London: Duckworth.

Sommerstein, A. H. (2005), 'Tragedy and Myth', in Bushnell, R. (ed.), *A Companion to Tragedy*, 163–80, Oxford: Blackwell.

Sommerstein, A. H. (2009), *Talking about Laughter: and Other Studies in Greek Comedy*, Oxford: Oxford University Press.

Spyropoulos, E. S. (1974), *L'Accumulation Verbale chez Aristophane: Recherches sur le Style d'Aristophane*, Thessaloniki: the author.

Squire, M. J. (2013a), 'Apparitions Apparent: Ekphrasis and the Parameters of Vision in the Elder Philostratus's *Imagines*', *Helios*, 40 (1–2): 97–140.

Squire, M. J. (2013b), 'Invertire l'*ekphrasis*. L'epigramma ellenistico e la traslazione di parola e immagine', *Estetica. Studi e ricerche*, 1/2013: 109–36.

Stewart, E. (2020), 'The Profession of *Mousikē* in Classical Greece', in Stewart, E., Harris, E. and Lewis, D. (eds), *Skilled Labour and Professionalism in Ancient Greece and Rome*, 269–92, Cambridge: Cambridge University Press.

Storey, I. C. (2003), *Eupolis: Poet of Old Comedy*, Oxford: Oxford University Press.

Storey, I. C. (2005), 'But Comedy has Satyrs too', in Harrison, G. W. M. (ed.), *Satyr Drama: Tragedy at Play*, 201–18, Swansea: Classical Press of Wales.

Storey, I. C. (2006a), 'Comedy, Euripides, and the War(s)', *BICS*, 49 (S87): 171–86.

Storey, I. C. (2006b), 'On First Looking into Kratinos' *Dionysalexandros*', in Kozak, L. and Rich, J. (eds), *Playing Around Aristophanes: Essays in Honour of Alan Sommerstein*, 105–25, Oxford: Aris & Phillips.

Storey, I. C. (2011), *Fragments of Old Comedy*, Vol. I: *Alcaeus to Diocles*, Cambridge, MA: Harvard University Press.

Storey, I. C. (2012), 'Angling in Archippos – The Webster Lecture 2008–09', *BICS*, 55 (2): 1–19.

Süß, W. (1967), 'Über den Chiron des Pherekrates', *Rh. Mus.*, 110 (1): 26–31.

Sutton, D. F. (1980), 'Plato Comicus Demoted: A Reconsideration', *ZPE*, 38: 59–63.

Sutton, D. F. (1990), 'Aristophanes and the Transition to Middle Comedy', *LCM*, 15 (6): 81–95.

Swallow, P. and Hall, E., eds (2020), *Aristophanic Humour: Theory and Practice*, London: Bloomsbury.

Taaffe, L. K. (1993), *Aristophanes and Women*, London: Routledge.

Taillardat, J. (1965), *Les Images d'Aristophane: Études de Langue et de Style*, Paris: Les Belles Lettres.

Taplin, O. (1980), 'The Shield Of Achilles Within The *Iliad*', *G&R*, 27 (1), 1–21.

Taplin, O. (1986), 'Fifth-Century Tragedy and Comedy: A *Synkrisis*', *JHS*, 106: 163–74.

Taplin, O. (1987), 'Phallology, *Phlyakes*, Iconography and Aristophanes', *PCPS*, 213 (New Series 33): 92–104.

Taplin, O. (1993), *Comic Angels: and Other Approaches to Greek Drama through Vase-Paintings*, Oxford: Clarendon Press.

Taplin, O. (2007), *Pots and Plays: Interactions between Tragedy and Greek Vase-Painting of the Fourth Century B.C.*, Los Angeles: J. Paul Getty Museum.

Telò, M. (2013), 'Epic, *Nostos* and Generic Genealogy in Aristophanes' *Peace*', in Bakola, E., Prauscello, L. and Telò, M. (eds), *Greek Comedy and the Discourse of Genres*, 129–52, Cambridge: Cambridge University Press.

Telò, M. (2016), *Aristophanes and the Cloak of Comedy: Affect, Aesthetics, and the Canon*, Chicago: University of Chicago Press.

Thomas, R. (2000), *Herodotus in Context: Ethnography, Science and the Art of Persuasion*, Cambridge: Cambridge University Press.

Thompson, D. W. (1947), *A Glossary of Greek Fishes*, London: Oxford University Press.

Torchio, M. C. (2021), *Aristofane* Nephelai protai – Proagon *(fr. 392–486): Traduzione e commento*, Göttingen: Verlag Antike.

Tordoff, R. (2011), 'Excrement, Sacrifice, Commensality: The Osphresiology of Aristophanes' *Peace*', *Arethusa*, 44 (2): 167–98.

Torrance, I. (2013), *Metapoetry in Euripides*, Oxford: Oxford University Press.

Urios-Aparisi, E. (1996), 'Old Comedy Pherecrates' Way', *Ítaca: Quaderns Catalans de Cultura Clàssica*, 12–13: 75–86.

Vaio, J. (1973), 'The Manipulation of Theme and Action in Aristophanes' *Lysistrata*', *GRBS*, 14 (4): 369–80.

Webb, R. (1999), '*Ekphrasis* Ancient and Modern: the Invention of a Genre', *Word & Image*, 15 (1): 7–18.

Webb, R. (2009), *Ekphrasis, Imagination and Persuasion in Ancient Rhetorical Theory and Practice*, Farnham: Ashgate.

Whitman, C. H. (1964), *Aristophanes and the Comic Hero*, Cambridge, MA: Harvard University Press.

Whittaker, M. (1935), 'The Comic Fragments in their Relation to the Structure of Old Attic Comedy', *CQ*, 29 (3–4): 181–91.

Wilamowitz-Möllendorff, U. von (1903), *Timotheos: Die Perser, aus einem Papyrus von Abusir im Auftrage der Deutschen Orientgesellschaft*, Leipzig: Hinrichs.

Wilkins, J. (2000a), 'Edible Choruses', in Harvey, D. and Wilkins, J. (eds), *The Rivals of Aristophanes: Studies in Athenian Old Comedy*, 341–54, London: Duckworth.

Wilkins, J. (2000b), *The Boastful Chef: The Discourse of Food in Ancient Greek Comedy*, Oxford: Oxford University Press.

Willi, A. (2003), *The Languages of Aristophanes: Aspects of Linguistic Variation in Classical Attic Greek*, Oxford: Oxford University Press.

Willis, W. H. (1991) [1993], 'Comoedia Dukiana', *GRBS*, 32 (4): 331–53.
Wilson, A. M. (1977), 'The Individualized Chorus in Old Comedy', *CQ*, 27 (2): 278–83.
Wilson, N. G. (2007), *Aristophanis Fabulae*, 2 vols, Oxford: Clarendon Press.
Wilson, P. and Taplin, O. (1994), 'The "Aetiology" of Tragedy in the *Oresteia*', *PCPS*, 39: 169–80.
Wohl, V. (2015), *Euripides and the Politics of Form*, Princeton: Princeton University Press.
Worman, N. (2015), *Landscape and the Spaces of Metaphor in Ancient Literary Theory and Criticism*, Cambridge: Cambridge University Press.
Wright, M. (2007), 'Comedy and the Trojan War', *CQ*, 57 (2): 412–31.
Wright, M. (2012), *The Comedian as Critic: Greek Old Comedy and Poetics*, London: Bristol Classical Press.
Wright, M. (2016), *The Lost Plays of Greek Tragedy*, Vol. I: *Neglected Authors*, London: Bloomsbury.
Xanthaki-Karamanou, G. and Mimidou, E. (2014), 'The *Aeolus* of Euripides: Concepts and Motifs', *BICS*, 57 (1): 49–60.
Zagari, E. (2018), 'Myth-making in Aristophanes: Innovation and Evolution in Attic Comedy', PhD thesis, University of Reading.
Zanker, G. (1981), 'Enargeia in the Ancient Criticism of Poetry', *Rh. Mus.*, 124 (3–4): 297–311.
Zanker, G. (2004), *Modes of Viewing in Hellenistic Poetry and Art*, Madison: University of Wisconsin Press.
Zeitlin, F. I. (1985), 'Playing the Other: Theater, Theatricality, and the Feminine in Greek Drama', *Representations*, 11: 63–94.
Zeitlin, F. I. (1994), 'The Artful Eye: Vision, Ecphrasis and Spectacle in Euripidean Theatre', in Goldhill, S. and Osborne, R. (eds), *Art and Text in Ancient Greek Culture*, 138–96, Cambridge: Cambridge University Press.
Zeitlin, F. I. (1999), 'Aristophanes: the performance of utopia in the *Ecclesiazousae*', in Goldhill, S. and Osborne, R. (eds), *Performance Culture and Athenian Democracy*, 167–97, Cambridge: Cambridge University Press.
Zimmermann, B. (1992), *Dithyrambos: Geschichte einer Gattung*, Göttingen: Vandenhoeck & Ruprecht.
Zimmermann, B. (1993), 'Comedy's Criticism of Music', in Slater, N. W. and Zimmermann, B. (eds), *Intertextualität in der griechisch-römischen Komödie*, 39–50, Stuttgart: M&P Verlag für Wissenschaft und Forschung.
Zimmermann, B. (1997), 'Parodie dithyrambischer Dichtung in den Komödien des Aristophanes', in Thiercy, P. and Menu, M. (eds), *Aristophane: la Langue, la Scène, la Cité. Actes du colloque de Toulouse, 17–19 mars 1994*, 87–93, Bari: Levante Editori.

Zogg, F. (2014), *Lust am Lesen: Literarische Anspielungen im* Frieden *des Aristophanes*, Munich: Beck.

Zweig, B. (1992), 'The Mute Nude Female Characters in Aristophanes' Plays', in Richlin, A. (ed.), *Pornography and Representation in Greece & Rome*, 73–89, New York: Oxford University Press.

Index

abstract entities
   and actor's body 66
   and other non-human characters 58–9
   nearly always female 66
abstract thought *vs.* sensual knowledge 9–10
absurdity
   of comic landscapes 41
   in jokes and metaphors 20
   of non-human characters on stage 58–9
      especially fish 63–4
   of theatrical make-believe 57, 60
Achilles, shield of 41
Aegisthus 16, 87, 114
Aeolus (god and character) 90, 92, 95–6
afterlife, and Golden Age 43–4
agon 45–6
Ameipsias 2
animal choruses 64, 75–80
animals
   birds
      and choral song 62
      as construction workers 51–2
      crows, going to the 47–8
      and other non-human characters 58–9
      thrushes 44
      of various species 98
      Zeus in the form of a swan 97–9
   fish
      difficulties in costuming them 63
      with feet 47, 60–4, 68, 80
      and other non-human characters 58–9
      sexual overtones of fish imagery 30
   frogs 62, 76, 119
   'horse-cocks' 121
   insects
      and choral song 62
      dung-beetle in *Peace* 81–4
      and other non-human characters 58–9
      wasps in the *Wasps* 75–80
   piglets 64–6, 108–9
   shrimp 30–1
   spiders 34
   swan, Zeus disguised as 97–9
Antiphanes 88–9
   The Man from Mt Cnoethideus or *The Potbelly* 37–8
   unknown play 84
Apollo 25
Araros, son of Aristophanes 97
Archilochus (poet and comic character) 26–7
Archippus 13
   Fishes 60–4, 68, 76, 80
Arguments, Good and Bad, as comic characters 32–3, 58
Aristophanes
   in the context of his contemporaries and competitors 13
   interest in standard metaphors 28
   works
      Acharnians 35–7, 64–6, 75, 80, 88, 91, 106–11, 114–15, 123
      Aeolosicon 88–90, 92–7, 107, 114
      Assemblywomen 94
      Birds 44, 47–53, 60, 67, 76, 99
      Clouds 76, 80
         arsehole jokes in 32–3
      Daedalus 87, 96–8, 102, 104–6, 114–15
      Frogs 76, 105, 109, 119, 121
         first joke 1–2, 8
      Islands 73
      Knights 21–5, 83, 88
      Lemnian Women 87
      Lysistrata 69
      Peace 69–70, 81–2, 91, 106, 111–15
      Seasons 45–7, 52

Wasps 75–80
    scholia on 101
Wealth 84–5
Women at the Thesmophoria 72
Aristophanocentrism, avoidance of 12
Aristotle
    on arrangement 89–90
    on jokes 3–4, 6
    on metaphors 12
    on the probable and necessary 89–90, 114
    works
        Poetics 39, 87, 90, 114
        Rhetoric 3–4, 12, 18, 20–1, 39, 53
arseholes, wide 32–3
Aspasia 100, 103, 109
Athenaeus 43–5
    abundance of quotable jokes in 12
Athens and its empire, in comedy 34, 48–51, 106
    fish as Athenian democrats 61–2
Attardo, Salvatore 4–5, 7
automatism in the Golden Age 46

baggage-carries in comedy 2
Bdelycleon 77
Bellerophon 81, 106, 111–12
Blackadder (television comedy) 57, 60
Blepsidemus 84–5
body
    body jokes not always sexual 73
    female, as a space to be occupied 68–9, 72
    human, on stage 66–75

Callias the Athenian (comic poet) 17
Canace 92
Catullus, and ekphrasis 41
characters, non-human 58–9
choruses
    of cities 66–8
    of clouds 73–6
    of islands 73
    of letters 17
    of satyrs and/or shepherds 102
    see also animal choruses
Chremylus 84–5
Cicero
    on Aristophanes 45

    on jokes 6, 20
    works
        De Legibus 45
        De Oratore 6, 20
Cinesias 70–1, 117, 119
Cleisthenes, effeminate politician 74
Cleon 21, 23, 107
    see also Paphlagonian
Cleonymus, Athenian shield-dropper, as tree 48–9, 51
cognitive theories of metaphor 19
comedy, *see* genre
Comedy (comic character) 21
cooks and chefs on the comic stage 95–6
costuming
    in Aristophanes' *Wasps* 77
    and Dionysus 2, 105–6
    bird costumes 98–9
    city costumes 68
    cloud costumes 74
    fish costumes 63–4
    Furies 85
    pig costumes 65, 68
    as a topic for jokes 12, 54
    tragic costuming in comedy 84–5, 107
country life, grand chracters suffer 114–15
Crates, *Wild Beasts* 43, 46–7, 67
Cratinus
    and the epic cycle 87, 89
    interest in standard metaphors 28
    piles up metaphor-puns 61, 120–1
    works
        Archilochoi 26–8
        Cheirones 98
        Didaskaliai 25–6
        Dionysalexandros 88–91, 97, 102–7, 111, 113–15
        Drapetides 34, 121
        Nemesis 90, 97–8, 100, 102–3, 106, 114
        Nomoi 31, 43
        Pytine 21–5, 30–1, 88
        Thrattai 98
        Wealth-Gods 43
Cratinus or Eupolis, obscene fragment 29–30
Cypria (epic) 97

Daedalus (character) 98, 101
defamiliarization
    by means of puns 33
    and metaphors (Aristotle) 4, 21
    in poetry and jokes 3, 7, 14
Demos (comic character) 21
deus ex machina 84
Dicaeopolis 36–7, 64–6, 88, 106–10, 115, 123
Dionysus 36, 88, 91, 97, 102–6
    Dionysiac themes in Cratinus 24
    disguised as Herakles 1–2, 105
    disguised as Paris 102–5
    songs for *(thriamboi)* 26
dithyrambic style 118, 121
Drunkenness (comic character) 21, 24

ekkyklema 59, 83
ekphrasis 42–53
    defined 18, 38–9
    and the Golden Age 42–7
    'obedient' *vs.* 'disobedient' 41
    and metaphor 17–19, 37–42, 53–5
entrances and exits 40
epirrhema 77–9
euphemism 28–9
Eupolis
    Cities 34, 66–70, 76, 80
    political, *ad hominem* style of 13
Eupolis or Cratinus, obscene fragment 29–30
Euripides
    and metapoetics 18
    works
        Aeolus 90, 92
        Bellerophon 83, 106, 111–12
        Electra 121
        Hecuba 93
        Medea 89
        Telephus 106

fictionality 50–1, 58–60, 63–4, 66–8, 75, 79–82
figurative speech, Aristotle on 3–4
fire and smoke, used against men or wasps 78
food
    anchovies 38
    apples 44
    celery 99–100
    cheese 31
        cheese-graters 92, 143
    chickpeas 65
    and comedy 95–6
    cucumbers 45–6, 108, 110
    figs 49, 65
    fruits and flowers in winter 45
    garlic 95, 108–10
    honey 38
        honeycomb 45
    mint 31, 99–100
    oil 31
    onion 95
    pancakes 43
    pickle-juice 27
    radish, punishment for adultery 32–3
    raisins, showers of 43
    sausages 42, 44, 72
    thrushes 44
    see also animals
form and meaning 2
    gap between 8–9
form, preeminence of, in jokes and poetry 10
fragmentariness 12–13
frames of reference, incompatible 19–20, 58
Freud, Sigmund, on jokes 6–8, 20
'frigid' puns 61, 63–4
Furies 85

gaps and fault-lines
    between convention and cliché 86
    between fictional identity and human body 76
    between fictional world of the play and the real theatre showing it 59, 85–6
    between form and meaning 9–10
    between language and representation 9–10, 14, 18–19
    between performance and imagination 54
    between poetic and historical systems of causality 91
    between representation and represented 75, 80–1

genitalia, female
   kusthos (cunt) 65–9
   piglet, slang for female genitalia 65–6, 110
genitalia, male
   acorn, and *glans penis* 34
   caterpillar as phallic euphemism 72
   chickpea as phallic euphemism, 65
   cock-and-balls, implied by the number three 30–1
   comic phallus
      and animal choruses 63, 144
      as part of the comic costume 30
   crustaceans as phallic euphemism 30
   cucumbers as phallic euphemism 110
   figs as phallic euphemism 65
   pine cone as phallic euphemism 72
   sausages as phallic euphemism 72
   shrimp as phallic euphemism 30–1
genre 10–12, 14–18, 33, 40–1, 53–5, 57–9, 83–90, 92, 96, 101–2, 107, 118–19, 122–3
Golden Age, in comedies 31, 41–7
   always relegated to the offstage space 42
   and ekphrasis 42–7
   list of plays set in 43
Gorgias (orator) 49–50
GTVH (General Theory of Verbal Humor) 4–5, 7

Helen 91, 102–6, 109
   conception of 97
   daughter of Nemesis and Zeus 97–8
Hellenistic literature 41
Herakles, Dionysus disguised as 2, 105
Hermes (god and character) 112–14
Hermippus
   Europa 87
   The Birth of Athena 87
Herodotus 97, 109
Hesiod (comic character) 26
history, role of chance in 115
Homer
   as comic character 26
   comic poets humorize his serious metaphors 28
   Iliad 22
   Odyssey 90, 104
Homeric Hymn to Apollo 25

Humor (journal) 4
hypotheses
   of Cratinus' *Dionysalexandros* 88, 102–3
   Hellenistic, dubious reliability of 102

Ilissus (river) 24–5
impossibility, in poetry and jokes 3
incongruity
   appropriate 5, 58
   balance of congruity and incongruity 6
   in ekphrasis on the comic stage 42–7
incongruity theory 3–4
   Schopenhauer's version of 9, 122–3
inference, in understanding jokes 8
instantiation, poetic 18
Iris (goddess) 52

joke theories 19
jokes
   adjacent to metaphors in Aristotle's theory 3, 20
      differences between 7
   as complete 'closed' texts 13
   entire play built on one joke 76
   inherent multiplicity of 74
   integral part of how comedy thinks about drama 80
   interpretative openness in 8
   inward-looking and outward-looking 86
   kinship with poetry 2–3, 11
   as a literary and poetic phenomenon 2–3
   metatheatrical, importance of 60
   as a mode of storytelling 6
   polyvalence, endlessly recursive 9
   as rulebreaking and -bending speech 11
   as a site of poetic experimentation 13
   spelling out rude words 17
   standalone *vs.* whole fictional world 5–6, 88
   stock 2
   thematic constellations of 13
   on tragic and epic storylines 11
   on tragic stagecraft 11
   types of 3
   see also puns
Judgment of Paris 97

Kant, Immanuel, on jokes 7, 9
KomFrag project, Freiburg 12

landscapes
  fantastical comic 41
  on and off-stage 40
language
  anti-representational potential of 14
  and representation, gap between 9–10, 14, 18–19
language, as visual force 53–4
Leda, mother or step-mother of Helen 97–8
letters of the alphabet, as chorus 17
linguistics, cognitive 19
Lycis 2
lyric poetry 10, 18

Macareus 92, 94
Marathon, Battle of 78
mechane 59, 81–4, 101
Megara and Megarians 108–10
Megarian decree 64, 113
Megarian merchant (character) 64–6
Melanippides 71–2, 117
metaliterary discourse 12
metaphor 17–42
  comic 19–21, 28
  and defamiliarizaton (Aristotle) 3–4
  and ekphrasis 17–19, 37–42, 53–5
  and euphemism 28–33
  and jokes
    adjacent in Aristotle's theory 3, 20–1
    forms of indirect representation 20
    obscene puns and metaphor 35
    similar underlying structures of 19
    slippage between 20–1, 54
  and metatheatre 75
  in prose 12
  specific metaphors
    bodies, ships, and landscapes mingled 121
    comedy and wine as wife and mistress 21
    drinking young wine as pederasty 30
    invective as salt or vinegar 27
    laws as spider webs 34

libation wine as bathwater 34
mosaic *vs.* painting 9
orators as grotesque monsters 50
Paphlagonian (Cleon) as cauldron 23–4
peacemaking as wine tasting 36–7
political misbehaviour as sexual misbehaviour 32–3
shrimp as leather thong as phallus 29–30
speech as barking of a dog 21–8
speech as liquid 21–8
  as flooding torrent 22–3
  as pickle-juice 27
spiders as human soldiers 34
state as household 21
theories as buildings 19
teach the reader/hearer (Aristotle) 3–4
metapoetics 10–11, 18, 26, 28, 40, 45, 95
metatheatre 10, 47, 57–60, 65–6, 73, 75, 95–6, 101, 104–5, 107
  jokes an essential tool of 85–6
  puns a tool of 80
mimesis 54
  as comic vocabulary word 95
  and play (*paideia*) 11–12
Music (character) 70–2
music-making 11

Nemesis (goddess) 97–8, 100
Nephelokokkygia 47–9, 52
'New Music' 70–1, 117–23

obscenity, comic 28–35
Oedipus 89
Orestes (Athenian mugger) 48–9
Orestes (mythic hero) 16, 87, 114
Oring, Elliott 5–7, 19–20, 58
Oxyrhynchus Papyri 102

Palmer, Jerry 5–7, 20
Paphlagonian (Cleon) 21, 23–4, 83
parabasis and pseudo-parabatic passages 10, 21–3, 77, 110
paratragedy 10, 15–16, 57–8, 81–2, 88, 96, 106, 111
Paris (Trojan prince) 91, 102–6, 109
  Judgment of 97

parody 10–11, 48, 89, 92–4, 106–7, 109, 118
Peace (goddess and character) 69, 113
Peace of Nikias 111
peace treaties 36–7
Peisetairos 48, 51–3, 63
Peloponnesian War 98, 106–11, 115
Penia, 'poverty' (character) 84
Pericles 90, 97–8, 100, 102–3, 109, 113
peripeteia, Aristotelian 6
Persian War 78, 109, 111
Pherecrates
   Chiron 70–2, 87, 117, 119
   Miners 43, 46
Philip (orator) 49–50
Philocleon 77, 79
Phrynichus 2
   Cronos 87
Phrynis 72
Plato Comicus
   Adonis 87
   Greece or *Islands* 34–5
   Io 87
   Menelaus 87
Plato, and mimesis 11–12
plausibility and implausibility 7
   in metaphors and jokes 20
Plutarch 70, 98, 100
poetics, spatial 40
poetry
   comic and serious 21
   interpretative openness in 8–9
   kinship with jokes 2–3, 11
   as rulebreaking and -bending speech 11
poetry and poetics, jokes in and as 2–3
Pollux, Julius 12
'portmanteau' play-titles 88
professionalization of performance culture 118–19
prostitutes, theft of 108–9
punchline, single with multiple pay-offs 13
puns
   frigid puns an effective literary device 63–4
   and non-human characters 58–9
   obscene double meanings 29–35, 65–6
   specific
      acorns and bathtubs 34
      agricultural landscape and pubic hair 67

atima as lacking moral and monetary value 110
atopos and *ektopos* both 'strange' and 'out of place' 49, 52
branch, dried fig, and *mechane* 83
bricks both baked and visible *(optais)* 51
cabbage, caterpillar, and penis 72
celestial sphere *(polos)* and city *(polis)* 48
crows, literal and metaphorical 47–8
fermented wine and putrid fish 38
figs and sycophancy 49
fire and smoke, used against men and wasps 78
fish and *hetairai* 62–3
on fish-names 61–3
fountain and water clock 49–50
Kardia (Greek colony) and heart as courage 49
kitchen utensils and theatrical props 47
libations and peace treaties 37
loins as virility, arse, or wasp's stinger 76–7
ménage à trois, implied by the number three 30–1
modern
   Jesus as footballer 5
   spring as source of water and mechanical device 5, 58
   time, bananas, and fruit flies 8
planting crops and begetting children 67
sex
   and athletics 69–70
   and instrumental music 71–2
   and ploughing 69
   sexual assault and military occupation 67–8
sharp stingers and harsh temperaments 76, 78
stonelessness and artlessness 22–3
whirlwind, pinecone, and penis 72
structurally integral to metaphor more than to ekphrasis 54–5
a tool of metatheatre 80
see also jokes

Raskin, Viktor 4–5, 7–9, 19, 58, 88
Reconciliation (character) 69
riddles, poetic *(griphoi)* 120–2
rivers
    flowing with wine 42
    Ilissus 24–5
    of porridge and soup 43–4
roses 99

Salamis, Battle of 120–2
scatology 1, 104–5
scene changes and *skenographia* 42
Schopenhauer, Arthur, on humour 9, 18, 40, 122–3
scripts
    in theatrical performance 80
    in theory of jokes 4, 58
sensual knowledge *vs.* abstract thought 9–10
Shakespeare, William 2
Sicilian soothsayers 61
Sicon (chef and character) 90, 92, 94–6
sight and blindness, in ekphrasis 46
signification, systems of 84, 86, 91
signifier and signified 7–8, 27, 54
slaves 1, 21, 46, 77
socio-political aspects of jokes 2
Socrates 48, 74
Solon, on the comic stage 31
space, fictional, beyond the stage 40, 50–1
Sparta and Spartans 36–7, 98, 103, 106–7
SSTH (Script-based Semantic Theory of Humor) 4–5, 7
stagecraft
    comic 60
    tragic jokes on, 11
    see also ekkyklema; mechane
storylines, tragic and epic, jokes on 11
Strattis 89
    Anthroporestes 88
    Atalantus 82, 101
    Phoenician Women 84
Strepsiades 73–4

technology, Daedalus' interest in 101
Teleclides, *Amphictyons* 43
Telephus 88, 107
tenor, *see* vehicle and tenor

Theocritus and his scholia 99
Theon, *Progymnasmata* 53
Theoria, 'Spectatorship' (character) 69–70
theories of humor
    cognitive theories 19–20
    formal semantic analysis in 4
    grounded in linguistics 4
    incongruity 3–4
    joke theory 19–20
    shortcomings of 7
Timotheus 70–1, 117–23
    and Old Comedy 120
    Persians 117, 119–20
tongue, cut out in animal sacrifice 50
tragedy 59, 81, 96
    see also paratragedy
Tragedy of Letters (Callias), actually a comedy 17
Trojan War
    origins of 97, 114–15
    paralleled with Peloponnesian War 98, 100, 111
    source of mythical plots 89
    trivial origins of 100–1
Trygaeus 69–70, 81–2, 111–13

Underworld, and Golden Age 43–4

vegetarianism 46
vehicle and tenor 19, 110
visuality
    in the language of comedy 53–4
    and vividness in ekphrasis 39
visualization, in poetry 18
vowels, characters in comedy 17

wall, aerial 51–2
walls, house and city 34
War (god) 113
Wealth (goddess and character) 84–5
wealth, value of 94–5

Xanthias 1, 77
Xerxes 78

Zeus
    and Nemesis 96–8
    and Pericles 98

Index Locorum

Antiphanes (PCG)
  The Man from Mt Cnoethideus or
    The Potbelly
    Fr. 123: 37–8
  unknown plays
    Fr. 189.5-6: 88–9
    Fr. 189.13-16: 84
Archippus (PCG)
  Fishes
    Fr. 14: 62
    Fr. 19: 62–3
    Fr. 25: 62–3
    Fr. 27: 62–3
    Fr. 28: 61
    Fr. 30: 61
    Frs. 15-16: 61–2
    Frs. 17-18: 61
Aristophanes
  fragments (PCG)
    1 *(Aeolosicon)*: 93, 96
    2 *(Aeolosicon)*: 92
    3 *(Aeolosicon)*: 93–5
    5 *(Aeolosicon)*: 95–6
    7, 14-16 *(Aeolosicon)*: 92
    192 *(Daedalus)*: 101
    199 *(Daedalus)*: 100–1
    201 *(Daedalus)*: 101
    403 *(Islands)*: 73
    410: 73
    581 *(Seasons)*: 45–6
  extant plays (OCT line numbers)
    Acharnians
      186-203: 35–7
      393-489: 107
      496-556: 106
      500: 14, 115, 123
      502-03: 107
      515-37: 107–10
      527: 103
      716: 32
      729-835: 110
      738-47: 64–5
      781-82: 65–6
    Assemblywomen
      816-22: 94
    Birds
      28: 47–8
      267-304: 67
      273: 98
      550-52: 51
      667-74: 63
      1122-63: 51–2
      1166-67: 52
      1171-74: 52
      1199: 52
      1210-14: 52
      1470-81: 48–9
      1471: 52
      1482-93: 48
      1553-64: 48
      1694-1705: 49–51
    Clouds
      276: 95
      340-45: 73–74
      538-39: 30
      1071-83: 32
      1088-94: 32–3
      1101: 33
    Frogs
      1-15: 1–2
      46: 105
      46-47: 2
      109: 95
      718-26: 109
      932: 121
    Knights
      44: 23
      526-28: 22–3
      526-36: 21
      919-22: 23–4
      1249: 83
    Lysistrata
      1114: 69
      1173: 69

Peace
  149-76: 81–2
  173-76: 101
  195-97: 112
  204-09: 112–13
  223: 113
  605-09: 113
  615: 113
  618: 113
  632-38: 113
  894-906: 69–70
Wasps
  105-07: 79
  129: 79
  140: 79
  191: 101
  207-08: 79
  223-26: 76–8
  241: 77
  366: 77
  407-08: 77
  420: 77
  422-25: 77
  457: 77–8
  1074: 79–80
  1075-90: 78–9
  1509: 35
Wealth
  Hypothesis IV: 92
  422-25: 84–5
Women at the Thesmophoria
  156: 95
  515-16: 72
Aristotle
  Poetics
    1447a2-3: 89
    1450b26: 89
    1451a-b: 90
    1451b: 114
    1451b9: 89
    1452a4: 89–90
    1453a35: 16, 114
    1453a35-39: 87
    1455a22-25: 39
  Rhetoric
    1406b10-11: 12
    1406b6-7: 3
    1410b: 20–21
    1410b10-13: 3–4

    1410b32-33: 4
    1411a: 53
    1411a26: 14
    1411a27-28: 18
    1411b: 39
    1412a11-12: 7
    1412a19: 20
    1412a19-22: 3, 7
Athenaeus, Deipnosophistae
  276a: 17
  448b: 17
  453c-454a: 17

Cicero
  De Legibus
    2.37: 45
  De Oratore
    2.240: 20
    2.240-255: 6
Crates (PCG)
  Wild Beasts
    Fr. 16.4-10: 46–7
Cratinus (PCG)
  Archilochoi
    Fr. 6.1: 26–8
  Cheirones
    Fr. 258: 98
  Daedalus
    Fr. 199: 98
  Didaskaliai
    Fr. 38: 25–6
  Dionysalexandros
    hypothesis (P.Oxy. 663) 11-47: 102–3, 105
    Fr. 40: 105–6
    Fr. 42: 104
    Fr. 43: 104–5
    Fr. 45: 105
  Drapetides
    Fr. 54: 34, 121
  Nemesis
    Frs. 114-15: 97–8
    Fr. 116: 99
    Fr. 117: 98
    Fr. 118: 98, 100
    Frs. 120-21: 98
  Nomoi
    Frs. 130-31: 43
  Pytine

Fr. 195: 30–1
Fr. 196: 31
Fr. 198: 24–5
Thrattai
Fr. 74: 98
unknown plays
Fr. 314: 29–30

Eupolis (PCG)
Cities
Fr. 244: 66–7
Fr. 245: 68
Fr. 246: 68
Fr. 247: 67–8, 70
unknown plays
Fr. 120: 29–30
Euripides
fragmentary plays (TGF)
Aeolus
Frs. 19, 20, 22: 92
Bellerophon
Fr. 285: 111–12
Fr. 286: 112
Fr. 311: 83
Hecuba (OCT line numbers)
1-2: 93

Herodotus
1.1: 97
1.2-4: 109
7.1.50: 78
Homer
Iliad
1.247-49: 22
Odyssey
10.1-79: 90
Homeric Hymn to Apollo

261-63: 25
379-87: 25

Pherecrates (PCG)
Chiron
Fr. 155: 70–2, 117
Miners
Fr. 113: 43–5
Plato Comicus (PCG)
Greece or *Islands*
Fr. 21: 34–5
Plutarch
Lives
Pericles
3.5: 98, 100
Moralia
1141d-42a *(De Musica)*: 70 + n.50

Sosipater (PCG)
Fr. 1: 90
Strattis (PCG)
Atalantus
Fr. 4: 82–3, 101
Phoenician Women
Fr. 311: 84

Theocritus
11.10 and scholion: 99
Theon, *Progymnasmata*
118, 1.7: 18, 53
Timotheus (PMG)
Persians
Fr. 791.88-93: 117, 120–1

Xenophon
Poroi
4.10-11: 110

www.ingramcontent.com/pod-product-compliance
Lightning Source LLC
Chambersburg PA
CBHW052122300426
44116CB00010B/1769